MW01050801

TRUE CRIME

Compulsion to Kill

BY
THE EDITORS OF
TIME-LIFE BOOKS
Alexandria, Virginia

Compulsion to Kill

Predators

In the twisted minds of men who murder again and again, life, sex, pain, and death are fashioned into a terrible compulsion to kill. Otherwise rather ordinary men, serial killers turn to violence and death in search of power over others and to explore their own monstrous sexual identity. That is what their killing is really all about, although it takes many different forms.

Some of these men view women as mere dolls to be terrorized, murdered, violated, and then callously dispersed, piece by piece, for wild animals to find. Others, through a perverse psychological chemistry, form a murderous composite entity—but remain relatively harmless on their own. Men may prey upon other men, often propelled by an aching loneliness. And there are those rare predators who, hunting with the cunning savagery of a forest wolf, stalk through the human herd and attack its weakest members: the homeless, the impaired, the young of both sexes.

Curiously, such men lead more or less normal lives in parallel with their murderous ones. They have parents, fiancées, wives, lovers, children, homes, jobs; they enjoy a drink with the boys, they fret about bills, and they aspire to better things—many yearn to be police officers. When apprehended they often reveal a host of "reasons" for their deadly acts: a tyrannical or missing parent, a prostitute's scornful laugh, demons murmuring secretly in their minds. They may even exhibit a self-pitying variant of remorse.

While their behavior has been insane, however, they are rarely locked away in mental institutions. To be judged legally insane, one cannot understand the wrongness or consequences of one's crimes. But these men plan and commit not one but a series of premeditated murders and then skillfully elude capture. They may indeed be compelled to kill, but they are not insane in the eyes of the law. When society finally sweeps up such predators, their very cunning ensures them a life behind bars—or a place on death row.

*S*omeday you're
going to hear from me
again. You'll see me,
or you will read about
me again.

JEFFREY DAHMER

1

Milwaukee Monster

Pain in every corner of his body roused the young man from his drunken stupor. With panic rising, he opened burning, bloodshot eyes and found that he was a prisoner in a cat's cradle of ropes, hooks, and straps that bound his wrists and ankles and stretched in opposite directions. At the center of the pain between his naked legs, the young man could make out his tormentor, a bearded, dark-haired man intent on extracting his own pleasure from the agonies of his young blond prey. The captive man screamed and cursed, convulsing wildly. But every pull produced an opposing push, and his efforts to ease his suffering only inflicted new tortures. His terror rose. He was helpless in this web, and he could die here.

The night had begun better. The two men had met, had talked, had drunk—Yukon Jack whiskey, probably, but there was no remembering now. Nor was there any recollection of coming to this apartment. Certainly the captive had not agreed to this. No, he shrieked. He pleaded. He threatened. Finally, his bearded torturer released the bonds and allowed the young man to slip to the floor.

Don't leave, implored the engineer of the web. Stay awhile and talk. But the victim wanted only to be gone from the torture chamber as fast as possible, to be out on the street, to escape from this predatory monster who had used him so brutally. The blond man gathered up his scattered clothing and fled, grateful for the bite of Milwaukee's November wind. It was the morning after Thanksgiving, 1989.

Recalling the terror of that morning two years later, the young man was indifferent to the details of the event. He could not remember, nor did he seem to care, who his tormentor had been or where the awful business had happened. Such nights were a risk he took, he told his interviewers, in an existence that easily mingled pleasure with pain. Satisfaction and suffering were twin demons that directed his life.

It was a life in which the notions of predator and prey might also intermix; a man could be the aggressor one night, the victim the next. So it surely was in his case, for the blond young man's name was Jeffrey Dahmer, and on the morning that he discovered that another's lust could kill him, Dahmer's own appetites had already taken the lives of five young men. After fleeing from his tormentor, he killed another dozen times. Before Milwaukee police stumbled across him, Jeffrey Dahmer had, by his own account, seduced 17 victims, murdered them, and taken his solitary pleasures with their lifeless bodies. He had butchered his victims, then enshrined their bones and, sometimes, even made meals of their flesh.

Once in the hands of police, Dahmer freely admitted his crimes. Always polite and agreeable, he described them in detail. Although he couldn't always remember his victims' names, or exactly when they died, he did recall *how* they died. He furnished ghastly particulars that helped authorities confirm his guilt and locate long-buried remains. He submitted to a battery of psychological tests and interviews, pleasantly answering the doctors' questions. He was a model monster.

Jeffrey Dahmer had become practiced at presenting to the world a variety of faces. As the audience warranted, he was genial, earnest, and compliant, or surly, ill-mannered, and stubborn. He was depressed. He was a clown. He was pious. He was a drunk. He was a wise guy, or a sincere penitent. He was dull or bright. The guises were mostly camouflage, artful decoration to disguise his carefully tended secret garden—a private place, lush with the sickly overgrowth of his fantasies. The world outside often snubbed Jeffrey Dahmer, shutting him out, making him lonely—but no matter; he could always find comfort and companionship within his fantasies. He had lived among them for many years.

Jeffrey Dahmer was born on May 21, 1960, at Deaconess Hospital in Milwaukee. At the time, his father, Lionel, was a graduate student in chemistry at Marquette University. His mother, Joyce, was a homemaker. From Milwaukee the Dahmers moved to Ames, Iowa, where Lionel earned a doctorate from Iowa State University. In 1966 the couple had a second child, David, and Lionel got a job with PPG Industries in Barberton, Ohio, a suburb of Akron. The family lived there and in nearby Doylestown until 1968, when they settled in Bath, a quiet country town north of Akron that was favored by the area's affluent. Their home provided an ideal site for raising two boys. Situated on two acres of land, the house's large rear windows overlooked a spring-fed pond and peaceful woods.

But while the setting might have seemed nearly perfect, something in young Jeffrey had already gone very much amiss. Like other Bath youngsters, he roamed the woods and carried home the things that interested him. For Jeffrey, however, those things were, invariably, dead. He was intrigued by animal remains, and he amassed a collection of bones that he called his "fiddlesticks." In a shed behind the house he kept a large collection of insects and dead animals—chipmunks, squirrels, woodchucks, raccoons, and other dead creatures found in the woods or by the side of the road. A friend years later described the collection as "tons and tons of jars of animals and pieces of animals. And he seemed to be fascinated by the decomposition." Once he came across a road-killed dog. He dismembered it, then cut the head off and impaled it on a stick near his house.

Playmates may have suspected that Jeffrey was more than a little peculiar, but teachers and other adults seldom saw anything unusual about him. They generally regarded him the way neighbor Georgia Scharenberg did: He was "a very nice, polite boy," she said. "We liked him."

Dahmer had only a few real friends as a teenager, but he was adept at being alone without being altogether a loner. Some of his classmates at Revere High School regarded him as an interesting curiosity. Smiling, pleasant Jeffrey Dahmer often drank Scotch whisky from a Styrofoam cup during class. All the kids knew it. The teachers never found out. One of his classmates, John Backderf, said that alcohol was "probably what made him act the way he did." That way was often bizarre—calculated to attract attention, if not ad-

Viewed from Lake Michigan, the Milwaukee skyline masks the seedy neighborhoods where Jeffrey Dahmer eased his fatal loneliness.

miration. So common was this behavior that it became known as "doing a Dahmer," or "Dahmer's Command Performance" in high-school circles. For a price, Jeffrey would get drunk and stumble through a local mall, harassing patrons, pretending to have seizures—in short, disrupting the adult world in a way that most of the youths following him would like to have done themselves at one time or another.

The performance was fun to watch—but more than a little frightening, said Backderf. "We were always a little bit wary of him. He was a big guy. We had this feeling that if he went off, you didn't want to be in his way."

There were many pranks. A mediocre student, Dahmer crashed the school's National Honor Society photo session, popping up at just the right time to include himself in the group picture. The editors blacked out his face before the photograph was printed. He reportedly also amused himself by chalking crime-scene outlines of bodies in the school corridors. To Backderf and his friends, Dahmer was "a sort of peripheral figure" who "never really let down his act."

Jeffrey Dahmer had reasons to maintain a facade. At an age when his male classmates could hardly restrain themselves around girls, Jeffrey was indifferent to females. His one sexual experience in high school, at about the age of 14, involved kissing and touching another boy.

He had dark fantasies, and they began to extrude from young Jeffrey Dahmer's mind into the real world. When Jeffrey was about 15 years old, he saw a jogger who ran past the Dahmer home. Jeffrey thought about how he'd like to know this attractive young man, but surely, he feared, the runner would reject his advances. So Jeffrey formulated a plan: He would hide in the shrubbery next to the jogger's path, and when the man appeared, he'd leap out, slug him with a baseball bat, drag the unconscious body off into the woods, and there have sex with it. But the fantasy went, for the time being, unfulfilled; the jogger never ran past the house again.

Struggling with his sexual identity, uncomfortable with the growing evidence that homosexuality was to be his lot in life, Dahmer staggered through high school in increasing isolation. His home was no haven. During his senior year, his warring parents divided the house, each occupying half. The demarcation line was a string stretched by Dahmer's father. Dangling from it were dozens of keys whose jingling was intended to alert Lionel if Joyce tried to trespass. It was never clear exactly where Jeffrey belonged in this extraordinarily partitioned household.

Ninth grader Jeffrey Dahmer *(right)* smiles in this yearbook portrait from Eastview Junior High School in Bath, Ohio. As a junior at Revere High School, Dahmer *(circled below)* crashes the school newspaper staff photograph in his lonely quest for more attention.

Dahmer retreated more and more into his inner universe of invention and fantasy—a world far more satisfying than the real one. One of his favorite visions—an immensely gratifying one—involved the possession of an unconscious, totally compliant male lover who would never leave him. Sometimes there was a disturbing but exciting overlay that intruded on this vision: In it Jeffrey's lovers were dead, dismembered, and disemboweled. There was no question that young Dahmer was capable of causing such carnage if he decided to act out his visions. By the time he graduated from high school he stood six feet tall and weighed a muscular 200 pounds. He lifted weights.

Revere High School's class of 1978 graduated on the evening of June 4. For most of the 280 members of the class, the time surrounding commencement was a signal event: There were dances, parties, farewell trysts. Not for Dahmer. He'd invited a girl to the senior prom but abandoned her there, decamping for a local fast-food restaurant where he passed most of the night. Nor, for him, were there the elaborate gifts that wealthy and indulgent parents gave some of his peers—the new cars, the trips to Europe. Jeffrey Dahmer remembered no particular celebration in his household to mark his departure from childhood. In fact, there no longer *was* any household. By graduation day Dahmer's father had moved out of the family home and into a nearby motel. His mother and brother had gone to Wisconsin. Jeffrey was alone in the house on Bath Road. He was nearly broke. There was very little food. The refrigerator was broken. His isolation continued for two weeks after graduation.

Then, one evening in mid-June, Dahmer was driving alone outside town when he encountered a slender, shirtless young hitchhiker. The youth, who gave his name as Steven Hicks, gratefully accepted a ride. Like Dahmer, Hicks was 18. He was thumbing his way home to Coventry Township from a rock concert at Chippewa Lake Park, about 40 miles east of Akron. It was his father's birthday, and Hicks had promised that he'd return in plenty of time for the scheduled party.

The two young men apparently hit it off well. Both enjoyed music. Both liked to drink beer and smoke pot. Dahmer disclosed that his parents were away from home. It was hot and muggy—why not stop and knock back a few cold ones? Hicks readily agreed.

While they talked, the two lifted weights, drank a dozen beers between them, and smoked some marijuana. Dahmer recalled that there was no homosexual encounter. "I didn't think he was gay," he explained. It was enough to have a friend. But a problem soon emerged: Dahmer's new friend wanted to leave. Hicks's father's party beckoned.

But as it turned out, the young man stayed with Dahmer after all. When Hicks turned his back, Dahmer knocked him unconscious with a barbell, then strangled him by pressing the bar into his throat. As Hicks's life ebbed, Dahmer found his own pleasure rising. His most exciting fantasy had suddenly come true: An attractive young man lay helpless beneath him. He found the satisfaction all he dreamed it could be.

Eventually the ecstasy receded, and fear of discovery took its place. The body, as attractive as it was to Dahmer, had to be disposed of. He dragged it into a crawlspace under the rear of the house and left it for two days before dismembering it with a large hunting knife and stuffing the pieces into plastic trash bags. Two more days passed before he summoned the boldness to load the bags into his father's car for a trip to the landfill.

On the road, Dahmer's luck nearly ran out. A police officer thought he was driving erratically and pulled him over on the suspicion that Dahmer might have been drinking. The officer shone his flashlight on the bags containing Hicks's mutilated body. Dahmer coolly explained that the bags held garbage that he was taking to a landfill. Satisfied that Dahmer was not drunk, the officer let him go with only a citation for driving in the wrong lane. Dahmer, shaken by the close brush with discovery, drove home and returned the bags to the crawlspace.

Although he was nervous about getting caught, Dahmer couldn't leave his victim's remains alone. He carried Hicks's decomposing head to his room, where it entered into his satisfying fantasies. The next morning he hid the bags in a drainage pipe in the woods behind the house, burned Hicks's clothing and identification, and threw the hunting knife and a necklace Hicks had been wearing into the nearby Cuyahoga River. He had gotten away with murder.

Apparently, success carried a price. After his arrest 13 years later, Dahmer told psychiatrists that memories of Steven Hicks's slaying tormented him for years. Perhaps the recollections were responsible for Dahmer's disastrous start at Ohio State University in Columbus. Soon after he arrived there he started drinking heavily, and he never stopped until he flunked out in December. His dormitory

As an average high-school senior in 1978, Jeff Dahmer *(left)* continued to play the role of class lunatic with such pranks as infiltrating the National Honor Society students' class photograph. So annoyed were the yearbook editors that they blacked out the intruder's face *(circled below)* before publication. The troubled young man's attempts at normal behavior were no more successful than his stunts in attracting congenial companions. For example, Dahmer arrived at his senior prom with a date *(right)* but soon abandoned her in favor of a nocturnal feast of fast-food burgers—and perhaps some time alone to feed his fantasies, which had already begun to fill with dead and mutilated male lovers.

Home alone after his warring parents left him in their suburban house *(right)* in Bath, Ohio, Dahmer picked up 18-year-old hitchhiker Steven Hicks *(inset),* who became the killer's first victim. Hicks's dismembered body was buried for years in this backyard.

STEVEN HICKS

room was decorated with an impressive collection of liquor bottles and beer cans.

Lionel Dahmer, dismayed at his son's out-of-control drinking, urged Jeffrey to join the army in the hope that the discipline of military life would straighten the youth out. On Christmas Eve Lionel married his second wife, Shari Virginia Jordan. Five days later, Jeffrey joined the army. After training in Alabama and Texas, he became a medical corpsman and was shipped to Baumholder, Germany.

For a time the young soldier fared well, showing interest in his chores as a medic. But then old habits returned, and he fell to lying on his bunk for as many hours as he could manage, sipping martinis and listening to tapes of heavy-metal bands. (A favorite was Black Sabbath, whose leader, Ozzy Osbourne, was notorious for biting the heads off small animals during his concert performances.) Hard liquor was off-limits in the barracks, but Jeffrey installed a clandestine bar in a briefcase.

Dahmer was no less an enigma to his army mates than he'd been to his high-school classmates. He seemed at times quite intelligent, a good conversationalist, a polite barracksmate. On the other hand, he could be boorish and hostile, and he was an obnoxious drunk. Most of his fellow soldiers, if they thought of him at all, saw him more or less as a mirror image of themselves—a young man trying to get through his service as easily as possible.

Dahmer's only family contact in those days seemed to be with his paternal grandmother, Catherine Dahmer, who lived in West Allis, Wisconsin, a suburb of Milwaukee. She wrote regularly, sending boxes of cookies. None of his army acquaintances noticed anything untoward in Dahmer's sex life. Nor could police find any evidence of misbehavior in his military days when they tried years later. Dahmer himself has said that alcohol abuse, homosexual pornography, masturbation, heavy-metal music, and a busy work schedule kept him out of serious trouble at the time.

He remained an outsider, seldom speaking of home or a girlfriend and rarely joining in the normal barracks banter. Apparently driven by his private torments, Dahmer's drinking increased during his second year in the army. He began skipping work assignments and when he did report for duty he had liquor on his breath. In March of 1981, less than 10 months short of his scheduled release, he was ejected from the army with a discharge stating that his drinking made him unsuitable for service.

Before leaving for home he told his platoon leader, David Goss, "Someday you're going to hear from me again. You'll see me, or you will read about me again." Goss took this as a sign that Jeffrey Dahmer had determined to put his life in order. Later, Dahmer's words would take on for Goss a different, chilling, cast.

Following his discharge Dahmer drifted to Miami Beach, Florida, with no more purpose, he said later, than to "live someplace warm." He found work at a sandwich shop on 163rd Street but was often so broke that he had to sleep on the beach. Lionel Dahmer, concerned over his son's aimless existence in Florida, urged him to move back to Ohio. Lionel and Shari seemed to have found peace with each other, and they hoped that some of their serenity would rub off on Jeffrey.

Jeffrey complied with his father's wishes, but his return to Bath Road was anything but tranquil. Almost immediately

he revisited the hiding place of Steven Hicks's remains. By now the flesh was mostly gone, so Dahmer took a sledgehammer and methodically smashed each bone and all of Hicks's teeth and scattered the pieces in dense brush on a steep, rocky hillside near the house.

He accomplished little else. Night after night Dahmer borrowed his father's car and drove from one local saloon to another, drinking vodka and picking fights. Often he forgot where he'd been or even where he'd left the car. On October 7, 1981, a few weeks after his return to Bath, he was thrown out of Maxwell's Lounge at the local Ramada Inn and arrested for disorderly conduct. The judge gave him a 10-day suspended sentence and fined him $60.

To Lionel and Shari Dahmer, the arrest was further proof that Jeffrey was beyond their help. There seemed to be no way to stop his self-destructive carousing. Desperate for a return to peace — theirs and his — Lionel contacted his mother in Wisconsin, who seemed to be the only person whom the troubled young man loved and respected without reservation. Catherine Dahmer, the devoted grandmother who'd sent him cookies and letters during his army hitch, agreed to let Jeffrey live with her. He arrived at her home shortly before Christmas of 1981.

For a time, the move seemed to possess the hoped-for curative powers. Within a month Dahmer found a job drawing blood at Milwaukee Blood Plasma, Inc., a local blood bank. He began attending church with his grandmother. He read the Bible regularly. In the spring he planted roses for Mrs. Dahmer. He mowed the lawn for her. He drank less. He later told police that during this period he was genuinely looking for an opportunity to live what he called the "straight and narrow life."

But Bible study and church were no match for Dahmer's fantasy world. Try as he might to avoid them — and he says

Photographed by a platoonmate, army medic Jeffrey Dahmer sprawls drunkenly on his barracks cot in Baumholder, Germany, wearing civilian clothes and cradling a bottle of Thunderbird. His drinking led to his early discharge from the military in March 1981.

he did try—he found pleasure in visions of homosexual activity and human mutilation. In the real world Dahmer was miserable—almost alone, friendless, empty. But his fantasies gave him unalloyed joy. With little effort he found endless rapture within his private world; there he could dance, and more, with the dead.

Dahmer's will was never strong. He gave up Christianity. He dabbled in the occult and Satanism but discarded them. His own fantasies were more satisfying than anything the outside world had to offer. So he set about augmenting those fantasies. At the blood bank, finding one donor attractive, Dahmer concealed a vial of the young man's blood so he could take it home and drink it. The experiment was a failure, however. Rather than expanding the frontiers of solitary sex, the blood was simply distasteful.

That incident aside, Dahmer stayed clear of trouble that winter and spring. But in the summer of 1982 the blood bank, in an economy move, laid him off. He had time on his hands, no prospects, and his unemployment checks provided just about enough money for cigarettes—Dahmer was a heavy smoker—and booze. He was chronically broke and depressed. On August 8 he went to the Wisconsin State Fair in Milwaukee and got drunk. More than 20 people complained that he exposed himself to them. He was fined $50 for drunk and disorderly conduct.

The arrest caused a pause in Dahmer's slide: He later claimed that he fought mightily against his homosexual impulses and more lethal urges—until sometime in 1983. Still unemployed, Dahmer spent many of his afternoons reading in the West Allis library. One day a man walked by and dropped a note in his lap; could they meet in the second-floor men's room for a brief sexual encounter? Dahmer managed to resist the offer, but the effort seemed to shred any remaining fibers of his will. Soon he took to cruising Milwaukee's adult bookstores and peep shows, and then the gay bars and bathhouses.

In Milwaukee, as in other cities during the 1970s and early 1980s, homosexuality had come out of the closet. With the enormity of the AIDS epidemic not yet fully recognized, gay liberation meant in some quarters that behavior that had once been suppressed was now indulged, and conduct once hidden was now public. Formerly discreet liaisons were conducted openly. Bars and other gathering places that had advertised only circumspectly, if at all, now flamboyantly displayed their patrons' preferences. And the clubs, bars, and bathhouses made it clear to their clientele that they would cater to any tastes. Sometimes those tastes ran toward violence. There were predators among those who lived the gay nightlife in the city, and there was vulnerable prey.

In Milwaukee's warehouse district along South Second Street, the favorite gay bars included La Cage aux Folles, the Phoenix, C'Est La Vie, and the Club 219, the last easily distinguished from its lackluster straight neighbors by a purple awning and a hot pink neon sign. Embraced by the bar's dark interior, a patron could sit for hours on one of the club's black barstools, gazing at pictures of bikini-clad men hanging on the nightclub's black walls, until he struck up a conversation with someone who, like himself, was looking for sex.

At the time that Jeffrey Dahmer entered the scene, one of the most popular meeting places for gay men in Milwaukee was the Club Baths. The place's dress code was simple: a towel loosely wrapped around the waist. In the steamy front rooms men drank and mingled. Pairing off, they retired to cozy, mirrored, private parlors where they could, for $10 a night, lock the door, forget the rest of the world, and pursue their own pleasures. Jeffrey Dahmer frequented the Club Baths and, like most patrons, found the facilities congenial.

Dahmer's months of unemployment ended in January of 1985, when he was hired as a mixer at the Ambrosia Chocolate Company in downtown Milwaukee. The job paid $8.25 per hour, more than he'd ever earned before. A semblance of order returned to his life, although his fantasies continued to take form and intrude on reality. On September 8, 1986, he was arrested for masturbating in front of two 12-year-old boys on the banks of Milwaukee's Kinnickinnic River. Dahmer confessed to this and five other

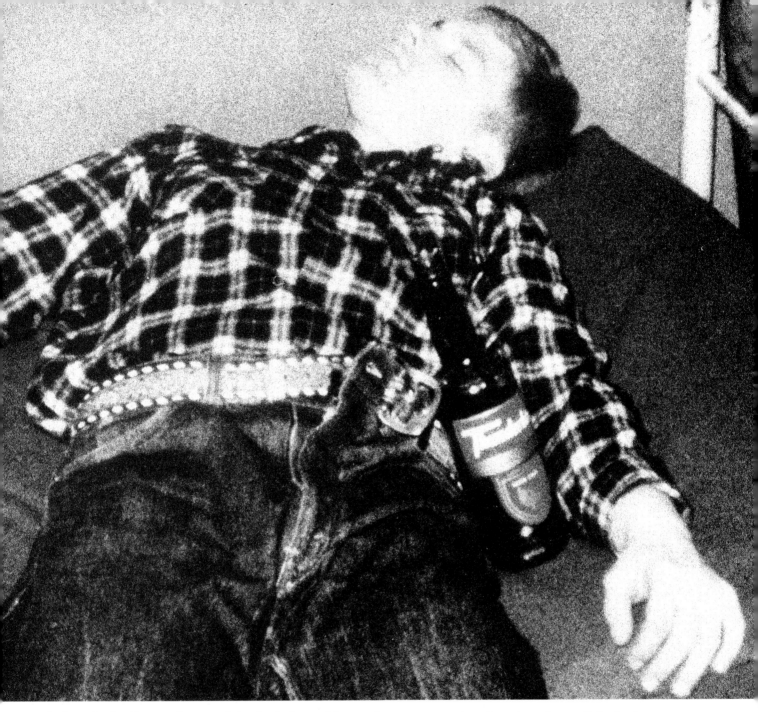

similar episodes. In court he agreed that he had a problem and promised to seek help. The charge of lewd and lascivious behavior was reduced to disorderly conduct and he was sentenced to one year's probation and required to enter therapy. (He would see the therapist for about a year, telling her nothing of importance.) He kept his job at the chocolate factory.

Dahmer continued to make the rounds of Milwaukee's gay nightspots. He frequented the Club Baths on weekends and occasionally during the week, going directly there after his night shift ended at the chocolate factory. In the course of a weekend, he customarily took three or four companions, one at a time, into the privacy of the back rooms. There his tastes grew increasingly exotic and aberrational. When their passion was spent, Dahmer's partners often fell asleep. It was then that he most enjoyed being with them. He listened to their hearts, and while they slept he found his most profound gratification.

Dahmer, however, desired a level of passivity that living, breathing companions couldn't quite offer. He stole a mannequin from a local department store and used it for two weeks until his grandmother made him get rid of it. He then turned from the merely lifeless to the formerly living: He began scanning the newspaper obituaries for likely com-

Home from the army, Jeffrey *(right)* joins his father, Lionel, and younger brother, David, for this portrait of the three Dahmer males.

Arrested for exposing himself at the Wisconsin State Fair, Jeffrey Dahmer poses for a Milwaukee County sheriff's office mug shot in August 1982.

panions. In January of 1985 he found one, an 18-year-old boy who had been killed in an automobile accident. He visited the funeral home, viewed the youth's body, liked what he saw, and—fantasies at full throttle—a few nights after the funeral took a shovel and a wheelbarrow to the cemetery to dig through the frozen ground and retrieve the corpse. The work was hard and slow, however, and Dahmer was frightened by the night noises—a dog barking, an owl hooting. He gave up and went home.

Dahmer then sought to impose passivity on his partners at the Club Baths. With a plausible story that his night work made sleeping difficult, he persuaded several doctors to prescribe sleeping pills. He rarely took the drugs himself, but added them to rum-and-coke cocktails that he mixed for his bathhouse companions. They fell unconscious quickly and quietly, and Jeffrey had never enjoyed himself so much.

But not all of Dahmer's partners appreciated the experience as much as he did. Several suspected they were being drugged and complained to the Club Baths management, which was slow to act. Then, during the summer of 1987, one of Dahmer's drugged companions couldn't be revived. Paramedics were called, and the man was hospitalized for two weeks. Dahmer was among those questioned by police in connection with the incident, but the victim was unwilling to press charges and the whole matter was dropped. However, the Baths management at last banned Dahmer from the premises. He began picking up his partners at bars and taking them to the Ambassador Hotel, a seedy, no-questions-asked establishment frequented by prostitutes.

One night a while after he'd been thrown out of the Club Baths, Dahmer dropped in at the Club 219, where he met Steven Tuomi, a 28-year-old aspiring artist who made his living as a short-order cook. Dahmer enticed Tuomi to the Ambassador, where the guest accepted one of Dahmer's distinctive cocktails—rum and coke laced with half a dozen crushed sleeping pills. Dahmer himself drank nondrugged booze heavily and eventually passed out. According to him, he remembered nothing more until he awoke, naked, lying on top of Tuomi. The artist's chest was bruised, and blood trickled from his mouth. He was dead. With that discovery, Dahmer slipped into his most grotesque fantasies. When he was satisfied, he began to confront reality. His own forearms were black and blue, so he concluded that he must have killed Steven Tuomi. It was September 15, 1987.

Dahmer stuffed the body into a closet and hurried to a nearby shopping mall, where he bought a large suitcase. Returning to the Ambassador he rented the room for one more night, stuffed Tuomi's remains into the suitcase, and took a cab to his grandmother's house. Slipping in through the separate outside entrance that led to his basement room, the killer hid the corpse in Catherine Dahmer's fruit cellar for about a week before beginning the grisly task of cutting it up. He later told a psychiatrist that he became aroused when he slit open Tuomi's abdomen and examined the colors and textures of his victim's entrails. Having extracted what awful delight he could from those parts, Dahmer got down to the business of dismemberment. He put chunks of flesh into large plastic trash bags and left them for the garbage collector. The bones, except for the skull, he wrapped in a sheet and crushed with a hammer. After calling a taxidermist for information on preserving bones, he bleached the skull and used it in his fantasies for about a week before putting it into the garbage. Tuomi's remains were never found.

Dahmer's public facade of calm if distant amiability remained intact. He stayed with his grandmother, went to work at the chocolate factory every afternoon, and remained a regular at Milwaukee's gay bars. In mid-January of 1988—four months after he did away with Steven Tuomi, Dahmer encountered 14-year-old James Doxtator at a bus stop near the Club 219. Doxtator, a six-foot-tall Native American, caught the older man's attention imme-

In the shadows of Milwaukee's glittering lakeside skyscrapers, an active and sometimes predatory gay life unfolds in such bars as Club 219 *(above)* and La Cage *(right)* on the city's run-down South Second Street, south of the rail yard. Dahmer drugged the companions he picked up on these streets—an experimental prelude to his practice of sedating the men he killed.

In September 1987 Dahmer woke up
in this seedy Milwaukee hotel, a site of
every kind of assignation, with Steven
Tuomi dead beside him.

diately: He was dark, slim, and attractive. Doxtator was also amenable to Dahmer's offer of money, so the two caught the next bus to West Allis and Catherine Dahmer's house.

Starting with Doxtator, Dahmer substituted rum and coffee for the customary rum-and-coke offering to his guests. The finishing touch—ground sleeping pills—remained unchanged. When Doxtator passed out, Dahmer strangled him, had sex with the corpse, then hid the body. By and large, the killing had followed the murderer's standard routine, but there was a difference far more telling than the switch from coke to coffee: Dahmer, although he'd hidden a body in his grandmother's house, had never before killed there. Death was coming closer to home.

Doxtator's remains ended up temporarily in the fruit cellar. A week after the murder, while Mrs. Dahmer attended church, Jeffrey, in a state of high excitement, dismembered his latest victim, keeping as a memento Jamie Doxtator's skull.

Jeffrey Dahmer continued to haunt the bars, and near closing time on March 24, 1988, he picked up 22-year-old Richard Guerrero at the Phoenix, just down the street from the Club 219. In Catherine Dahmer's basement Guerrero succumbed to Dahmer's drugged drinks. Dahmer then killed him, defiled the body, cut it up, threw the pieces in the garbage, and kept the skull as a remembrance.

Dahmer's routine took on the trappings of a twisted liturgy. The drink ingredients were kept ready. A leather belt was at hand for garroting his victims; a set of knives stood by for dismembering them. He performed his dissections naked: It was, he confessed later, so much tidier that way.

Not all who ended up in Jeffrey Dahmer's company ended up dead. Soon after Richard Guerrero became Dahmer's fourth victim, Ronald Flowers drank from Jeffrey's cup. But the host concluded that Flowers was unattractive—too big for his taste—and when the drugs and alcohol wore off, Flowers simply left. One or two other visitors—the names withheld by authorities or forgotten by the killer himself—enjoyed a similar reprieve.

Ever since Jeffrey had come to live with her, Catherine Dahmer had played the role of loving, understanding grandparent. If she couldn't ignore his drinking, his frequent absences, and his sordid sideswipes with the law, the odd hours he kept and the even odder company, she did her best to be tolerant and understanding. But Dahmer didn't always make it easy for her to live with him. Once she started down the stairs to his basement room when he was entertaining a guest and Dahmer shouted, "Don't come down here! You don't want to come down here!" She later said that she thought Jeffrey and his friend were both naked.

In early 1988 an unfamiliar smell began to rise from the basement, and Catherine called her son, Jeffrey's father, to come to Wisconsin and investigate. Lionel Dahmer searched the premises—for what, he had no idea—but found nothing but an unidentifiable glob of black sludge oozing from a garbage can. Jeffrey soothed his father with a story about bleaching a chicken carcass to see what the bones looked like, and leaving the flesh in the garbage. Then he changed the story, saying he'd dissected and discarded a raccoon that he'd found dead in the street. Lionel, remembering similar projects from his son's childhood, accepted the second yarn, but told Jeffrey that he thought such behavior was weird.

Even though he could find nothing too terribly alarming in his son's behavior, it was clear to Lionel Dahmer that it was time for Jeffrey to leave Catherine Dahmer's house. The younger Dahmer was nearly 28 years old, after all, employed, and apparently healthy. It was time for him to find his own place. In September of 1988 Jeffrey moved to a run-down brown brick building at 808 North 24th Street—and soon gave his father reason to question the wisdom of the relocation.

At about 3:30 on the afternoon after he moved, Dahmer was walking about a block away from his apartment when he encountered a young Laotian boy who was returning home from school. He approached the boy, saying that he wanted to try out a new camera. Would the boy pose for $50? The youngster would, and he followed Dahmer to his apartment. Once they were inside, Dahmer fondled the youth and plied him with a cup of coffee mixed with Irish Cream liqueur and crushed sleeping pills. Dahmer shot two Polaroid photos and then sent the youngster on his way.

The lad arrived home safely, but soon began mumbling incoherently. Then he lapsed into unconsciousness. His parents took him to the hospital, where doctors detected drugs and called the police. Meanwhile, Dahmer had reported for work as usual at the Ambrosia chocolate factory, and it was there at his giant mixing machine that police arrested him early the next morning. He was charged with sexual exploitation of a child and second-degree assault. Dahmer calmly explained away the evidence. The drugging had been accidental, he told police. The boy happened to use a cup that Dahmer ordinarily used to take his own prescription sleeping pills. The suspect insisted that he had no idea how young the boy was and, at any rate, he hadn't molested him. The police didn't buy it all, but the charges were nevertheless eventually reduced. The exploitation charge was changed to enticing a child for immoral purposes; the assault charge stayed the same. Dahmer's father guaranteed his $10,000 bail, and Jeffrey was free.

In less than a year, three victims had been sacrificed to Jeffrey Dahmer's cravings, two had narrowly missed the same fate, and the killer's pace seemed to be accelerating. But the brush with the law brought on a pause of nearly a year—until March 25, 1989, when Dahmer encountered 24-year-old Anthony Sears, a handsome black restaurant manager and aspiring male model. They met around closing time at La Cage, one of the gay bars clustered along South Second Street at the edge of the city's downtown. Sears was described by family members as a "photo fanatic," and perhaps Dahmer persuaded him to pose. Maybe, as he told police, he merely offered Sears money for sex.

Whatever the enticement, later that night a friend of Sears dropped the pair off at a bar in West Allis near Catherine Dahmer's house. They walked the rest of the way to Jeffrey's former basement room, where the familiar ritual of drugged drink, necrophilic sex, and butchery was played out. Dahmer worked through the night to clean up the evidence, finishing up by boiling the flesh from Sears's head and painting the skull. He also kept his guest's scalp and genitals. As Dahmer put the final touches to his latest horror the sun was rising. It was Easter Sunday.

On January 30, 1989, a court had convicted Dahmer of molesting the Laotian youth, and on May 23 he was sentenced. At the sentencing hearing his attorney, Gerald Boyle, argued that the case was a single incident, unlikely to be repeated. Dahmer spoke to Judge William Gardner on his own behalf, begging the jurist, "Please don't destroy my life. I know I deserve a great deal of punishment. I do want help. I want to turn my life around despite what the prosecution has told you." Prosecutor Gale Shelton, pointing out Dahmer's earlier arrests for public exposure, argued that the man belonged in jail. Judge Gardner didn't entirely agree. He imposed a one-year work-release sentence.

The arrangement allowed Dahmer to continue working at the chocolate factory while spending his nights in the Milwaukee House of Corrections. He was considered a model prisoner—so untroublesome that he received a 12-hour pass to visit his family on Thanksgiving Day. After dinner at Catherine Dahmer's house with his father, stepmother, and grandmother, he fled first to a local bar, then to his favorite haunts along South Second Street. Drinking heavily, he eventually wandered into the Club 219.

Sometime after blacking out from drinking too much, Dahmer apparently found a kindred spirit, someone nearly as predatory and depraved as himself. It was the bearded, dark-haired companion who took him home and trussed him up for some kinky, painful sex. When Dahmer escaped from his host's spider web he rushed back to jail, hours overdue. He was penalized

ANTHONY SEARS

Picked up at La Cage, Anthony Sears was Dahmer's fifth murder, just two months before his sentencing for molesting a boy.

After he was released from prison in 1990, Dahmer moved into number 213 at the Oxford Apartments *(right),* to which he lured men like Raymond Lamont Smith *(inset)* with promises of booze and money for posing nude.

two days of good behavior time. Nevertheless, he received a pass for Christmas Day and again returned with liquor on his breath. But with two months off for good behavior, Dahmer was freed on March 2, 1990. He moved back in with his grandmother. By early May, however, he was back on his own, having rented unit 213 in the Oxford Apartments at 924 North 25th Street.

On May 29 Dahmer encountered his sixth victim, Raymond Lamont "Cash D" Smith, a small-time burglar and hustler who also went by the name Ricky Beeks and several other aliases. Smith's fate followed the established ritual, and Dahmer added Smith's preserved skull, which he later painted gray, to his growing collection.

On his release from jail, Dahmer began reporting regularly to a probation officer, Donna Chester, whose notes revealed, if not a murderous Jeffrey Dahmer, at least a decidedly unappealing one: She described him as a self-pitying whiner who did nothing to take control of his life. He complained about his parents. He told Chester that he'd been mugged several times, was hospitalized after one incident, and was now beset by the hospital, which was threatening to sue over the bill. He was even considering suicide, he told Chester. She suggested declaring bankruptcy instead.

Dahmer griped to Chester about having to live in a dangerous neighborhood. In fact, the area around the Oxford Apartments did fall far short of Milwaukee's finest; it regularly led the city's crime statistics. Many of its buildings were run-down—once-proud mansions now converted to seedy rooming houses, apartments, halfway houses, and group homes for the indigent aged and the mentally ill. Although the neighborhood housed a high proportion of the unemployed, the unemployable, and transients, Milwaukee's highly segregated housing market also forced many respectable black working families to live there too. The Oxford and its residents were considered a cut above other buildings and tenants in the area. Police seldom had to make calls at the Oxford.

Chester—perhaps influenced by Dahmer's tales of woe—considered the neighborhood so dangerous that she never visited apartment 213 at the Oxford. If she had, its appearance would not have set off any alarms. The door opened on a neat living room containing a sofa, chairs, dining table, television, and lamps. A fish tank stood on a table in one corner, and a potted plant decorated a pedestal by the window. The kitchen occupied a niche off the living room, with

a stove, refrigerator, and sink. Dahmer added a low freezer. The bedroom contained a nondescript but neatly kept collection of furniture.

Chester would have had little use for Dahmer's taste in literature and the arts: Audiotapes ran to heavy-metal music, and there was an extensive collection of videos of hardcore gay pornography. There were also tapes of four of Dahmer's favorite movies, *The Exorcist I* and *II* (these films suggested to him the yellow contact lenses he took to wearing in order to look satanic) and *Hellraiser I* and *II.* Sandwiched among the other works were a recorded version of the King James Bible and two books on numerology.

Dahmer's dissatisfaction with his new environs was probably aggravated by the fact that they were all the way across town from his favorite gay-bar haunts. He didn't own a car, and late at night, when the city buses had stopped running, he was forced to ride cabs from the South Second Street strip to his home. When he had a potential victim in tow, Dahmer had to take an extra precaution against being identified: He always had the cab drop them at an all-night store a couple of blocks from the Oxford. After he bought cigarettes or beer, Dahmer would walk his victim to his fate.

That is what he did on the night of June 14, 1990, after Dahmer met Eddie "the Sheik" Smith at the Phoenix bar. Smith, a 24-year-old tall and flamboyant ex-dancer, enjoyed flaunting his gay lifestyle by wearing makeup and the turban that prompted his nickname. Promising Smith that he'd take his picture, Dahmer led him to apartment 213. The Sheik was victim number seven. And Dahmer did, indeed, take his picture. He took five photographs of Smith's dismemberment, then put four of them in plastic bags that also held body parts. The bags were left behind the Oxford to be picked up by the garbage collector.

About a month after dispatching Smith, Dahmer picked up a 15-year-old boy outside the Phoenix and offered him $200 to pose for nude photographs. The two went to Dahmer's apartment where, the killer later said, they had "normal homosexual sex," then agreed to meet the following evening at the Phoenix. Ordinarily, on that second night, the host would have plied his guest with sleeping pills and liquor. But Dahmer's prescription had run out and he prepared a more cost-effective method of subduing his prey: While the boy lay on his stomach on the bed, Dahmer hit him in the back of the head with a rubber mallet.

Instead of losing consciousness, the boy jumped to his feet

RAYMOND LAMONT SMITH

This joined pair of police photographs shows the inside of Oxford Apartment 213, the stage on which Dahmer played out his gruesome variations of passion and murder 12 more times. Praised by his landlord as a neat housekeeper, Dahmer added such homey touches as a fish tank *(far right)* and a lava lamp *(center)*. A wall-mounted dummy video camera *(right, above portrait)* reassured visitors with an illusion of tight security. Although a freezer *(below)* was used to preserve some severed body parts, the apartment so reeked of death that Dahmer's neighbors often complained.

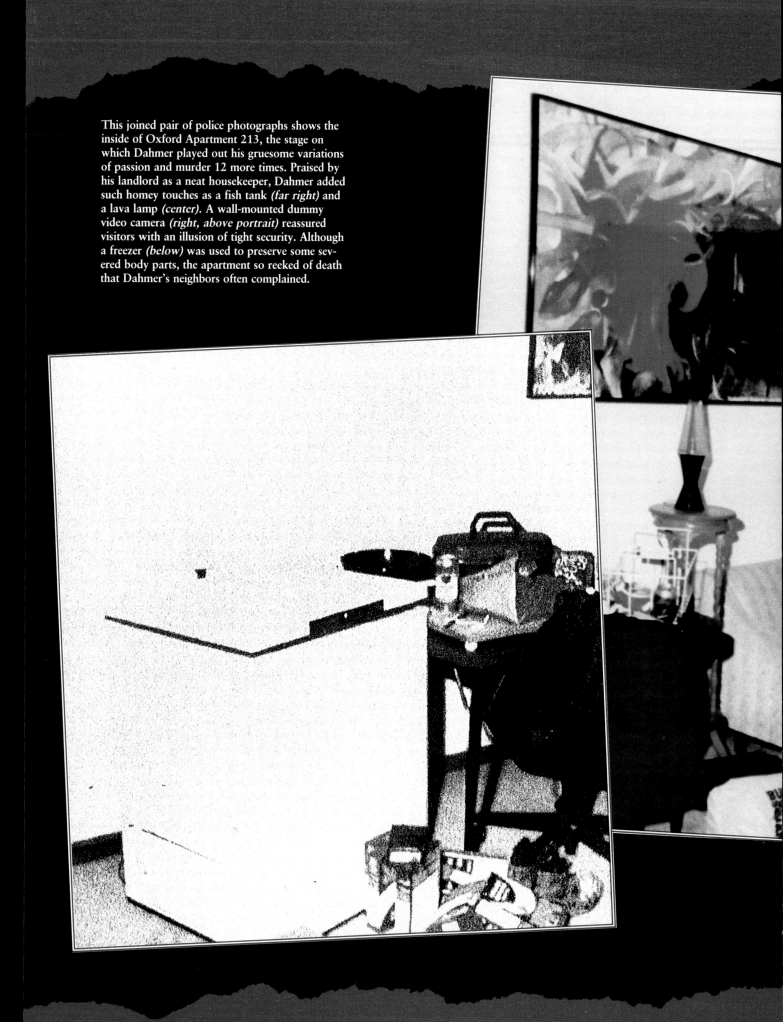

and began fighting. He and Dahmer wrestled to the floor, and eventually Dahmer got the youngster under control. He told the boy that he'd hit him because he was afraid the boy would run off with Dahmer's money before he could take any more photos. After a night of cajolery, Dahmer felt confident that there would be no police report, and he allowed the boy to leave early the next morning. Although the boy's foster mother reported the assault to police, the youngster himself claimed he couldn't remember where Dahmer lived. Once again, the monster escaped detection.

As he met and dispatched his eighth victim that September, Dahmer's fantasies launched him toward new levels of depravity. Ernest Miller was a handsome, muscular 23-year-old dancer who was lured by Dahmer with an offer of money for sex and modeling services. But once he'd drugged his guest, Dahmer revised his ritual. Rather than strangling Miller, he slit his throat, then slipped his body into the bathtub for dismemberment. When the murderer had removed most of the flesh, he hung Miller's skeleton from the shower head and photographed it. Another memento.

But evidently a photo alone was not enough to properly memorialize the marvelous muscles and the energy that had first attracted Dahmer to Miller. The liturgy of death required revision. Although the flesh had been stripped from Miller's frame, it need not be wasted, Dahmer reasoned. What better way to remember this remarkable person—to help him find a new life—than to eat his flesh?

The idea alone may have been the most arousing event in Dahmer's experience. Awash in his obsessions, he found Miller's heart and biceps—sources of life and strength—treated them with meat tenderizer, fried them, added a steak sauce, and ate them. As he dined, Dahmer drank and drank, and watched a pornographic video. Much later he remembered that Miller's flesh tasted somewhat like beef.

Victim nine followed that same September. He was David Thomas, a 22-year-old black man with a reputation as a street hustler.

In October Dahmer may have made a feeble attempt to stop the carnage when he walked into the Milwaukee County Mental Health Center and asked to see a counselor. But the facility was busy, as usual, and Dahmer was asked to wait. His fervor for reform—if such it was—lasted only 15 minutes before he returned to the street.

In a regular visit to Donna Chester, his probation officer, in January 1991 Dahmer seemed again to sound a subtle

theme of change. He told Chester that he wouldn't be getting into any more trouble because he was afraid of returning to jail. Anyway, he was too busy: Twelve-hour shifts at the chocolate factory left him with little time or energy for misbehavior.

Whatever the sincerity of these sentiments, they didn't match Dahmer's actions. On February 18 Curtis Straughter, a handsome 17-year-old high-school dropout who dabbled in songwriting and dreamed of a modeling career, became an easy target for Dahmer's offer of money for posing. After the killer had dispatched victim 10, he kept Straughter's skull, hands, and genitals as mementos. By now Dahmer had acquired two plastic vats that he filled with acid; Straughter's remaining flesh and bones went into them.

During Dahmer's March visit to Chester—about a month after the Straughter killing—the probation officer noted that his spirits had improved greatly. After a five-year estrangement, Dahmer's mother had telephoned him from Fresno, California, where she was working as an AIDS counselor. It had been a good conversation, Dahmer said, and he felt that he and his mother would continue to improve their relationship. But if the familial contact cheered him, it did nothing to stop the killing. In fact, the murders accelerated. Dahmer killed three more young men during the next two months—slayings with new derangements.

The first of the three victims was a jovial, outgoing 19-year-old named Errol Lindsey, whom Dahmer met on April 7, 1991. Lindsey quickly succumbed to the combination of money, sex, and knockout pills. But he didn't die quickly. Dahmer's fantasy world had always been peopled by compliant slaves who would willingly carry out his every wish—mindless zombies who were at once dead and alive. And the luckless Lindsey became the guinea pig for a gruesome experiment aimed at fulfilling the killer's sick dream. Intending to eradicate Lindsey's will and transform him into the ultimate passive love slave, Dahmer set about to perform a lobotomy on his drugged guest.

With a small electric drill, Dahmer bored two holes in Lindsey's head, then used a culinary syringe—a turkey baster—to inject acid into the victim's brain cavity. To Dahmer's amazement and distress, Lindsey awoke after the bizarre procedure and complained of a headache. Disappointed in the failure of his experiment, Dahmer gave Lindsey some more sleeping pills and strangled him. After performing his usual rites, the murderer preserved the skull,

After murdering Ernest Miller *(top)*, Dahmer ate the dancer's heart and biceps. He drilled a hole in the head of Errol Lindsey *(middle)* and filled it with acid; but when the amateur lobotomy failed to turn Lindsey into a love slave, Dahmer killed him. Popular deaf-mute Tony Hughes *(bottom)* was Dahmer's 12th victim.

ERNEST MILLER

ERROL LINDSEY

TONY HUGHES

took photographs, and consigned Lindsey's flesh and bones to the acid vats.

As he cultivated his vision of a zombie harem, Dahmer also dreamed up a use for his growing collection of skulls and body parts. They would become elements in what he would later describe as a "temple"—an altar on which would be arrayed the carefully cleaned and painted skulls, bones, and other parts of his victims. Black paint, cloth, and candles would decorate the display. A skeleton would guard either end. Immersed in his grotesque fantasies, Dahmer saw the arrangement as a shrine. The skulls, he said, were no mere trophies but contained the "true essence" of his prey. By keeping the heads he could sustain his relationships with the men and boys he'd killed.

Less than two months after dispatching Lindsey, Dahmer killed Tony Hughes, an enormously popular, cheerful deaf-mute who used sign language, lipreading, and pen and paper to keep up lively conversations with his many friends at the gay bars. As peaceable as he was affable, Hughes went to great lengths to avoid violence. In July of 1990, following the murder of a neighbor in his Milwaukee apartment building, he'd moved to Madison, Wisconsin, to be safer. Returning to Milwaukee to visit his mother in May 1991, Hughes decided to work in a little time with his old friends on the club circuit. Unfortunately, Dahmer happened to be among those old friends.

One of the notes that passed between Dahmer and Hughes contained an offer of $50 for sex. Dahmer told police that he couldn't remember if the two had actually consummated their arrangement. He did, however, remember that both he and Hughes passed out in Dahmer's apartment, and when Dahmer woke up, he found that his intended victim had died. Dahmer, who was never able to account for how Hughes expired, laid the body out on his bed and went on with his life. It was May 24.

Hughes's corpse was still in the bedroom two days later when Dahmer went to the Grand Avenue Mall and there he discovered Konerak Sinthasomphone, a 14-year-old Laotian whose family had settled in Milwaukee after fleeing Laos 10 years earlier. Konerak was a child of the streets. Although his family described him as a shy boy who enjoyed fishing with his father and roaming the inner city on his bike, police knew him as a juvenile prostitute.

Perhaps Dahmer did, too, because these boys tended to prowl the streets of the strip. Maybe he knew the boy be-

cause the family lived in his neighborhood. Perhaps Dahmer even knew that Konerak was the younger brother of the Laotian boy whom he'd molested back in 1988. That incident had led to Dahmer's arrest and conviction; the encounter with Konerak nearly had a similar result.

On May 26, 1991, Konerak was supposed to have been on his way to Mitchell Park to play in a soccer match. Instead, he accepted an invitation to Dahmer's apartment. There Dahmer had the boy pose for two photographs. The two watched a video, and Dahmer slipped Konerak a drug-spiked drink. With the boy unconscious, Dahmer had sex with him, drank beer, and watched videos. At some point he once again attempted his zombie experiment by drilling small holes in Konerak's head and injecting acid.

In the course of the evening, Dahmer ran out of beer and decided to leave his unconscious guest to buy more. But instead he went to the Care Bear Tavern on North 27th Street and drank until closing time. When he returned to the Oxford, he found Kon-

Hunting in the Grand Avenue Mall *(right)*, Jeffrey Dahmer picked up 14-year-old Konerak Sinthasomphone. When the drugged Laotian boy escaped, the killer persuaded police that the problem was just a lovers' spat. Once he had the boy back in 213, Dahmer strangled him.

erak sitting on the curb, dazed and naked. Before he could get the boy on his feet and back into the apartment, a crowd gathered. Someone called 911, and police and firefighters soon arrived. Dahmer, smiling and confident, convinced the police that the Laotian was an adult, and that the pair were homosexual lovers who were having a domestic spat.

Konerak, staggering and jabbering incoherently after his ordeal, could neither do nor say anything to defend himself. Some of the bystanders were insisting that Dahmer had injured the boy, and asked the police to rescue him from Dahmer. Nevertheless, the officers and firefighters apparently concluded that Konerak was not seriously injured, despite the fact that he was, according to witnesses, bleeding from the rectum. The authorities also seem to have missed any evidence of a lobotomy. Over the neighbors' protests, police made ready to let Konerak and Dahmer go. But first they wanted to check out Dahmer's apartment.

As the body of Tony Hughes lay rotting on the bed in the next room, Dahmer led the officers into his living room, where he calmly showed them Konerak's neatly folded clothes and the Polaroid photographs he had taken earlier. One cop commented that the apartment smelled like someone had defecated there. Then the police left. Dahmer immediately strangled Konerak, making the youth his 13th victim. He completed his fantasy rituals, stashing the boy's skull with others and dissolving the rest of his corpse in acid. While he was at it, he also disposed of Hughes's remains in an acid vat.

Saturday, June 29, 1991, found Jeffrey Dahmer in Chicago at the annual Gay Pride Parade—certainly, for him, a staggering bounty of potential victims. And so it proved. At the Greyhound bus station in Chicago's Loop, Dahmer met a slender young black man who introduced himself as Donald Montrell. A 20-year-old runaway whose real name was Matt Turner, Montrell had been living at a halfway house on Chicago's North Side. Dahmer, lavishly complimenting the destitute man's physique, offered to pay him to pose nude. After the 90-mile bus ride to Milwaukee, the two ended up in Dahmer's apartment, where Turner downed Dahmer's deadly potion and became his 14th victim.

A few days later Dahmer returned to Chicago for the long Fourth of July weekend. At 4 p.m. on Saturday, July 6, he left a gay bar called Carol's Speakeasy with 23-year-old Jeremiah Weinberger in tow. Weinberger, who worked as a customer service representative for a gay adult film com-

pany, fell for Dahmer's money-for-posing offer and went willingly to the killer's Milwaukee slaughterhouse at the Oxford Apartments.

Dahmer later offered two conflicting accounts of how Weinberger died. In his confession to police, he said that the pair spent the better part of two days together in his apartment—an incredible feat on Weinberger's part, considering the vile smells that permeated the place. On the second day Weinberger wanted to leave, and it was then, said Dahmer, that he administered the doped drink and then strangled his sleeping guest.

But later Dahmer told a psychologist that he doped Weinberger early on the first day and attempted another zombie experiment, this time using the drill and boiling water. Astonishingly, Weinberger survived the ordeal and regained partial consciousness. Dahmer tried the experiment again, this time managing to put his guest into a coma. Dahmer then went off to work. On his return, Weinberger was dead—a severe disappointment, since Dahmer had looked forward to a conversation with his guest.

Whatever the details of the murder, Weinberger's head wound up in Dahmer's freezer next to that of Matt Turner. Weinberger's body went into the bathtub. Dahmer planned to dispose of it later. Weinberger was victim number 15, the fourth in a month and a half.

The rate of killing created a host of difficulties for the murderer. He was running out of storage space, for one thing. Boiled skulls filled his closet. Decapitated heads and body parts crowded his refrigerator and freezer. Weinberger's corpse lay in his bathtub. By now Dahmer had replaced his two plastic vats with one 57-gallon drum of acid. Its contents had become a sludgy mess of flesh and bones. Worse, Dahmer's neighbors were beginning to wonder about the smell emanating from apartment 213. He told one that his freezer had broken down and that all its contents had spoiled. Another neighbor noted that the cats that frequented the building's Dumpster seemed particularly interested in Dahmer's garbage.

As Dahmer devoted more and more time to his deadly fantasies, real life began to close in on him. He was often late for work. Sometimes he never showed up. When he called in sick on the Monday after murdering Weinberger, the management at the Ambrosia Chocolate Company, finally fed up with his absenteeism, fired him from the job he'd held for seven years. He hadn't paid his rent for several

KONERAK SINTHASOMPHONE

months, and he was being evicted from his apartment at the end of July. His grandmother—the one person who'd shown consistent regard for him—was in the hospital. Dahmer called probation officer Donna Chester to tell her that he'd lost his job, was deeply depressed, and was thinking of committing suicide. Concerned, she set up an appointment for the two of them to meet and discuss what she called his "relapse."

But if Dahmer's firing depressed him, it also left him free to follow his morbid pursuits. A few days after he was let go by Ambrosia, he picked up Oliver Lacy, a 24-year-old bodybuilder and former high-school track star, near a bar and liquor store on 27th Street, a few blocks from the Oxford. Dahmer's polished routine began with an offer of money for posing and ended a few hours later with death and sex. Lacy's head, heart, and biceps were preserved in the refrigerator; the rest of his remains went into the garbage. He was victim number 16.

With his eviction looming, Dahmer was told by his probation officer to start a serious job hunt and report back before the end of the month. That may be why he was riding a downtown bus on Friday afternoon, July 19, when he spotted Joseph Bradehoft standing at a bus stop with a six-pack of beer under his arm. Dahmer jumped from his own bus, approached the gangly young man, and offered his standard—and apparently foolproof—modeling come-on. Soon the two were on their way to the Oxford Apartments. At about 6 p.m., while Dahmer's neighbors were eating their suppers, Bradehoft's head went into the freezer. He was number 17.

Dahmer had now been killing at the rate of almost one victim every week. With an apparently seamless portrayal of normality, Dahmer lured males from bars, street corners, bus stations, and shopping centers. Many of his victims were African Americans or other people of color. Most were homosexual hustlers, small-time criminals, or poor people susceptible to an offer of a little easy money. They were borderline lives whose marginality not only made them easy marks for Dahmer, but probably helped explain why their disappearance caused so little stir in Milwaukee. By most measures, Jeffrey Dahmer was a one-man crime wave, but no one seemed to notice.

Until the night of Monday, July 22, 1991. Cruising the Grand Avenue Mall, Dahmer ran into 32-year-old Tracy Edwards, a small-time grifter who was himself cruising the mall with two friends. He knew Dahmer from the neighborhood where they both lived, and he considered him harmless, soft-spoken, and friendly—a regular guy, likable enough despite his phony claim of being a professional photographer.

When Dahmer asked the three if they'd be interested in earning $100 each for posing for a few pictures, Edwards and his friends hedged; they'd think about it. Fine, Dahmer said. In the meantime maybe they should all get together for a party. He'd buy the beer and rum.

Free drinks and easy money worked their usual magic. Off they all went to a local liquor store, where they stocked up for the party. Edwards's two friends left to pick up their girlfriends while Edwards himself helped Dahmer carry the supplies back to the Oxford. From there the scenario played as if Dahmer had written it from the beginning. He'd given Edwards's friends the wrong address; he wouldn't be bothered by them again.

Even before he entered Dahmer's apartment, Edwards noticed the stench and joked that it smelled "like someone died in there." Dahmer told him that a sewer pipe had broken, an explanation that Edwards, a former construction worker, found plausible. Except for the smell, Edwards would relate later, he thought that unit 213 looked "like a normal apartment." He was curious, however, about some acid boxes he saw near the door. Dahmer explained that he sometimes used acid to clean bricks. Again, Edwards thought the explanation made sense. The two sat on the sofa talking amiably about military life. Edwards, the son of a career air force man, had grown up on military bases. Dahmer asked again if Edwards was interested in posing for some photographs, and again the guest put him off. Unoffended, Dahmer presented Edwards with a beer and his special rum-and-coke-and-drugs cocktail. Edwards sipped the mixed drink politely.

The drama that Dahmer had so carefully constructed—that he'd no doubt rehearsed and relished in fantasy—was beginning to stall. None of his previous guests had failed to gulp down the doped drink. The killer was running out of ideas. The amiable facade that lulled his other guests was having no effect on Edwards. Unaccustomed to having things go wrong, Dahmer grew increasingly tense. Finally he snapped. From nowhere, it seemed, he pulled out a pair of handcuffs and slapped one cuff onto Edwards's left wrist, taking him completely by surprise. Dahmer then brandished a large military knife and screamed, "Do exactly what I tell you or I'll kill you."

Dahmer guided Edwards into the bedroom, where a videotape of *Exorcist II* was playing. Rocking back and forth and chanting gibberish, Dahmer interrupted himself long enough to threaten Edwards and try cuffing his other wrist. He made Edwards lie on the floor so he could listen to his heartbeat. He told Edwards that he intended to eat his heart. At first the visitor was nearly paralyzed with terror. Then, recovering his wits, he tried to calm his captor. As he looked for a way out, Edwards soothingly told Dahmer that he was his friend.

Edwards's chance for escape came when Dahmer, still slipping in and out of incoherence, gave him permission to use the bathroom. Edwards got off the floor, slugged Dahmer in the head with his fist, kicked him in the chest, and ran for the door. Fumbling with the multiple locks, he finally managed to get out of the deathtrap before Dahmer could recover.

A few blocks away on West Kilbourn, police officers Rolf Mueller and Robert Rauth were sitting in their squad car when they saw something that was, even for police in a high-crime area, a strange sight: Edwards, clothes awry and eyes wild with fear, was sprinting toward them, screaming and waving his arms. From his left wrist flapped Dahmer's handcuffs.

"Which one of us did you escape from?" asked one of the officers, assuming that the runner had somehow broken away from another policeman. Instead of an answer, Rauth and Mueller received a wild, rambling account of a "freak" who'd tried to eat Edwards's heart. Edwards seemed more like an unstable kook than a victim, but the police decided to take him back to the apartment and separate fact from fancy.

The rank smell assaulted the officers as soon as they entered the Oxford. Edwards led them up the steps to apartment 213. They banged on the door, and after a few moments it swung open to reveal Jeffrey Dahmer—calm, smiling, and ready to explain away his latest lovers' quarrel. Inside, the officers asked Dahmer for the handcuff keys. They were in the bedroom, he replied, and as he turned to get them Edwards spoke up. The knife was there, too, he said. Officer Mueller told Dahmer to remain in the living room; he would search for the keys and knife.

The search was short. Glancing into an open dresser drawer, Mueller spotted Dahmer's Polaroid gallery of dismembered bodies, skulls, and Ernest Miller's skeleton hanging from the shower spigot. He yelled to his partner to arrest and handcuff Dahmer. The killer, realizing that his secret was uncovered, tried to resist, but Rauth quickly subdued him. Mueller came out of the bedroom waving a handful of photographs at the badly shaken Edwards. "You're one lucky son of a bitch, buddy," Mueller said, showing him a photo of a severed head. "This could have been you."

Soon Dahmer's apartment was crowded with police officers, forensic experts, photographers, and other technicians. Out of the closet emerged seven skulls and a complete skeleton. In the refrigerator and the freezer the investigators discovered four heads with flesh still on them. And Dahmer's blue plastic barrel contained the acid-bathed torsos of three victims.

The Milwaukee County medical examiner also cataloged a kettle containing decomposed hands and a genital organ, a filing cabinet that held three skulls in the top drawer and assorted bones in the bottom, a computer box holding two skulls and a photographic diary of Dahmer's deeds, and three heads in plastic garbage bags.

News of Dahmer's atrocities quickly spread around the world via television and newspapers. Reporters flocked to Milwaukee in search of details, crowding outside Dahmer's apartment in hopes of interviewing neighbors or anyone else who might know the monster.

As more of the story came out, there were certain local repercussions. Dahmer's penchant for Afri-

After escaping from Dahmer, Tracy Edwards caused the killer's arrest—and his own as well. Edwards is seen here in a Mississippi mug shot after his extradition for rape.

Wearing protective clothing and air tanks, two hazardous-materials specialists gingerly remove a blue 57-gallon drum filled with hydrochloric acid and body parts from Oxford Apartment 213 after Jeffrey Dahmer's arrest.

can American victims abraded racial tensions, which were further aggravated by accounts of how the police had sent Laotian teenager Konerak Sinthasomphone back into apartment 213 to die at Jeffrey Dahmer's hands. Gays and racial minority groups held vigils for victims and protests against the police department. The central complaint was that if the victims had been white, straight, and middle-class, the killer would have been caught a lot sooner. Milwaukee Mayor John Norquist formed a commission to look into this allegation.

Although he escaped with his life, the man who blew the whistle on Dahmer, Tracy Edwards, talked himself into trouble of a different kind. Tabloid newspapers paid Edwards several thousand dollars for interviews, and each was more fantastic than the last. He told wild tales to radio and television talk show audiences—and among those audiences were police from Tupelo, Mississippi, where he was wanted on rape charges. Edwards returned to the South, pleaded guilty to a sexual battery charge, and drew a 10-year sentence—suspended as long as he left Mississippi and never came back. Unaccountably, he did go back, and a warrant was issued for his arrest. As of early 1993, he was still eluding it.

Dahmer's three-week trial began in January of 1992, not to determine whether he'd murdered nearly a score of young men—this Dahmer admitted—but to decide whether he was sane when he killed. As he listened impassively, defense attorney Gerald Boyle had a succession of police officers recite the ghastly details of Dahmer's crimes. He hoped to convince the jury that only a madman was capable of committing such acts. Prosecutor Michael McCann argued that only a sane man could prepare as carefully as Dahmer had and disguise his acts so well. On February 14, after five hours of deliberation, the jury decided that Dahmer was both sane and guilty.

Judge Laurence Gram sentenced him to 15 consecutive life sentences, or roughly 950 years behind bars, with no possibility of parole. There is no capital punishment in Wisconsin. Dahmer subsequently pleaded guilty in Akron, Ohio, to the murder of his first victim, Steven Hicks. He got a 16th life sentence for that crime.

On February 18, 1992, Jeffrey Dahmer began serving his sentence at the Columbia County Correctional Institution, a maximum-security facility in Portage, Wisconsin.

Milwaukee's monster had at last been tamed. ◆

Painted skeletons

A pensive Jeffrey Dahmer enters a Milwaukee County courtroom in August 1991 for the second hearing following his arrest. Charged with 15 counts of first-degree murder he eventually pleaded guilty but insane.

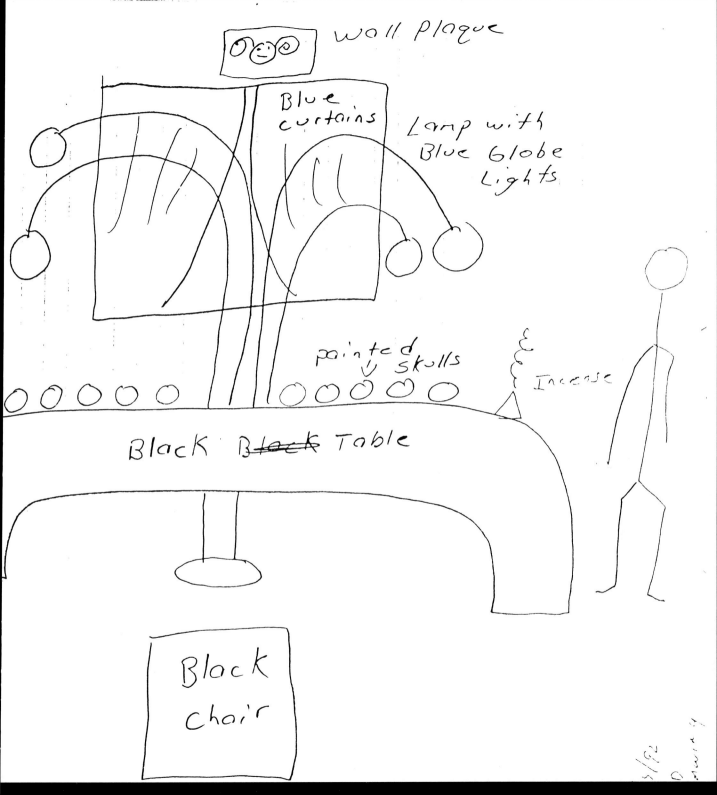

In this "temple," sketched by Dahmer for a psychiatrist, blue globes illuminate skeletons and a rank of painted skulls flanked by incense urns.

During a lighter moment in his 1992 trial, a bemused Jeffrey Dahmer hands an observer a copy of *The Journal,* whose tabloid headline trumpets one murder he did not commit: "Milwaukee Cannibal Kills His Cellmate."

I can't find the
words to express
the sorrow for what
I have done.

KENNETH BIANCHI

2

Cousins

In a bigger city than Bellingham, Washington, the police would have shrugged off the report: Two adult college girls missing for a few hours? Call back in a day or so. Los Angeles police, for instance, had a rule that anyone over the age of 10 had to be gone for at least 24 hours to make the Missing Persons list. But Bellingham had not yet acquired such sophistication. Nestled up against the Canadian border among the inlets of Georgia Strait, the seat of Whatcom County was more a town than a metropolis, with a large aluminum plant and two oil refineries, a thriving tourist trade, and a population of around 46,000. People in Bellingham knew one another, and when someone turned up missing, somebody cared.

Karen Mandic and Diane Wilder were the kind of young women one might expect in such a community—friendly, fresh-faced, lively but conscientious. Both were students at Western Washington University. Mandic, 22, a business major, was a self-reliant sort who insisted on working her way through school even though her parents could have paid her expenses. She shared an off-campus house with her friend Wilder, who at 27 had saved up the money to pursue her passion for Middle Eastern studies. With Wilder's savings and Mandic's evening job at Fred Meyer's department store, the pair did all right, although they still watched their pennies: Mandic even cultivated a summer vegetable garden to hold down the grocery bills.

So it looked like a real windfall when, in early January 1979, a new acquaintance of Mandic's—a young man named Kenneth Bianchi—offered the women $100 each for a couple of hours' housesitting on his behalf. Mandic had met Bianchi when he'd worked as a security guard at the department store. He seemed nice enough—in his middle twenties, handsome, polite. His coworkers at Fred Meyer's knew that he'd come up from Los Angeles the year before, proved himself a whiz at nailing shoplifters, and moved on to Whatcom Security, one of the area's leading guard services. At Whatcom Bianchi had leaped up the chain of command to become operations captain, and he wore an impressively official-looking uniform topped by a captain's double silver bars. A neat police-academy-style mustache completed the effect of a young officer exuding professional know-how.

Bianchi's housesitting pitch to Mandic had been irresistible. A home in the city's affluent Edgemoor section needed some shopwork on its alarm system while the owners were away, he said. The repairs would take about two hours, during which the house and its valuables would be vulnerable to thieves if left unoccupied. Could the two women stay in the place during that short interval? Delighted by the prospect of earning some easy extra cash, Mandic said yes for both of them, and Bianchi made a date for 7 p.m. on Thursday, January 11. He cautioned Mandic not to say anything about the job. Security, he confided. He would meet them at the house.

But Mandic couldn't keep the secret. She had to tell someone about the bit of good luck that had befallen her and Diane, and she picked a friend, Steve Hardwick, himself an officer with the university campus police. Hardwick wondered why anybody would pay so much for so little work, but he more or less accepted Mandic's explanation that the man making the offer was a friend who'd come up with the chore to be helpful.

On Thursday evening Mandic arranged to have a two-hour dinner break, starting at 7. But 9 o'clock came and went and she didn't return. This was highly unusual; Karen was the sort who would call from a roadside pay phone if traffic made her so much as five minutes late. When 11 o'clock rolled around without word from her, the store manager's unease hardened into concern. Not knowing what else to do, he phoned Steve Hardwick. Careful campus cop that he was, Hardwick drove to her house and also to the Edgemoor address that she'd given him—and found no one. Around midnight he called the police to report that two women were missing. This being Bellingham, the desk sergeant took the matter seriously. Police cruisers quietly began looking for Mandic's green Mercury Bobcat

41

as they made their rounds. They also began looking into the housesitting job, which was starting to seem less and less like a lucky break.

A call to one of the partners at Whatcom Security quickly turned up the name of the captain who'd made the job offer: Kenneth Bianchi. The Whatcom partner contacted Bianchi by phone, and Ken explained that he'd spent the evening in a classroom session of the Whatcom County sheriff's auxiliary. The Whatcom man passed this story along to the police. But no sooner had he hung up the phone than Bianchi began to think about his story, which would be easy to check—and to discredit. He called the police and arranged to meet two Bellingham detectives at the Whatcom offices. The cops arrived at 2:30 a.m. and listened politely while Bianchi told them that he'd actually played hooky, cutting the auxiliary meeting in favor of driving around all evening. He was already up on the subject matter that was on the meeting's agenda, he confided, and besides, driving around relaxed him. The police officers left, thinking that Captain Bianchi was a transparent liar—and a frightened one.

When morning came with still no sign of Mandic or Wilder, Bellingham police chief Terry Mangan, a much-admired one-time Roman Catholic priest, and Duane Schenck, his top detective, drove over to the house that the women shared. The porch light was still on and Wilder's cat was yowling for food—a bad sign, for Wilder had been crazy about her pet. She never let it go hungry, or lonely; whenever she planned to be away for more than a few hours, she'd take the cat with her.

Another check with Whatcom Security revealed that the information card and keys for the Edgemoor house were missing. As supervisor, Ken Bianchi was responsible for those items. The police called a locksmith to let them into the house and started searching—slowly and methodically, as they would have combed a murder scene, even though there was still a chance that the missing women were merely off on a spur-of-the-moment skiing jaunt. When detectives talked to a neighborhood woman who'd been coming in to water the houseplants, they learned that Ken Bianchi had called her with a warning to stay away on Thursday evening. Special work was being done on the alarm system, he'd told her, and armed guards might mistake her for an intruder. To the police, the Edgemoor house began to smell like a deadly trap.

By noon Friday a statewide police teletype had gone out describing Mandic and Wilder, and Terry Mangan had personally called the area's radio and TV stations with a de-

An operations captain for a local security firm, Kenneth Bianchi lured college students Karen Mandic and Diane Wilder to this Bellingham, Washington, house—and to their deaths—on January 11, 1979, with a generous cash offer for two hours' housesitting. A day later, the strangled women's bodies were found in Mandic's green Mercury Bobcat *(inset)* about a mile from the house.

scription of the women and of Mandic's Mercury. At about 4:30 p.m. a Bellingham woman listening to the radio suddenly remembered seeing such a car parked in a cul-de-sac near her home as she'd driven off to work that morning. It was still there, she said.

It took only a few minutes for the first cruisers to reach the scene. Next came floodlight-equipped fire trucks and police photographers, some of them carrying camcorders to videotape everything; tapes always helped juries visualize what had happened. The Bellingham P.D. might be small, with only 68 men, one woman, and four dogs, but it was razor sharp and very thorough. At last, when all was in place, some officers approached the car and looked inside. As loose-limbed and lifeless as a pair of carelessly tossed rag dolls, the two women lay on the car's hatchback deck, Karen Mandic atop Diane Wilder. The coroner reported that they both had been strangled with some sort of ligature.

In the Edgemoor neighborhood, Ken Bianchi was making his Whatcom Security rounds in a company truck when his radio dispatcher directed him to a guard shack down by the docks. He would receive further instructions by telephone there, the dispatcher said. This was standard procedure — nothing out of the ordinary. Bianchi did as he was told and headed for the shack. Minutes later detective Terry Wight

arrived, studied the place for a moment, then went in fast, his .357 magnum pointed straight at the good-looking young guy standing at a window. Bianchi didn't flinch, and he offered no resistance. "He was very self-assured about the whole thing," Wight said later. "He was positive we weren't going to be able to prove a damn thing. His attitude was, well, you guys just made a mistake and I know you'll get it straightened out pretty soon, so I'll just go along."

It was all a terrible mistake. That would be Ken Bianchi's explanation off and on for years after his arrest in Bellingham — one of the few consistent things about him. The cops were in error, he would tell the legions of police, psychiatrists, and lawyers eventually drawn to his case. Another pet phrase of Bianchi's was that he couldn't remember. Memory lapse was his explanation as abominations came to light that made the Bellingham horror seem mild by comparison. Then he remembered that he'd had an accomplice. He implicated a cousin, a man as coarse as Bianchi was clean-cut. Their day in court would become the longest criminal trial in American history. At the end of it, Kenneth Bianchi would still be lying, still claiming to be innocent, amnesiac, or mad.

Bianchi began his odyssey through the justice system on

the evening of January 12, 1979, at Bellingham police headquarters. His opening gambit was to vigorously disavow any involvement with Karen Mandic and Diane Wilder, denying even that he'd known them. Their murderer must have been an impostor, he said, with such apparent sincerity that the police half believed him. Kelli Boyd, Bianchi's common-law wife and the mother of his infant son, was the daughter of a respectable Bellingham family. She rushed to police headquarters, aghast and unbelieving. She and Ken had their problems, she told police, but he'd been a gentle lover, an adoring father. Well, he'd hit her once a year or so ago in a fit of pique, but he'd been so sorry afterward. Ken was not a violent man.

By way of reinforcing his claim of innocence, Bianchi readily gave the police permission to search his house. In the basement they found a cache of stolen goods: expensive telephones, clothes, canned salmon and canned shrimp, chain saws and other tools. The stuff had been heisted from various stores that Bianchi was supposedly guarding. He would later complain that he'd cooperated to show that he was a thief, not a murderer. "I steal," he once told a psychiatrist. "It beats me why. I don't use the items and I don't sell them either. I mean, that was my line of work, to pick up shoplifters." Police booked him for grand theft and took him to the city jail.

As Chief Mangan turned over the elements of Bianchi's

After Bianchi's arrest for stealing such items as these power tools *(inset)* from places he guarded, police impounded this Whatcom Security truck, which Bianchi was driving on the night that Karen Mandic and Diane Wilder died.

Kelli Boyd, Bianchi's common-law wife and the mother of his baby son, was shocked that her husband was suspected of murder, insisting he was a gentle lover who would not harm anyone.

case—the thievery, the likelihood that he'd murdered two young women—he began to make the subtle connections that underlie good police work. Bianchi still carried a California driver's license bearing an address in the Los Angeles area. Los Angeles had recently been racked by a sudden, baffling rash of sex murders. Ten young women had been lured to their deaths in the space of scarcely four months, between October of 1977 and February of 1978. All of the victims had been raped; all had been strangled; all but one of them had been left nude in the foothills of the San Gabriel range, the rough, wrinkled ground of northern Los Angeles suburbs such as Pasadena, Eagle Rock, Burbank, and Glendale.

At that time, an ordinary year brought more than 800 murders to the sprawling metropolitan cluster of cities that constitute Los Angeles. Angelenos killed one another with a kind of gusto, it seemed, using almost everything imaginable. But strangulation was rare, with only a score of cases a year. Thus the methodical throttlings of young women, and the sexual brutality that evidently preceded their deaths, brought a great collective shudder to the jaded city. L.A. had seen everything—except this.

The first nude body, that of a 19-year-old black prostitute, was found on October, 18, 1977, sprawled on a hillside near the entrance to Glendale's Forest Lawn cemetery. Her death scarcely rated a mention in the newspapers, nor did the second nude body get much attention when an early riser stumbled across it on the morning of November 1. This victim was another streetwalker, a white 15-year-old, a child really; she'd been raped and strangled before being dumped by a flower bed on Alta Terrace Drive in the foothill city of La Crescenta. About a week later a morning jogger happened upon a third nude corpse, near the Chevy Chase Country Club in Glendale. The victim had been a 21-year-old dancer and Hollywood hopeful who had worked as a waitress to make ends meet. By the end of November, five more women had been raped and strangled,

their naked bodies left to be found by passersby.

The newspapers finally snapped alert. Forensic examination and other evidence, they reported, suggested that two murderous men were at work: the "Hillside Stranglers." As the headlines blared, the city slipped toward panic. Though the killers had shown a distinct taste for youth, women of all ages dreaded leaving the security of their homes or offices; they hurried, some actually running, to and from their cars. If they could, they traveled in groups or with male escorts. Self-defense classes for women suddenly filled to overflowing. Sales of Mace, tear gas, and pistols skyrocketed. "Everyone I talk to is petrified," said one woman, and another added: "I sleep with a hammer under my pillow and carry a steak knife." Headlined the Los Angeles Times: The Southland's New Neighbor: Fear.

Meaning to be helpful, the L.A.P.D. and Los Angeles County Sheriff's Department nevertheless added a further element of terror with a warning: Certain aspects of the rape-murders indicated that the killers might be impersonating policemen. Don't pull over if a cop flags you down, the departments advised. Keep driving to the nearest police substation; the officer, if he's a real policeman, will follow you there. This advice seemed to confirm everyone's deepest dread: The killers could be anyone, anywhere.

As a kind of evil punctuation mark, in mid-December the naked, ravished, strangled body of victim number nine was found spread-eagle in a vacant hillside lot overlooking downtown Los Angeles. January 1978 passed without another strangling, but on February 17 a traffic-helicopter pilot spotted a car halfway down a cliff by a turnout on the Angeles Crest Highway. In the trunk police found the nude body of the Hillside Stranglers' 10th victim, a 20-year-old part-time waitress.

Then, as suddenly as they'd begun, the murders stopped. And three months later, Kenneth Bianchi turned up in Bellingham, Washington, now the death site for two young women who'd been strangled like their California sisters. Chief Mangan wondered at such coincidence, and he asked his detectives to call Los Angeles. Two days after Bianchi's arrest, two L.A. detectives were on their way north to Bellingham.

Frank Salerno and Dudley Varney were members of a joint Hillside Stranglers task force formed by several traditionally competing jurisdictions—the Los Angeles Police Department, the L.A. County Sheriff's Department, and the Glendale police. At its peak the task force employed no fewer than 130 investigators. A bank of 24 hotlines funneled thousands of tips into a mainframe computer, where they were logged, classified, and, for the most part, checked out by task-force operatives. The pressure on the police had become so great that scarcely a week went by in November and December without a press conference to announce some development in the case. Twice suspects were arrested, only to be swiftly released for lack of evidence. On one memorable occasion, a dead man was named as a suspect.

When the murders stopped, the police, in reduced force, plodded on, adding thousands of work hours to the hundreds of thousands already expended. But all the labor was to little effect until Bellingham gave them the name of Kenneth A. Bianchi. The L.A. detectives found him in the computer, under clues numbered 6111, 6458, 7598, and 7745: A tip had told them that he owned handcuffs and a badge; he looked like one of the Hillside composite drawings; he'd applied to, and been rejected by, the L.A.P.D. and sheriff's

Diane Wilder's wadded winter coat lies where Kenneth Bianchi concealed it under a pipe near the guard shack where he was arrested. The garment became an important piece of evidence in an airtight textbook case developed by the Bellingham police against Bianchi, despite the glib killer's numerous ploys and phony alibis.

department; he'd lived in the same apartment complex as one victim and across the street from another. A detective had talked to him, but nothing had come of the interview, and Bianchi had vanished into the wilderness of data.

Bellingham restored him to police scrutiny. By the time the L.A. detectives got there, a Bellingham police search of the Whatcom Security truck that Bianchi had been driving had turned up the keys to the Edgemoor house that figured in the two murders. There was also a woman's scarf in the truck; the police could not immediately identify the owner, but friends said that Diane Wilder loved scarfs and collected dozens of them.

More evidence accumulated in the days and weeks that followed. Searchers came across Wilder's coat hidden in the grass near the guard shack where Bianchi had been arrested. One of his business cards turned up in the Mandic-Wilder house, and a note with Mandic's name and telephone number on it was found in Bianchi's house. Combing the place, Bellingham detectives came up with a turquoise ring that had belonged to the Stranglers' first victim. That stunning discovery was not enough to prove that Bianchi had killed her, only that he'd known her. But, for the Hillside task-force detectives, it was the first bright light they'd seen—a positive link between the Bellingham suspect and an L.A. victim.

At the Bellingham police garage, investigators discovered a fresh scrape on the gas tank of Karen Mandic's Bobcat. The striations exactly matched a chunk of broken rock in some heather alongside the driveway of the Edgemoor house. The weight of the two women would not have been

Five days after his arrest for grand theft, a manacled but confident Kenneth Bianchi strides into Whatcom County Superior Court for a pretrial hearing. Thirteen days later Bianchi pleaded innocent to two counts of murder.

enough to lower the Bobcat to the level of the rock, but the weight of their bodies plus that of 193-pound Ken Bianchi would have done it.

Detectives went through the Edgemoor house with tweezers and magnifying glasses and sent off a packet to the FBI crime lab in Washington, D.C. The report came back: A pubic hair gleaned from the stairwell of the house matched a sample taken from Bianchi. The same stairwell produced blond hairs from Mandic's head.

Cooperating with police—though still unable to believe her husband could be involved in the killings—Kelli Boyd turned over the clothes Bianchi had worn on the evening of the murders. Semen stains had been found on the dead women's underclothing. Bianchi's shorts showed semen stains as well—and some menstrual blood. The autopsy report stated that Diane Wilder had been having her period when she was slain. There was more forensic evidence: Light-yellow nylon fibers from the stairwell carpet turned up on the shoes and clothing of both women; identical fibers were found on the shirt and pants worn that night by Kenneth Bianchi. The clues were circumstantial, to be sure—but, in the view of the Bellingham police, they were more than enough to place Bianchi with the two women on the night they were murdered.

In late January, Bianchi was formally charged with first-degree murder in the deaths of Karen Mandic and Diane Wilder. The ultimate penalty on conviction for that crime in the state of Washington was death. With nothing to lose, Bianchi pleaded innocent and continued to deny any knowledge of the killings. But he was careful in the way he proclaimed his innocence. He didn't rave about false arrest or police harassment; instead, he seemed puzzled by the accusations and calmly insisted that he simply had no memory of such things. Total amnesia, he called it. Later he would explain that he'd suffered from memory loss all his life.

But Bianchi did change one part of his original story. He admitted that he'd lied when he said he spent the evening of the murders just driving around to relax his mind; actually, he now told police, he'd been out with a woman and had cooked up the driving-around story to spare Kelli's feelings. A Bellingham detective got on a plane and flew out to Grand Forks, North Dakota, to interview the woman in question. The detective returned with a sworn statement from her flatly denying any date with Bianchi.

In fact, in supplying the bogus alibi Bianchi had only

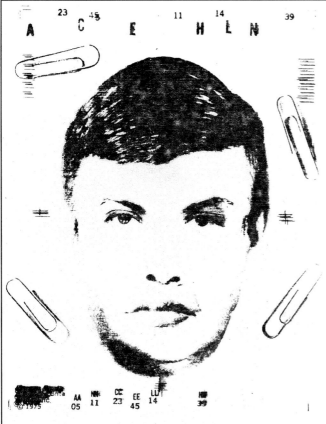

While in the Whatcom County jail during 1979, Bianchi used police Identikit facial features to produce these portraits of his two secret personalities: Steve *(top)*, a foul-mouthed confessed killer of 12, and Billy, a mild-mannered con man and hustler.

followed his powerful reflex for falsehood. The easy use of the unblinking lie increasingly seemed to be the only stable element in his personality. He lied about everything; it was habitual and, it seemed, pathological. Kelli Boyd offered a telling case in point. Once, she told police, she'd caught him in a lie about his whereabouts. Oozing tenderness and sincerity, Bianchi had confessed that, yes, he supposed he had fibbed to her, but it was just that he'd developed this cancer, and he'd been at the hospital getting his radiation treatment. He knew how much she'd worry, he said, and he couldn't bear that, so he'd told her a white lie. A tearful Kelli had prayed for his recovery.

Listening to the man, investigating him, the Bellingham and Los Angeles police figured Ken Bianchi for one of the smoothest liars they'd ever encountered. They put no stock whatever in his so-called amnesia or his claims of innocence. In the view of his court-appointed lawyer, Bianchi was probably a goner, almost sure to be convicted. Accordingly, the counsel for the defense began to look for ways to rescue his glib client.

Attorney Dean Brett was a Washington State native, a solid, intelligent, caring counsel who'd practiced law in Bellingham since graduating from Stanford University in 1972. He'd handled several homicide defenses before but had never been involved with anything like the impenetrable puzzle offered by Kenneth Bianchi. Despite the overwhelming strength of the case developing against Bianchi, the man just sat there declaring his innocence, saying over and over again that he remembered no killings. At the beginning of March, faced with his client's feeble and erratic testimony, Brett raised the issue of Bianchi's sanity.

Over the next five months no fewer than six eminent experts visited the case, two summoned by the prosecution, two by the defense, and two by the judge, to probe Bianchi's mental state and determine whether he was legally sane and competent to be tried for murder. The doctors interviewed him extensively, even using hypnosis in hopes of exploring his unconscious mind. Sixty hours of the sessions were videotaped, another 35 hours recorded audially but not filmed. The experts assessed his intelligence quotient—a "bright-normal" 116—pored over his inkblot Rorschach personality projections, delved into his past associations, and studied what school and medical records were available.

In the end, the doctors offered the court something like

400 pages of diverse professional opinion. Two of the examiners, backed by computer analysis of the tests, diagnosed Kenneth Bianchi as a type 300.1 psychoneurotic, characterized by "hysteria, disassociation reaction." In other words, he suffered, they said, from an affliction that blocked his control over his own actions and that resulted in amnesia. But he also exhibited signs of a more exotic affliction, two of the doctors said—a condition that his lawyer thought might save him after all.

One day, while supposedly under hypnosis, Bianchi suddenly changed almost beyond recognition. Mannerly, pleasant, sincere, cooperative, gentle Ken became his own virtual antithesis, a brazen, foul-mouthed, demanding, hyperactive, dangerously hostile and aggressive man who said his name was Steve. Steve, it seemed, was a whole new personality, and that suggested that Ken was suffering from a rare mental disability called multiple personality disorder, or MPD.

The emergent personality, if such it was, had no problem with amnesia and found nothing surprising in the charges of murder. Far from denying the Bellingham and Los Angeles killings, Steve boasted of them, informing the doctors that he hadn't been alone—he'd had a partner in Los Angeles, an older cousin named Angelo Buono.

Steve was extremely fond of Buono; in fact, he seemed to be modeled on the man. "There ought to be more people like Angelo in the world," Steve told the doctors. But Ken was another matter. Steve detested Ken, and he wanted the doctors to know how cleverly he'd framed his corporeal host. "I wanted him out of the way so — — — bad that I left myself a nice little trail," he said, "and I left him a nice little trail, and I thought I had the asshole cooked."

The doctor who'd put Bianchi under hypnosis was convinced. "The changes in total personality were such that even the most seasoned actor could hardly have malingered them," wrote John G. Watkins, a psychology professor at the University of Montana and a widely published authority on multiple personalities. "Mildness changed to violence; reticence to talk about the crimes changed to bragging about them; soft voice changed to shouting; respectful words in talking about women changed to crude obscenities; good use of English changed to short, ignorant verbalisms; solid cognitive reasoning became concrete, childish exclamations. The personality changed in all modalities—perceptual, intellectual, emotional and motor." Watkins concluded that Ken Bianchi had no control over alter ego Steve, was not responsible for Steve's actions, and was therefore insane.

A second psychiatrist concurred with Watkins's multiple-personality diagnosis. Two other psychiatrists agreed that Bianchi was insane—though not suffering from MPD. But the final two—Martin T. Orne, a distinguished clinician from the University of Pennsylvania, and Saul Faerstein, a Beverly Hills psychiatrist—believed that the alleged MPD was merely one of the defendant's expertly crafted lies. Kenneth Bianchi, they argued, had been clever enough to defeat the hypnosis and to dupe the psychiatrists into thinking that he was mentally not responsible for his actions. "Contrary to popular assumptions," Orne wrote, "it is possible for untrained naive subjects to simulate deep hypnosis and fool even very experienced hypnotists by behaving in ways they think the hypnotist wants."

By way of demonstrating this, Orne advised Bianchi in one session that something about the emergence of Steve had not rung quite true. Real multiples, he said, always evidenced at least three personalities. Bianchi took the bait. Later that same day, "Billy" emerged. Billy was a hail-fellow-well-met hustler, an eager, enthusiastic chap whose specialty seemed to be getting his own way and squirming out of scrapes by lying.

Billy's emergence and numerous other reasons—there was no evidence to support Bianchi's claims of chronic amnesia and no history of multiple personality disorder—led Orne to conclude that Kenneth Bianchi knew precisely what he was doing, currently and at the time of the murders. He was sick, true enough, but his sickness, wrote Orne, was not insanity. Rather, it was "an antisocial personality disorder with sexual sadism." Bianchi, said the doctor, had a "perverted sexual need which allows him to obtain gratification from killing women." In most states, legal insanity requires evidence showing that, at the time of the crime, the defendant's mental condition kept him from understanding the nature of the act and obscured the difference between right and wrong. Bianchi, according to Orne, was accountable for his actions; he could stand trial.

But by the time the doctors finished their examinations in July, defense lawyer Brett had already made his move. On March 29 the attorney had amended his client's innocent plea to innocent by reason of insanity. The Bellingham and L.A. police were outraged at this tactic. "Okay, I got a great idea," growled an L.A.P.D. homicide sergeant. "The judge says to Bianchi, 'Mr. Bianchi, I tell you what I'm going to do. I am going to let Ken off. Ken is acquitted. But Steve gets the chair.' " Steve, and perhaps somebody else—the cousin identified by Steve as the other Hillside Strangler.

The Los Angeles police were not totally ignorant of Angelo Buono. He had a modest record of small-time brushes with the law, and, because Bianchi had once lived with him, he'd been under quiet police surveillance ever since his young cousin's arrest in Bellingham on January 12. If Buono knew he was being watched he gave no sign, and he made no false moves, quietly running his auto upholstery shop in Glendale like any other entrepreneur. But after Steve's remarks about an accomplice, the L.A.P.D. began looking at Buono more closely. The harder they looked, the more appalling he appeared.

Meticulously clean and house-proud, Buono had a good reputation as a craftsman and a businessman, with a loyal clientele that included a few celebrities. A slight speech impediment had rendered him uncommunicative, not much given to small talk. He fancied himself a figure in the Sicilian brotherhood of tough guys and racketeers. In fact, the strong, silent Buono appears to have been interested in very little besides running his business—and sex. He liked to call himself the Italian Stallion, after a pornographic film of that name, and he was said to hold a strong attraction for some women. Buono saw himself as the world's greatest stud, and he spent much of his life seeking to prove it. But, in his view, sex was not the tender exploration of another person; it was a cruel and brutalizing attack on a female object—the younger the better.

This self-styled stallion was born on October 5, 1934, in Rochester, New York, to Angelo Buono and Jenny Sciolino Buono, first-generation Americans of Sicilian ancestry. The parents were divorced when Angelo was four, and Jenny took him and her 10-year-old daughter to Los Angeles, where the mother eked out a living as a stitcher in a shoe factory. The family occupied a small house in a run-down part of Glendale, one of the cities in L.A.'s northeastern quadrant and Buono's hilly turf for the next 40 years.

The boy grew up to be lean and wiry, about five feet ten inches and outsize at the extremities—big head, big feet, apelike arms, huge hands. He cared nothing for education and made it to high school only through the generosity—or indifference—of his teachers. He quit school at the age

of 16 in any case, hardly able to read or write but with highly developed street smarts. His ideas about women had congealed even before he left school. Upset by his mother's divorce, Buono had started referring to her by filthy epithets when he was 14. He asserted himself by calling her a whore and worse, and by accusing her of sleeping with anyone who might grant some small favor. In later years, he would tell acquaintances that she'd carted him along on her trysts and had left him waiting outside while she performed with the men.

Avoiding school, looking for trouble, Buono started running with a gang of toughs and petty thieves. He was first nailed for stealing a car in his mid-teens. He went to reform school, escaped, got caught, and was sent up again. In 1951, the year his cousin Ken was born, Buono spent his 17th birthday in the Paso Robles School for Boys. In the reformatory but not much reformed, Buono found an idol: Caryl Chessman, the so-called Red Light Bandit who'd been convicted in 1948 on charges of kidnapping and sexual assault. His technique was the sort that would have appealed to Angelo Buono: Chessman had installed a police-style flashing red light on his car and prowled the lovers' lanes in the hills above Los Angeles. When he found a suitable couple, the flashing light would blaze to life, and the flustered lovers would roll down their car window on command. When they did, Chessman would stick a .45 automatic in their faces, force the girl into his car, and take her to a secluded place for rape and other abuses.

Chessman had something else going for him as far as Angelo Buono was concerned. Kidnapping was punishable by death in California. But Chessman, acting as his own lawyer, had successfully fended off the executioner for three years by means of one clever appeal after another and would continue for nine more years before finally losing out to the gas chamber—a real hero, in Buono's view, a gutsy guy with the brains to stick it to the system.

Despite his contempt for the system, it was treating Buono pretty well. After his youthful troubles, he turned his powerful hamlike hands to plastering and fireplace masonry before becoming a deft upholsterer of car interiors and enjoying some success. Much of the money he made went toward reinforcing his image of himself as a tough guy and a world-class lover. Keenly aware of his Sicilian heritage, he liked to dress gangster-style in flashy suits, dark shirts, and garish ties. He drove a Cadillac and exuded a kind of coarse

In a rare family portrait, a teenage Angelo Buono sits with his divorced mother, Jenny, whom he characteristically described with sexual slurs.

charm that attracted young girls. There were a lot of them. By the time he was 21, Angelo Buono had a reputation as a sexual athlete.

In April 1955 Buono made one of his sex objects pregnant. For some reason he married the girl, 17-year-old Geraldine Yvonne Vinal, but he left within a week of the wedding and never supported either her or the son she bore. Nevertheless, he must have liked something about family life, for in the next 17 years he married or otherwise lived with three more women and fathered seven additional children, six boys and one girl. Of course, none of this domesticity changed Buono's attitude toward women.

Mary Catherine Castillo was 17 when she married Buono on April 15, 1957, already pregnant with her second son by him. Over the next seven years, Candy, as she was called, bore her husband another three children—and absorbed far more than her share of sexual cruelty in the course of it. One night during their first year of marriage, Buono had pounced on his new wife, tied her hands and legs to the bedposts, and raped her so brutally that she feared she might die. Pain and humiliation were the currency of their

marriage. Once in 1963, when she tried to deflect his advances, he dragged her into the living room, threw her prone on the floor, and assaulted her while his children, aged one to seven, looked on in frightened bewilderment.

Finally, in May 1964, Candy filed for divorce, citing extreme cruelty. The court responded by awarding her $150 a month in support money for all five children. Buono temporarily changed his name to Bono and ignored the support order. Shortly thereafter he found another companion, Nanette Campina, a 25-year-old transplanted New Yorker with two children, Annette and Danny, from a previous arrangement. Buono didn't marry Campina in the seven years they were together. But he brutalized her as severely as he had Candy, and he told her that he'd kill her or have her killed if she even thought of leaving him. He said he had powerful friends—"the boys," he called them, hinting at a Mob connection—who'd be only too happy to do the job for him. He also fathered two more sons, making four children in that unhappy household.

Buono's brushes with the law continued. In March 1968 some police on auto-theft stakeout caught him and a friend

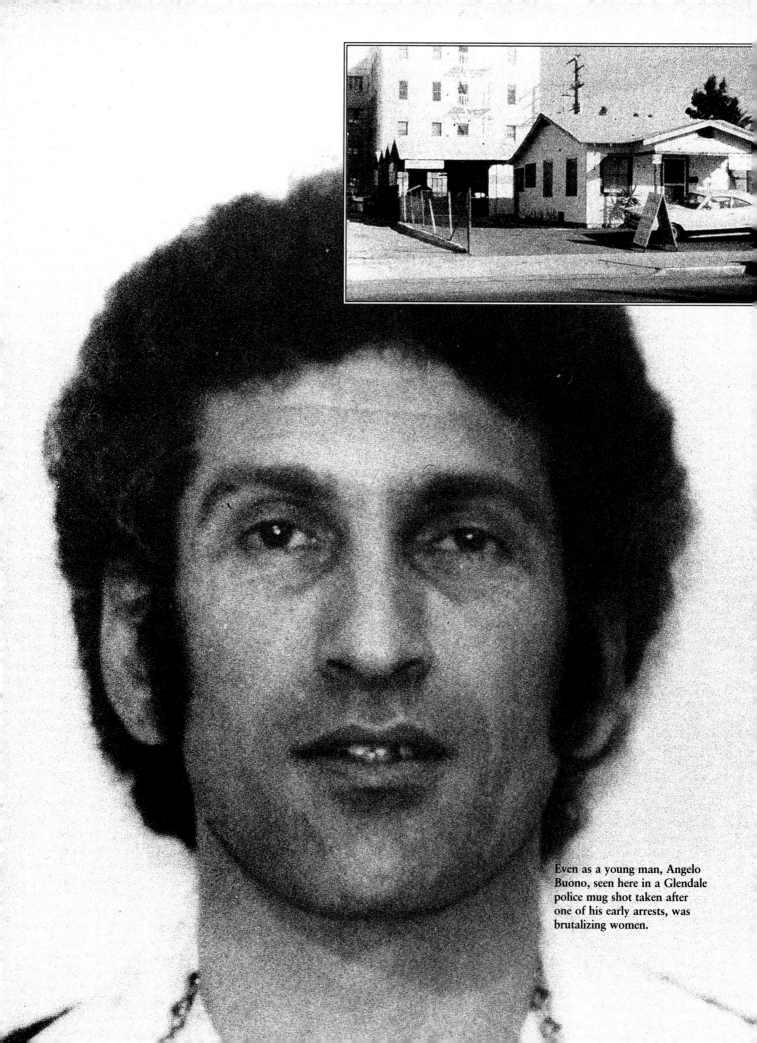

Even as a young man, Angelo Buono, seen here in a Glendale police mug shot taken after one of his early arrests, was brutalizing women.

Buono was proud of his Glendale home *(inset, left)*, bought in the early 1970s, and ran his upholstery business, Angelo's Trim Shop, from its garage. The fastidious housekeeper, seen through his living-room door *(below, top)*, decorated his walls with banners, oil-on-velvet paintings, and photos of the girls who trooped to this waterbed-equipped bedroom *(bottom)*.

trying to remove the hardtop from a Ford Thunderbird. Because he was a family man with kids to support, a lenient judge gave him a suspended sentence. But the family-man thing backfired that September, when the courts finally recognized Bono as Buono and socked him with a one-year sentence for failure to support his five children by Candy. He got lucky again when a second charitable judge suspended that sentence, provided that he pay Candy $190 a month in child support. True to form, Buono disregarded the new order, and the law somehow managed to forget about him again.

Another three years passed. At last, poor, battered Nanette Campina decided that death might be preferable to life with Buono. For one thing among so many, her daughter Annette was growing up—she had just turned 14—and the stallion had begun fondling her. One day, Nanette quietly bought plane tickets to Florida for herself and the kids and took off, never to return.

Left to himself, Buono moved around a good deal in the next few years. At one point he shared an apartment with a Hollywood bit player and through him met a lot of movie people with fancy cars. This was good for business. Very good at auto upholstery, Buono once worked on a sportscar owned by Frank Sinatra and a limousine supposedly belonging to Mafia kingpin Joe Bonanno. The money helped Buono achieve his lifelong ambition of owning a combination house and shop, where everything he cared about could come together in one place.

Buono found the ideal location in Glendale at 703 East Colorado Street, the western end of the boulevard that linked the town with Pasadena, Burbank, and other suburbs in the foothills. The property lay in a triangle that was walled by freeways and sandwiched between a glass shop and a car wash. It offered commercial exposure during business hours and privacy at night, when the urban sidewalks were largely deserted.

Angelo's Trim Shop, as he named it, was behind the house, and he put up a metal awning to shield the space between the two from anyone looking out an upstairs window of the nearby Orange Grove apartments. Having secured complete privacy, he populated it with a parade of young girls drawn to this mature macho man and his brutal appetites. Buono filled a bulging wallet with their pictures: Tonya and her pal Twyla; 13-year-old Melinda; 16-year-old Dawn; a youngster named Julie whom he shared with

Preschooler Kenneth *(left)* stands within the protective grasp of his adoptive mother, Frances Bianchi, and her quiet, hardworking husband, Nicholas, outside their Rochester, New York, home. At this point, the parents are unaware that the disturbing behavioral patterns they have seen in Ken will intensify during his teens *(inset)*—or that they signal the emergence of a vicious serial killer.

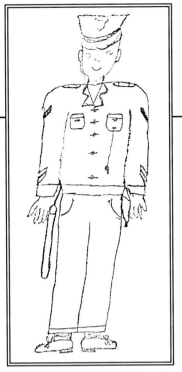

Asked by doctors at Rochester's DePaul Clinic to draw anyone he wanted, 11-year-old Kenneth Bianchi made this somewhat precocious sketch, foreshadowing his ambition to become a cop.

his sons Danny and Peter; Antoinette, a 16-year-old who prayed that she would one day settle down with Angelo.

As Buono approached his 40th birthday in 1974, he took steps to keep age at bay. He began dyeing the gray out of his shaggy black mane and made a couple of other adjustments designed to enhance his image. He took to wearing a big turquoise ring, hung a gold chain around his neck, and added red silk underpants to his flashy wardrobe. The girls were impressed. And so was the newest addition to his lively household: 24-year-old cousin Kenneth Alessio Bianchi, who arrived from Rochester in January 1976.

The guest had been sent west by Frances Buono Bianchi, the sister of Angelo Buono's father. She'd asked her rough-cut nephew to give her adored son, Ken, a place to stay until he got on his feet in Los Angeles.

From the time the boy had come into Frances's life as a kind of healing angel, he'd been the center of her formerly childless universe. She and her husband, Nicholas Bianchi, had been good people, gentle and loving to each other, hardworking, church-going, wanting nothing more than a decent house in a nice neighborhood where their days would be filled with lots of little Bianchis tumbling around. But Frances did not conceive. After months of failure and rising panic, she discovered that her reproductive organs were faulty and had to be removed. The hysterectomy was devastating; she became severely depressed, lost respect for herself, saw every minor ache and pain as some terminal illness. Her life lost its meaning until friends persuaded her and Nicholas to adopt a child.

The boy they took into their lives was born on May 22, 1951, the illegitimate son of a troubled Rochester teenage girl whom the agency described as attractive and promiscuous. The father was a good-looking young Italo-American who decamped before the baby was born. The mother gave up the infant at birth, and three months later the baby crawled into the arms of Frances Bianchi. She guarded her new son like a she-wolf, worrying that the authorities might steal him back before the adoption be-

came permanent, or that his health was precarious. Her concern for him spawned endless anxiety. Kenneth had four different doctors in his first year of life; one of them saw him eight times for spitting up milk and baby food. Nothing particularly serious was ever wrong, but that didn't relieve the adoptive mother. The fussing and fretting grew worse. In 1954 the family moved to the warmer climate of Los Angeles for the boy's health. But almost at once, his health suffered. At the start of Kenny's kindergarten year, he fell from the playground junglegym and banged himself up; his mother, furious at the lack of adequate supervision, kept him home all the rest of that school year. The family returned to Rochester in late 1957.

Things began to go wrong. Little Kenny developed asthma, wet his pants continually, and had a tendency to roll his eyeballs back into his head in moments of stress. Starting at about the age of five, the boy began the lying that would become his stock in trade, and now and then he staged scary temper tantrums. Frances Bianchi was beside herself with worry. She became openly hostile when doctors suggested that much of the lad's trouble was psychological, and that perhaps both he and his mother would benefit from counseling. At one point Frances found herself crying so much that she did visit a psychiatrist. Two hour-long sessions and one 20-minute meeting did little to reassure her. The doctor, she recalled later, had done nothing but pick his nose and clean out his ears.

When Ken was 11 a psychological workup at Rochester's DePaul Clinic diagnosed him as "a deeply hostile boy who has extremely dependent needs which his mother fulfills. He depends upon his mother for his very survival and expends a great deal of energy keeping his hostility under control." The report continued that the youngster was "a severely repressed boy who is very anxious and very lonely. He felt that the only outlet whereby he could get back at his mother was through his psychosomatic complaints." In other words, Ken's behavior indicated that he bitterly resented the one person in the world on whom he most depended.

Nicholas Bianchi, meanwhile, faded to an almost ghostly

A clean-cut senior in this 1970 yearbook portrait, Bianchi used his student days at Rochester's Gates-Chili High School to hone the spurious smooth-talking sincerity and flattery and the ability to lie that would become the tools of his dubious trade.

presence in the house, and a hostage to the spiraling costs of his son's medical needs. The father worked massive amounts of overtime as a foundry molder for Rochester American Brake Shoe, but he always ran just ahead of a breaking wave of debt. His family moved rootlessly around Rochester, sometimes changing residences three times a year. By 1965 they'd come down to an apartment on Jay Street in Rochester's old Italian neighborhood.

In her obsession to make a perfect world for her adopted boy, Frances Bianchi began to abuse her mild-mannered husband, both verbally and physically. She once gave him a bloody nose during a particularly angry fight. "My dad spent cold winter nights in the car," wrote Ken years later, "sleeping, because Mom threw him out. We almost didn't have a Christmas one year because of Dad's gambling. There was a lot of turmoil in that house." Nicholas labored doggedly on, and his son focused on him more and more while retreating emotionally from the overbearing, smothering Frances.

The boy keenly felt the absence of his always-working father, and thus a Maine fishing trip that father and son took together was the high point of 13-year-old Ken Bianchi's life. But a few days after their return, young Bianchi's world collapsed. Two policemen came to the apartment: Nicholas, they said, had been found dead at work of a heart attack—so much stress, all that overtime. Frances Bianchi became hysterical. One witness said that Ken tried to attack the officers, another that he cried out miserably and ran up to his room. At the funeral the boy wore a pair of Nicholas's best shoes; he'd been very proud of the fact that, even as a 13-year-old, he could wear his father's shoes. Long after, Ken spent hours up in the attic gloom, weeping and talking to the mental specter of his dead father.

No one can say how or whether that loss helped create Kenneth Bianchi the murderer. However much he missed his father, young Bianchi did enjoy a material improvement in his life after Nicholas's death. His mother moved her son and herself into a suburban home that she apparently bought with the insurance money from her husband's death. In the most stable, comfortable circumstances of his life thus far, Ken was praised by teachers for his verbal abilities and creative writing. These natural communicative skills provided the foundation for what would become the trademark Bianchi gift of gab, the patter characteristic of small-time con men.

Bianchi had a way of making things parodies of themselves. Just as fluency was debased in his mouth to mere glibness, so chivalry became sham. He approached girls with an old-fashioned sort of courtliness, said nice things, wrote them poems, sent flowers. He frowned on their wearing tight jeans and showy sweaters, and he demanded utter fidelity in return for his love. But it was all an act. Bianchi routinely pursued several girls at once, lying to each one about the others.

Soon after graduating from Rochester's Gates-Chili High School, the 18-year-old Bianchi married a girl he'd known since childhood, but the union was annulled about six months later. Other disappointments followed, and Ken's temper sometimes ran away with him. Once when a girl refused to see him, he broke through her window while she fled out the door and called the police. His subsequent contrition played so well at the station house that the young woman withdrew the charges.

Deciding to be a policeman himself, young Bianchi started taking police science and psychology courses at Monroe Community College. But he attended classes too erratically and learned too little. Despite his beaming personality, he just failed to make the cut at the sheriff's department, where he was 25th on a list of candidates for 21 jobs. Bitter but undaunted, Bianchi became a security guard.

The job appealed to both sides of the man. It put him into law enforcement with relatively little training, and it offered plenty of opportunities to steal. Bianchi had been notably light-fingered since childhood. Now, suddenly, the courtly young guard could shower his ladies with hundreds of dollars worth of costume jewelry. The only problem was that the girl he liked best, Susan Moore, worked in the same store he both guarded and robbed. She knew he was stealing; she could even tell him what counter the stuff had come from. She advised him to straighten up. If he did, she hinted, then she might listen to his adoring pleas.

Bianchi's urgent need to impress took surprising turns. Introduced to a motorcycle club called Satan's Own by another girlfriend, he donned its satyr-blazed denim jacket and got a tattoo. "Ken just always wanted to be part of something, to be important to somebody," the girlfriend told reporters later.

In 1972 and just 21, Bianchi wrote yet another girlfriend, Janice Duchong, confiding that he'd once killed a man—but not to worry, he'd made it look like heart failure. And he was sure, he told Duchong, that the police suspected him of the so-called Double Initial Murders. Three little girls— Carmen Colon, 10, Wanda Walkowicz, 11, and Michelle Maenza, 11—had been found raped and strangled over the past two years.

Rochester was outraged. Thousands of dollars in reward money had been posted—and the police, whispered Ken, were looking for a young guy in a small blue car. It happened that Duchong sometimes let Bianchi borrow her own small blue car. Even so, she put no stock at all in her suitor's stories of being a murderer or a murder suspect. A crazy young guy with crazy stories, thought Duchong, but really a sweet guy—just a trifle off the wall when he wanted a woman's undivided attention. Some years later, investigators would wonder how much Ken Bianchi had really known about the Double Initial Murders, but nobody could ever develop any evidence. The case was never solved.

Like so much else in Bianchi's life, Rochester now began to look like a mistake. He was 24 years old and had drifted through a succession of nothing jobs, in what felt more and more

like a nothing town. Certainly Rochester was no place for a guy destined for an exciting, important life, a young man with Bianchi's kind of hustle. He needed swifter currents; California looked like the scene. Through his mother and Aunt Jenny Buono, Bianchi made contact with his cousin Angelo, who seemed to have lots going for him out in Glendale. At the time, Ken had no memory of having ever met Angelo. For his part, Buono remembered Bianchi only as a pants-wetting brat from 19 years back. Nevertheless, coaxed by his Aunt Frances, Buono reluctantly agreed to let his young relative move into the spare bedroom temporarily. Bianchi headed west.

Tonya, Twyla, Melinda, Dawn, Antoinette—Buono's junior harem made Bianchi's head spin. The younger man had never imagined anything like this; he hadn't known a big, rough, inarticulate guy like Angelo could have such a lifestyle. The visitor from Rochester enthusiastically joined in. He found a blonde named Sheryl for himself, one who passed the Italian Stallion's cold appraisal. Peter and Danny Buono had grown up like their dad, and they brought over their girls, opening fresh avenues for the father and his out-of-town guest. One evening when Peter was stoned on the powerful drug PCP, Bianchi managed to cajole Peter's girl April into bed after telling her that he was an even better lover than Angelo.

Buono soon tired of having his cousin around 24 hours a day, however, and after seven months he practically threw him out of the house. Bianchi took eviction with his customary good grace. He had places to go—and sharp wheels to take him to them: His mother had just sent him enough money for a down payment on a 1972 four-door Cadillac sedan—just as she continued to send him everything, right down to his underwear. And the apartment he found in a complex at 809 East Garfield Avenue suited

"Official Local Sex Instructor" Ken Bianchi mugs with a customer's Rolls Royce in Angelo's Trim Shop.

Bianchi to a tee. For one thing, it was only about six blocks from Buono's; for another, it was filled with women.

When Bianchi approached one of them, a pretty 20-year-old art student named Kristina Weckler, he was told to get lost. But a second neighbor, Angie Holt, bought his Mr. Politeness routine—until he got too possessive, and Angie brought in a young man to live with her. Bianchi was furious. One day he broke into her apartment and ransacked it until he found her diaphragm. He punched a hole in the birth-control device, threw it on the floor, and urinated on it. Next he stole her new boyfriend's TV set. Finally, to make his point crystal clear, he hung a used condom over Holt's doorknob.

While not pursuing or persecuting women, Bianchi was busy applying to and being rejected by various police forces. On his application for the L.A.P.D. Reserves, he wrote: "The main concern is to be exemplary in conduct *off duty* as well as on." Whether in uniform or not, said Bianchi, a police officer had to remember that *"he is always representing the Department."* The sentiments sounded fine, but the L.A.P.D. checked some of his Rochester references and found them wanting.

Law enforcement wasn't Bianchi's only potential profession, however. He thought he might make a good psychologist, and, to that end, he somehow acquired a fake Master of Science degree from Columbia University, a sham Certificate of Accomplishment from New York's Strong Memorial Hospital, a bogus Doctor of Psychology diploma from the Psychiatric Association of America, and a spurious credential certifying him as a sex therapist. He installed his La Brea Counseling Services in a Hollywood office, took out some ads, and, while waiting for the phone to ring, distributed in the neighborhood some handwritten letters whose personalized charm couldn't fully offset their dubious syntax and carnival barker's tone.

"Hi," he would write. "First let me introduce myself. My name is Ken Bianchi. I'm a 1974 graduate of Columbia University, served an internship at a major New York hospital and over 2 years of private practice." Instead of charging an outrageous $20 an hour or more like other psychologists, he said, he would be a confidential counselor for the nominal fee of $10 for up to five questions. Hardly anyone replied. One of the few who did was a man on the verge of suicide; Bianchi had the sense to refer him to a hotline that specialized in such cases.

Business was bad, but, always persistent, Bianchi sent out flyers advertising himself as a psychologist trained at California State University, Northridge, and Pepperdine University. While waiting to see if fake West Coast credentials would be more of a draw than the fake East Coast ones, he pursued a sideline scam, posing as a major Hollywood studio's talent scout. The main thrust of this hustle was to help him meet women.

As tilted as his approach to life usually was, Bianchi could be remarkably competent at times. He found a job with a real-estate outfit called the California Land Title Company. His duties involved researching property ownership at the Hall of Records in downtown Los Angeles. The work was important and sometimes complicated, for every real-estate transfer hinged on there being a clear title to the property in question. So expert did Bianchi become at the job that he was soon promoted to junior title officer making $675 monthly at Cal Land's main office near Universal City in the San Fernando Valley.

Such success gave him fresh ideas about Susan Moore, the girl back home who'd told him to shape up. During his first year in California he'd phoned and written her, using the self-deprecating style that had worked for him in high school. "I've included an extra picture," he wrote, "which you may use at your next picture burning ceremony. I just wanted to show you what I looked like now." He also sought to demonstrate that he was a solid citizen—with a solid income. "I now drive a midnight blue Cadillac Sedan de Ville with a white vinyl top," he related. "I work for a title company and I have a part-time business on the side." Then, between happy news of his job and a doctoral degree that he'd recently obtained, he inserted a wholly preposterous medical bulletin: "The temporary prognosis now is that I'm dying of cancer."

Somehow, his lie-dotted communiqués persuaded Moore to give him yet another chance. That summer, Bianchi met her at Los Angeles International in the big Caddy. She seemed impressed. But she observed that the doctor of psychology diploma on the apartment wall was a fake, and that did not sit well. It reminded her of the old Ken Bianchi. And she knew he was lying when he swore that he wasn't dating anyone else. Well, she told him frankly, she'd been dating some boys in Rochester—at which news Bianchi flew into a jealous rage, called her a slut, and said she was no better than the California whores.

KENNETH BIANCHI, M.S.E.D.
DIRECTOR
Ph. D. DIPLOMATE

LCS

La Brea Counseling Services
COUNSELING AND PSYCHOTHERAPY

(213) 796-8835

LOS ANGELES, CALIFORNIA

Kenneth A. Bianchi, Ph.D.
PSYCHOLOGIST

10850 RIVERSIDE DR.
SUITE 612
NORTH HOLLYWOOD
CA 91602

(213) 469-2359
(213) 985-7445

The National Psychiatric Association
MEMBER OF

MENTAL HEALTH CENTER

KENNETH A. BIANCHI, M.S.ED.
Psychologist

10350 riverside drive, suite 612
north hollywood, ca 91602

(213) 935 7445

KEN A. BIANCHI
TITLE OFFICER

CALIFORNIA LAND TITLE COMPANY
90 UNIVERSAL CITY PLAZA / UNIVERSAL CITY, CALIFORNIA 91608
(213) 760-2700

Ever ambitious but with scant interest in real work, Kenneth Bianchi rented an office on North Hollywood's Riverside Drive, sent out promotional flyers, and had these business cards printed up to support his false claims of being a professional psychologist— a credential that attracted him almost as powerfully as a policeman's badge. His one legitimate card *(bottom left)* identifies Bianchi as a property-title researcher, a line of work for which he possessed enough real aptitude to rise to junior title officer with a San Fernando Valley firm.

THE TRUSTEES OF COLUMBIA UNIVERSITY
IN THE CITY OF NEW YORK
TO ALL PERSONS TO WHOM THESE PRESENTS MAY COME GREETING
BE IT KNOWN THAT

KENNETH ALESSIO BIANCHI

HAVING COMPLETED THE STUDIES AND SATISFIED THE REQUIREMENTS
FOR THE DEGREE OF

MASTER OF SCIENCE

HAS ACCORDINGLY BEEN ADMITTED TO THAT DEGREE WITH ALL THE
RIGHTS PRIVILEGES AND IMMUNITIES THEREUNTO APPERTAINING
IN WITNESS WHEREOF WE HAVE CAUSED THIS DIPLOMA TO BE SIGNED
BY THE PRESIDENT OF THE UNIVERSITY AND
BY THE DEAN OF THE FACULTY OF MEDICINE AND
OUR CORPORATE SEAL TO BE HERETO AFFIXED IN THE CITY OF NEW YORK
ON THE   FIRST   DAY OF   JUNE   IN THE YEAR OF OUR LORD

1974

DEAN

ACTING PRESIDENT

Bianchi festooned his office walls with these fake credentials: a Master of Science degree from New York's Columbia University *(above)*, a Certificate of Accomplishment from Rochester's Strong Memorial Hospital *(right)*, and a sex-therapist credential from the American Association of Sex Educators, Counselors and Therapists. In fact, Bianchi possessed considerable psychiatric cunning, which, prosecutors later claimed, he skillfully used to fake multiple personalities and insanity, fooling even some experts.

The American Association of Sex Educators, Counselors and Therapists

Washington, D.C.

hereby confers upon

Kenneth A. Bianchi, M.A.

the title of

AASECT Certified Sex Therapist

in recognition of attaining the required standards of competency as a sex therapist.

December 27, 1977

Date

AASECT

Michael A. Car...

Certificate of Accomplishment

Kenneth A. Bianchi

Has completed the study, and satisfactorily passed our prescribed

Intern in Residence

and is therefore awarded this

Award of Merit

in acknowledgment of achievements and in testimony of capabilities

STRONG MEMORIAL HOSPITAL

W.W. Malphy, MD Director of Training

Janet Bosley R.N. President

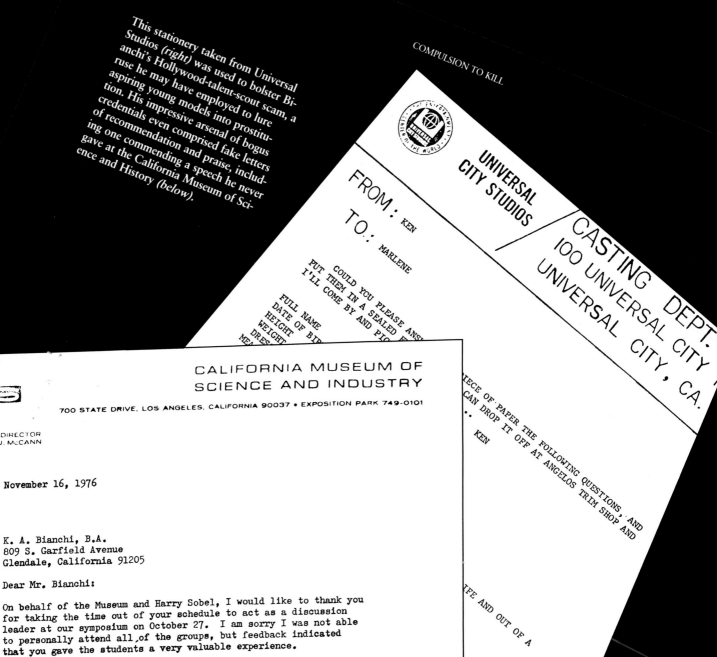

This stationery taken from Universal Studios (right) was used to bolster Bianchi's Hollywood-talent-scout scam, a ruse he may have employed to lure aspiring young models into prostitution. His impressive arsenal of bogus credentials even comprised fake letters of recommendation and praise, including one commending a speech he never gave at the California Museum of Science and History (below).

UNIVERSAL
CITY STUDIOS

CASTING DEPT.
100 UNIVERSAL CITY
UNIVERSAL CITY, CA.

FROM: KEN

TO: MARLENE

COULD YOU PLEASE ANS
PUT THEM IN A SEALED E
I'LL COME BY AND PIC

FULL NAME
DATE OF BIR
HEIGHT
WEIGHT
DRES
MEA

...IECE OF PAPER THE FOLLOWING QUESTIONS. AND
...CAN DROP IT OFF AT ANGELOS TRIM SHOP AND

KEN

...FE AND OUT OF A

....

...Y FOR

CALIFORNIA MUSEUM OF
SCIENCE AND INDUSTRY

700 STATE DRIVE, LOS ANGELES, CALIFORNIA 90037 • EXPOSITION PARK 749-0101

MUSEUM DIRECTOR
WILLIAM J. McCANN

November 16, 1976

K. A. Bianchi, B.A.
809 S. Garfield Avenue
Glendale, California 91205

Dear Mr. Bianchi:

On behalf of the Museum and Harry Sobel, I would like to thank you for taking the time out of your schedule to act as a discussion leader at our symposium on October 27. I am sorry I was not able to personally attend all of the groups, but feedback indicated that you gave the students a very valuable experience.

I hope you found the symposium enjoyable and perhaps would consider speaking at one of our symposiums in the future. This is one of the few times that students can meet with professionals in the field that they are interested in pursuing.

I was very pleased with how the day turned out. Again, thank you very much for helping make the symposium the success that it was.

If you should get a chance call us and let us know of not only your availability in the near future, but also any ideas you may have to develop possibly better symposiums.

Sincerely,

Lisa Hutchinson

Lisa Hutchinson

LH:rd

P.S. you will be receiving
some $ but red tape
takes a while Hope
I see you again soon.

LISA

Susan Moore left in the morning, with Bianchi alternating between sulks and whimpering attempts to make amends. At the airport he sat morosely in the departure lounge until it was nearly time for her flight, then started to weep and wail, thumping his head down onto her lap like a forlorn child. The embarrassed young woman fled to the plane and away from Kenneth Bianchi forever.

The jilted Bianchi hung on to his job into 1977, until his boss happened to see some marijuana in his desk and fired him. But Bianchi had a real knack for title search and quickly found a better-paying job with Stewart West Coast Title in downtown L.A. He also recovered quickly from Susan Moore, finding solace at Angelo Buono's and with a new girl he'd met on New Year's Eve. She was Kelli Boyd, from Washington State, blond and hazel-eyed, a bit chubby, totally smitten by Bianchi. She moved in with him a few weeks after they met and by May was pregnant. In August the pair moved to a Hollywood apartment at 1950 Tamarind Avenue, which was cleaner and closer to their jobs.

But something was changing in Bianchi's complicated and fantasy-laden world. A strange, destructive chemistry was evolving between him and his cousin, despite their being virtual opposites—one glib, one tongue-tied; one young and polite, the other a middle-aged vulgarian. Whatever their differences, the cousins shared one trait: an astonishing inner cruelty and contempt for women—traits that had emerged long ago in Buono and had just begun to show in the younger man. One September day, that bond solidified around an idea that was put forth by Buono: Maybe, he told Bianchi, they should get a couple of whores and go into the pimping business.

Not that there was any crying need; greater Los Angeles had a surfeit of prostitutes. The climate, the movie business, the wealth and glitter, the very size of the place attracted women of all ages, colors, sizes, and shapes, for whom legitimate livings could be hard to find. For the runaway kids, small-town beauty queens, new divorcées, and aspirants to stardom, turning tricks was a way of surviving in an economically cold climate. Many plied their dangerous trade from the sidewalks and doorways at the east end of Sunset Boulevard, where the broad strip decayed from the affluence of Beverly Hills to the nervous squalor of modern Hollywood.

It took Ken Bianchi no time at all to find a likely looking young woman to press into sexual service. At a party given by a pot-smoking girlfriend, he met 16-year-old Sabra, a classy-looking, well-formed girl with big round eyes and a sexy, pouty smile. She was escaping a mundane existence in Phoenix, Arizona, and yearned for a career as a model. Easy pickings for a smoothie like Bianchi. He had terrific contacts, he boasted. She could make $500 a week with no trouble at all.

Sabra went off on a visit to Texas and home to Phoenix for a couple of weeks. When her money ran out, she phoned Bianchi. He sent her a plane ticket, picked her up in his Cadillac, and per Buono's orders, put her up in a hotel for her first night. The next morning he took her back to Buono's upholstery shop, where the proprietor peeled off about $100 for her to buy clothes and cosmetics. She could even stay for a few days in his spare bedroom, he said.

The cousins' kindness began to curdle a few days later. Sabra swallowed hard when Bianchi said that he'd found her a job requiring a few nude poses. Artistic stuff, nothing dirty, he insisted, and would she mind if he and Angelo snapped a couple of samples to show the client? So the luckless teenager took off her clothes and lay down on a waterbed while her benefactors took a few Polaroids.

A day or so later, Bianchi was back with bad news. Unfortunately, he said, the job had fallen through. But since she needed money—indeed, she owed them a hundred bucks—had she ever considered prostitution? Never, she said angrily. But she soon would consider it. A couple of days later Buono and Bianchi stripped her, beat her with a wet towel—a technique that left no bruises—and forced her into oral sex with them. She was their whore, they told her, without hope of escape: If Angelo's Mafia pals couldn't find her, his cop friends would. Her arms and legs would be chopped off. The rest of her would be stuffed into a box and dumped in the desert.

Between beatings, administered mainly by Bianchi, the terrified girl turned tricks in Buono's house. It was gratifying to him how the upholstery business picked up when customers realized the parlay he had going. In time, Sabra was graduated to outside jobs. On one notable occasion, she and Buono's ever-loving, ever-hopeful Antoinette worked an orgy involving seven men, among them a local police chief, an out-of-town city councilman, and an aide to a member of the Los Angeles Board of Supervisors. For that triumph of endurance, Sabra received an unprecedented $60. Usually, Buono and Bianchi gave her nothing; sometimes they even refused her food.

Sabra's slavery lasted about three months. Then, one September day, she simply vanished—disappeared without a word or a trace. That made Buono and Bianchi very angry, especially as they had just been betrayed by another recruit, tiny, frail, 15-year-old Becky. No doubt pushed to a point of no return by Buono's incessant brutality, Becky had blurted out her story of threats, beatings, and forced prostitution to a customer she'd been sent to entertain. The customer happened to be a wealthy lawyer; he was so sickened that he put Becky on a plane out of L.A. with fatherly advice never to return.

Buono, furious, made the mistake of threatening Becky's benefactor, who happened to have connections with some of the city's rougher elements. The next thing the Italian Stallion knew, a 300-pound bouncer named Tiny and four imposing buddies appeared at Angelo's Trim Shop. "Buono was working on a car, detailing it, and I kept talking to him and he kept ignoring me," Tiny later recalled in an interview. "So I reached in the window and jerked him out through the window so fast, so hard, he left his shoes in there, and while I had him up in the air I asked him if he don't mind paying attention to me. So while I was dangling him in the air he paid full attention, so I lowered him back down on the ground. And I gave him one of the lawyer's cards and I told him, I said: 'Don't be offering to kill him no more, 'cause the last thing in the world you want's an instant replay of me.' "

Bianchi had run behind a locked security door upon the bouncer's approach. "Bianchi's a little sniveling poo-butt," Tiny declared later, adding an interesting note on how the two pimps kept their women in line. "His job was if girls were scared of snakes, he put snakes on 'em. He done that to make sure they brought the money home, he worked on their morbid fears." Tiny went on: "We knew they were into something heavy, but we didn't know what. But if I'd a known he was killing those little young girls—I got four daughters of my own—I'd a snapped their neck like a twig and not had no remorse for it."

In fact, the idea of killing had not yet coalesced between Buono and Bianchi, although the seeds of murder had been sown, and were nourished, by the defections of Becky and Sabra. As Bianchi later related it in both his own and Steve's

voices, he and Angelo had started talking about the possibility of killing someone. Cruising over to Hollywood one evening, the cousins picked up a couple of teenage prostitutes, had sex with them, and shoved them naked from the Cadillac without paying. Steve claimed that Buono had meant to murder them.

The next night, cruising Hollywood's Highland Street, Buono flashed an L.A. police badge that he'd somehow managed to buy illegally at a tiny girl with glasses. Bianchi snapped, "Vice squad," and demanded to see her I.D. It read, "Catherine Lorre." She was the daughter of film star Peter Lorre, and when they found a picture of father and daughter in the girl's wallet, the cousins hastily backed off. The father who'd originally gained fame as a serial child killer on screen in the movie *M* had probably saved his daughter's life.

In early October Bianchi and Buono suffered another slap from prostitutes. Hoping to expand his pimping business, Buono bought a list of outcall clients—men who preferred to have prostitutes come to them. The trick list had 175 names on it and cost $1 a name. The prostitute who sold it to Buono delivered the list in company with three friends. One of them, a tall, well-dressed 19-year-old named Yolanda Washington, said that she regularly worked the north side of Sunset near Highland Street.

Buono and Bianchi soon discovered that the list, supposedly a gold mine, was a scam: The names were of men who wanted to come to Buono's house, not men who wanted call girls to come to them. Enraged, Buono would have liked to take his revenge on the woman who'd sold him the useless roster, but she had wisely vanished. Now the pair remembered Yolanda Washington. Unless Washington had been lying, she'd be hustling on the corner of Sunset and Highland. They went looking for her.

No one really knows precisely how this first deadly night unfolded, or how the other nights of rape, torture, and murder would pass. The victims were silenced by death. Angelo Buono has denied all knowledge of the murders and, beyond a few inarticulate outbursts in court and prison, has kept his silence. Only Kenneth Bianchi, in his own well-modulated voice or in the obscene, hate-filled discourse he attributed to his other personality, Steve, has told of those horrible events. Bianchi has described, even lingered over, every hideous detail, often providing an exact fit

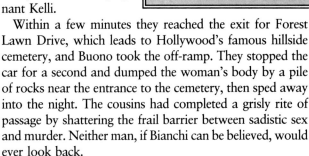

Cruising along Hollywood's Sunset Strip in Bianchi's blue-and-white Cadillac sedan *(above)* on October 17, 1977, the cousins picked up and murdered their first victim: prostitute Yolanda Washington *(inset)*, who was raped and strangled by Bianchi while Buono drove.

YOLANDA WASHINGTON

for what only the police—and the murderers—could know about the crimes. But sometimes Bianchi's roving, rambling voices got things wrong, or denied knowledge of events already described, or took a new tack altogether. The only vocal witness to the hillside stranglings is an accomplished, lifelong liar. Still, experts and investigators have extracted what looks and feels like truth from Bianchi's obscuring cloud of contradictions and impossibilities.

According to this record, Buono was driving the blue-and-white Cadillac four-door that evening of October 17. He let Bianchi out, then picked up Washington from her Sunset corner, had sex with her in the car, and drove back for his cousin. Then Buono whipped out his police badge and told the girl that they were taking her in. The two men put her in the backseat and Bianchi climbed in with her. The sudden turnabout from lustful Johns to arresting police did not convince Washington, who began to scream as Buono wheeled the big sedan onto the Hollywood Freeway. Quickly, Buono pulled over to the shoulder and lunged into the backseat to cuff her hands behind her. That quieted her.

While his cousin drove north along the freeway, Bianchi stripped Washington, raped her, and finally, carried away by the possibilities of cruelty, began to strangle her—a more difficult way to kill than he'd thought. First, he tried pulling back on her throat with his forearm, but Washington writhed and fought and he couldn't choke off her air. Buono, still driving, passed him a rag, which Bianchi rolled up into a garrote and twisted around the young woman's neck. Legs flailing, she still managed to kick the driver in the head. Cursing, Buono pinned her legs to the front seat with

his right arm, while steering with his left, and Bianchi throttled the life out of her. He also looted the body, secretly removing the woman's pretty turquoise ring. He thought it might make a nice present for his pregnant Kelli.

Within a few minutes they reached the exit for Forest Lawn Drive, which leads to Hollywood's famous hillside cemetery, and Buono took the off-ramp. They stopped the car for a second and dumped the woman's body by a pile of rocks near the entrance to the cemetery, then sped away into the night. The cousins had completed a grisly rite of passage by shattering the frail barrier between sadistic sex and murder. Neither man, if Bianchi can be believed, would ever look back.

Two weeks later, on Sunday, October 31, Bianchi showed up at his cousin's to regale Buono with the story of how he, Kelli, and some friends had gone to a Halloween party at a gay hangout called the Circus Maximus. It was a costume thing, he chortled. "We all dressed up as slugs. And we went there and we had green paint on our faces and we were in green garbage bags and it was hard to recognize who was who."

But Bianchi hadn't dropped by merely to chat. As he would tell the story later, he and Buono were restless, and Bianchi suggested that they go looking for another whore.

Buono objected: Last time had been sloppy and rushed. The meticulous upholsterer wanted them to plan this one out, find a place where they could take their time, do it right. Bianchi knew just the spot: Why not right here, in Buono's house? Buono saw the possibilities immediately. The neighborhood was largely deserted at night. Nobody could see much anyway because of the metal awning out back between the house and the shop. He and Bianchi could come and go as they pleased, with anybody.

They found their second victim on the Sunset Strip, standing in a driveway by Carney's Express Unlimited diner. She was in her mid-teens, small and slender, with straight brown hair. She was wearing slacks, a blouse, and a suede jacket. Buono said that he'd pick her up; Bianchi should wait across the street. Buono handed Bianchi the handcuffs and the wallet with the L.A.P.D. shield. Bianchi watched his cousin pull the Caddy into Carney's driveway. The small girl went up to the car's window. After a moment or two she walked around and got in beside Buono. He drove off slowly, made a U-turn—and there was Bianchi, yanking open the passenger door, flashing the police badge, and telling her that she was under arrest. The handcuffs came next. From that moment, Judy Miller, a 15-year-old Los Angeles runaway without even a pimp to look after her, never had a chance.

They drove quickly to Buono's house on Colorado Street and kept up the con, telling her that it was a satellite police station. But she knew that was a lie when they hustled her inside and she spotted Buono's aquarium. The two men dropped all pretense. Buono went into the shop and returned with some foamy polyester material he used in upholstering automobile seats. They taped the stuff over her eyes. When she started to scream, they gagged her with an orange work rag. Next they took off the handcuffs, undressed her, and cuffed her again. Buono pushed her into a spare bedroom, a space with a bed and no other furniture, separated from his own bedroom by a beaded curtain. It had seen much use.

The two men flipped a coin. Buono won and joined the trembling girl, while Bianchi rifled through her purse, finding a couple of dollars and some change in her wallet, along with a snapshot of what looked like two younger brothers. As he assaulted the handcuffed girl, Buono demanded a photograph of himself in action. Bianchi stood next to the bed and snapped a Polaroid, which his cousin declared to

be not bad. In time, it was the younger man's turn, and he followed Buono's lead.

Before they killed Judy Miller, they put her slacks back on: Buono didn't want her soiling his rug if her sphincters gave way at the moment of death, as is usual with strangulation. The girl was shaking violently but made little sound because the gag, which had come loose in her earlier struggles, had been taped firmly back in place. Bianchi tied her ankles together with heavy white nylon cord. The inventive Buono left the room and returned with a plastic supermarket vegetable bag that he jammed over the girl's head and sealed with a loop of white nylon cord around her neck. Bianchi sat on her legs to hold her still while Buono knelt behind her head and tugged at the two ends of the nylon cord. The vegetable bag puffed in and out. She started to buck so frantically that she threw Buono off. He cursed and redoubled his efforts. At last, the puffing and arching ceased. The child was dead.

They removed the handcuffs, the cords, the plastic bag, the foamy blindfold, the gag. They carefully slid off her slacks and put them in a green plastic trash bag along with her remaining clothes, her shoes, and her purse. Buono tossed the bag into a Dumpster outside the shop and arranged some rubbish on top of it. Pickup was Monday, the next day. Together, the pair carried the girl's pale, nude body out to the Cadillac standing under the metal awning and loaded her into the spacious trunk. Buono did the driving as they headed up into the hills, where they dumped Judy Miller's body on Alta Terrace Drive, alongside a flower bed, a few feet in from the curb. After viewing the corpse the next day, a TV reporter recalled the dead girl's "look of absolute horror. You could see it in her eyes. It was absolute, blank horror."

Judy Miller's death, like Yolanda Washington's, rated little mention in the media. No one had connected the two. Bianchi later admitted being disappointed; he'd expected it to be all over the papers and the airwaves. On the other hand, the killings—and the apparent absence of attention—built confidence. Having demonstrated how easy it was to prey along the fringes of L.A. society, they began edging toward the mainstream. The city was crawling with young women waiting to be killed. The cousins waited less than a week before testing this broader strategy.

Cruising Glendale not far from Bianchi's apartment they spotted 21-year-old Lissa Kastin driving home from her job as a waitress in a Hollywood health-food restaurant. When she parked her lime green Volkswagen convertible in front of an apartment house on quiet Argyle Avenue, Bianchi pulled the Cadillac in behind her, cop-style. By now he had his own badge, the star of the California Highway Patrolman. Although Buono had derided this—did Bianchi think he was writing traffic tickets?—they decided that few women would know the difference between a CHP star and an L.A.P.D. shield.

The police con worked like a charm. Bianchi held out his star and asked for her I.D. He told the dark-haired young woman that there had been a robbery and that witnesses had identified her car as being involved. She argued but reluctantly got into the Cadillac for the trip to headquarters. Then the handcuffs went on, and nothing could save her—not even the fact that her captors found her sexually unappealing. After some half-hearted abuse, the killers went straight to murder, but they made sure that Lissa Kastin died very, very slowly.

It took a surprisingly long time—perhaps 15 minutes, perhaps an hour, Bianchi later told one of the examining psychiatrists; he wasn't exactly sure. Tightening the cord around Kastin's throat, Buono brought her to the point of death. Her face turned first a grayish blue that deepened to a mottled purple. Then he suddenly released the ligature. Gasping and coughing, she gulped in air and slowly began to come around—until Buono tightened the cord once more. He did this again and again, rescuing some pleasure from the night. Looking on, Bianchi asked to trade places with his cousin, and it was he who finally throttled all life out of Lissa Kastin, while Angelo sat on her twitching, twisting legs. They liked the added touch—the grand implications of absolute power—of delaying a victim's death. The tactic became part of their repertoire.

As they'd done after Judy Miller's murder, Bianchi and Buono disposed of Lissa Kastin's belongings in the Dumpster. Then they bundled her body into the trunk of the car and drove into the hills searching for a place to dump her. They found the spot on East Chevy Chase Place in Glendale overlooking the ritzy Chevy Chase Country Club. There they hurled the corpse over a guardrail and watched it tumble grotesquely down a steep embankment and into a drainage ditch by the country-club fence.

For several days, according to Bianchi's rambling confessions, the men critiqued this third murder. They talked about being more selective, not being so eager, not jumping at the first chance that came along. On November 9 they were ready to try again. Bianchi drove and thought of cruising over to Westwood to forage for a terrific-looking U.C.L.A. cheerleader. But Buono wanted them to stay closer to home, and they kept to Hollywood near Bianchi's Tamarind Avenue apartment. It got to be 11 p.m.

Jane King was standing at the bus stop on the corner of Franklin and Bronson streets, a slender blonde wearing tight jeans. As they drove past, they could see that she was beautiful. When they came around the block, she was sitting on a bench at the bus stop, long legs stretched out in front of her, their form accented by a pair of silvery, spike-heeled shoes. Buono circled the block again, letting Bianchi out some distance from the bus stop. He casually ambled in the blonde's direction. Suave and friendly, he easily engaged her in conversation. Within a few minutes, Jane King had told him that she was an aspiring actress and a believer in scientology; she had just come from a drama workshop in the nearby scientology school. Bianchi feigned interest. Then Buono drove up.

Hey, said Ken, there's my old cousin, Angelo. Maybe he'll give us a ride. We won't have to wait for the bus. King was a trifle dubious—until Bianchi showed her his CHP badge and told her that both he and his cousin were L.A.P.D. Reservists. Her apprehension melted away. She got into the car, glad for the lift, and rode away to Colorado Street, rape, and death. This time the men took their time with the rape because their victim was so pretty. But the murder followed the same savage pattern as Lissa Kastin's—the deadly tease of the ligature tightening, loosening, tightening, loosening. Bianchi later claimed that he was still copulating with the woman when she died.

Looting King's purse, the cousins were surprised to discover from her driver's license that she was 28, born in 1949, two years before Bianchi. He observed that she was remarkably well preserved. Buono offered the benediction that they'd done her a big favor, letting her die beautiful. They reflected on that bit of philosophy for a moment before shoving her into the trunk of the Cadillac and driving to the Los Feliz off-ramp of the Golden State Freeway. There they tumbled her nude body down into some bushes where it would not be found for two weeks.

The next victims were much younger than King. They were, in fact, children. Dolores Cepeda, 12, and Sonja

Police cordon off the area near the Golden State Freeway where the nude body of aspiring actress Jane King *(inset),* victim number four, was discovered in a grove of trees. Bianchi and Buono had driven her there after raping and strangling King in Buono's home.

JANE KING

SONJA JOHNSON

DOLORES CEPEDA

The bodies of victims five and six, Sonja Johnson, 14 *(left)*, and Dolores Cepeda, 12 *(below)*—and those of two other young women—were found during a four-day period in November 1977, making "Hillside Stranglers" a household term in Los Angeles.

Johnson, 14, were clambering aboard a bus in the Eagle Rock part of L.A. on Sunday, November 13, when the cruising cousins caught sight of them. The idea of picking up a pair was instantly appealing. Bianchi happened to be driving Kelli's Mazda station wagon that day, and he tooled along after the bus, ready to play cop. When the two kids got off at York Boulevard, they almost fainted at the sight of the badges: Dolores and Sonja were junior shoplifters and had just stolen $100 worth of costume jewelry from a boutique at Eagle Rock Plaza. Now here came these big, stern-looking policemen. But they weren't after them for anything like that. They told the girls that a dangerous burglar was on the loose nearby and offered them a ride home. Limp with relief, Dolores and Sonja jumped into the Mazda.

Soon they were at Buono's "satellite police station," and that scared them about shoplifting all over again. The fear grew when they were ordered to strip down: They thought they were going to be searched. Then Sonja was taken into the spare bedroom, raped, and slowly strangled to death. When it came time for Dolores, she asked plaintively where her friend was. Buono replied that she'd be seeing her soon. She went to the bedroom, the pain, the prolonged death. Bianchi wanted her junk jewelry, but Buono tossed it into the Dumpster, along with the girls' clothes and the murder blindfolds, gags, tapes, and heavy white nylon cords. The cousins then laid the bodies out on the cargo area of the Mazda and covered them with a blanket. Having spent most of his life in the foothills, Buono knew just where to

dump them—down among the detritus of a landfill below a lovers' lane that he'd frequented as a youth.

What to do next? The cousins pondered for almost a week. Then Bianchi remembered Kristina Weckler, the art student who'd snubbed him when he first moved into the East Garfield apartments the year before. He reminded her of a sleazy used-car salesman, she'd told him. It was time for the payback.

Bianchi would give investigators two versions of how he got in touch with Weckler. One was that he picked her up at a party. A more likely account involved using his cop persona. On Saturday night, November 19, 1977, Bianchi knocked on her door, produced his badge and a smile, and announced that he was now in the L.A.P.D. Reserve. He handed her a slick line about an accident involving her car. He'd been patrolling the area, he said, and noticed that someone had smashed into her parked Volkswagen. He was really sorry. It would help speed the insurance claim if she'd come down and help him fill out police forms so he could write up a report. Soon Weckler found herself in the Cadillac, her hands cuffed. After that came the tiny hell at Angelo's Trim Shop.

As always, the sexual assaults were many and varied, but nonetheless routine; this time, Bianchi recalled, the ingenuity lay in the act of murder. Instead of immediately strangling Kristina Weckler, Buono brought out a hypodermic syringe, loaded it with Windex—a blue, ammonia-based cleaning fluid—and pumped the stuff into the captive's neck and arm veins. Weckler went into convulsions but didn't die. Buono became even more creative. In the kitchen, he'd recently installed a flexible gas pipe for a yet-to-be-purchased stove. The two cousins dragged Weckler over to the pipe, jammed it against her neck, covered her head with a plastic vegetable bag, and tied everything tight with nylon cord. Then, while Bianchi throttled the girl with the cord, Buono manipulated the gas, turning it on and off until the young woman eventually died.

Weckler's body was found the next morning on Ranons Way in Eagle Rock, only a few hours before the corpses of Dolores Cepeda and Sonja Johnson turned up in the landfill. Three days later, someone found Jane King.

Los Angeles began to buzz about the Hillside Stranglers. And the Stranglers, according to Bianchi, reveled in the sensation they'd stirred. Reward money quickly mounted to $100,000, and the media seemed to credit them with

every one of the area's thrice-daily killings, including that of a girl way out in Pomona, 20 miles east of Glendale.

Despite the fun of fame and murder, however, there were problems in Bianchi's personal life. On Thanksgiving, November 24th, something Kelli said enraged him and he hit her in the face with his fist. She moved out of the Tamarind Avenue place and in with her brother. Bianchi may have cared, but he had his consoling distractions: Four days later he and Buono were out in the Cadillac again, this time prowling the San Fernando Valley, northwest of their usual hunting ground.

Northbound on Sepulveda Boulevard, Buono noticed Lauren Wagner getting out of her two-tone Ford Mustang by a doughnut shop. She was 18, a pretty redhead, a business student. The cousins followed her as she drove to her home on Lemona Street in Sepulveda. There they stuck a .45 automatic as well as a badge into her face and dragged her out of her car into Bianchi's Cadillac.

Wagner was a smart, courageous young woman who played hard for her life. She told her captors she adored sex and had spent hours making love with her boyfriend earlier in the evening. Anything they wanted would be great with her. Buono and Bianchi liked her attitude, but not enough to spare her. After multiple rape by both men, Buono tried to electrocute her by taping live wires to her hands. The jolts made her jump when he jockeyed the plug in and out of the socket. Her flesh smoked and burned. But, like the Windex experiment, the electric shocks were not fatal. In the end, the cousins went back to their tried-and-true technique: a

Police gather along a hillside over-looking downtown Los Angeles, where the nude remains of Kimberly Diane Martin *(visible at lower right)* were dumped by the two cousins after the customary brutal rape, torture, and gradual strangulation.

nylon cord around the throat. They left her body on Cliff Drive near the Pasadena Freeway.

Even dead, brave Lauren Wagner managed to give her killers a scare. When her body was found the next day, the media reported that a woman had witnessed the forcible abduction. She said that one of the kidnappers was "Latin-looking" and described the car as black and white, like an L.A.P.D. cruiser. She got it wrong; the Cadillac was blue and white. But the law, the whole city, was now onto the plain-clothes police scam. The cousins had been careless.

Buono and Bianchi were not a whole lot smarter next time out, on December 13. Bianchi thought he was being extraclever by arranging to have a call girl sent to a vacant apartment he knew about—a safe place to pounce. But 17-year-old Kimberly Diane Martin was a husky five feet eight inches, and even with cuffs on she started fighting and hollering for help. Her abductors were lucky to quiet her down and lie low until the neighbors, disturbed by the racket, returned to their apartments. After they'd moved her over to Buono's, Martin tried to apologize for making a fuss, but they raped and strangled her as they had the others and dumped her nude body where it was sure to be found.

Curiously, Bianchi still wanted to join the Los Angeles police force, and he went on a civilian ride-along in a police car three days after he and Buono had killed Martin. Bianchi even asked the police to show him some of the Hillside Strangler sites. Buono couldn't believe it, according to Bianchi, and he told his girlfriends to stay away from the

A Los Angeles coroner's office technician helps recover an orange Datsun rolled off the Angeles Crest Highway by Bianchi and Buono. The bare knee of the car's owner, Cindy Hudspeth—the Hillside Stranglers' last victim in Los Angeles—can be seen in the trunk.

nutty cousin. Angelo was getting nervous. He began to want Bianchi out of Los Angeles.

And Bianchi himself wasn't having much of a life there. After Kelli left him he bounced around, first staying with male friends of hers, then in an apartment on Corona Street in the Glendale hills, then in a place on Verdugo Road. Then he lost his wheels; in early February 1978 the blue-and-white Sedan de Ville was repossessed. Everything seemed suspended. Two months passed without a Stranglers murder. Los Angeles began to breathe easier—but the respite was short. The cousins had been temporarily immobilized by caution, but fate handed them an irresistible opportunity to kill again.

Just before closing time on the afternoon of February 17, 20-year-old Cindy Hudspeth pulled into the driveway of Angelo's Trim Shop. She'd waited on Buono at a nearby restaurant called Robin Hood's and had taken his card. Now she wanted him to make some floor mats for her spiffy new orange Datsun. Bianchi was hanging around the shop. Hudspeth looked great to him: long, shiny, strawberry blond hair, great figure in black slacks. He and Buono went to work. They lured her into the house, tied her spread-eagle to the bed, and took their time raping her. Two hours later they finally strangled Cindy Hudspeth. It was dark by then.

Wearing rubber surgical gloves to eliminate any possibility of fingerprints, Bianchi got behind the wheel of Hudspeth's Datsun and drove away, with the dead woman's naked body jammed into the trunk. Buono followed in a customer's Mustang. Up they went to a turnout on Angeles Crest Highway, high above the city. A month earlier Bianchi had made out with a 14-year-old girl at the site. The cousins pushed the Datsun front-first over the lip of the steep embankment and watched the car flip once before coming to rest halfway down the hill. On the way home Bianchi dropped the rubber gloves into a trash receptacle when Buono stopped to buy some cigarettes.

Exactly one week later, Kelli Boyd gave birth to Ken Bianchi's son. They called the infant Ryan, and Bianchi was as proud as any new father could be, holding the baby while a photographer memorialized the blessed event. But Boyd was still unsure of her man and loath to move back in with him. Instead, that March she left Los Angeles for her hometown, Bellingham, Washington, to be near her parents. Bianchi, apparently miserable, deluged her with

73

such a flood of poems, letters, and phone calls that she finally relented and agreed to let him join her and their son.

In late May, Bianchi drove a $400 junker with a trailer attached up the Pacific coast to be reunited with his new family, leaving Buono to his never-ending parade of teenage playmates. The strange bond, the psychic chemistry binding the two men, dissolved; the composite entity that had unleashed the hillside stranglings ceased to exist, and Los Angeles saw no more of the grisly murders. In Bellingham, Bianchi more or less mended his ways—until the night of January 11, 1979.

In fact, the murders Bianchi committed on that night lacked the cleverness—if it could be called that—of the Hillside Stranglers' work. In Los Angeles, the cousins had been camouflaged by the very randomness of their crimes. The victims were struck down as if they had been chosen by lottery: one in a thousand prostitutes, one in 50 thousand students, one in a hundred thousand 12-year-olds. The police never had a crime scene to comb over, or much in the way of relationships or motives to study. Only four of the 10,000 or so clues in the big computer touched Bianchi, and then quite inconclusively. In Bellingham, on the other hand, Bianchi had killed two popular women, one an acquaintance of his, and had left a trail that put him in their company on the night of their deaths. Police were able to prove that he was the murderer. But the details of that night came from what Kenneth Bianchi finally told psychiatrists and investigating officers.

Speaking mostly as tough-guy alter ego Steve, salting every sentence with obscenities, Bianchi said that Karen Mandic and Diane Wilder had arrived at the Edgemoor residence around 7 p.m. for the promised housesitting job. He described how he'd conducted them down the carpeted stairs to the finished basement, and how he'd pulled out a handgun that he'd hidden earlier under the cushion of a chair. He told how he'd then bound and gagged his captives and taken them to different rooms: Mandic to a spare basement bedroom, Wilder to a nearby bathroom.

Ken/Steve claimed to have raped them, although there was no forensic evidence of this beyond a spatter of Bianchi's semen on their clothing and Wilder's menstrual blood on Bianchi's shorts. In the bathroom, Bianchi said, he'd untied Diane Wilder, removed her clothes, raped her, then ordered her to get dressed and bound and gagged her once more. He did the same with Karen Mandic in the bedroom.

When he was finished, he returned to the bathroom, led Wilder to another basement room, and strangled her there with a length of cord.

Then it was Mandic's time to die. Bianchi brought her into the room where her friend's body lay and strangled her. Afterward he hauled one body, then the other up the basement stairs and out to Mandic's Mercury Bobcat. He drove to the deserted cul-de-sac nearby, parked the Bobcat, and walked back to the Edgemoor house, where his Whatcom Security pickup truck was parked. At about 9 p.m. Bianchi stopped by at the Whatcom office for a few minutes, went home, watched some TV with Kelli, and went to bed.

All this Kenneth Bianchi had confessed to—in one voice or another. Yet throughout the months of psychiatric evaluation and police interrogation, the personality of Ken—strait-laced, eager-to-please, would-be cop Ken—had continued declaring himself stunned and revolted by the disclosures, unbelieving, amnesiac about the rapes and stranglings. Early in the proceedings, a psychiatrist had asked Bianchi if he thought he was capable of committing such crimes.

"No, I really don't think I am," responded Bianchi.

"Ever been violent?" the psychiatrist persisted.

"Not violent enough to kill anybody," said Bianchi, adding that in his late teens he'd parted company with a motorcycle club because of the fights. "That wasn't my thing."

The doctor asked Kenneth Bianchi

Confessing that he murdered two Bellingham university students in this comfortably finished basement suite, Bianchi said that he raped one victim in the bathroom *(inset, right),* the other in a spare bedroom. The women were strangled, he said, in a separate room, possibly this adjoining storage and laundry area *(inset, above).* But Bellingham police found no definite evidence of rape and developed another theory, suggesting that Bianchi had garroted his victims on the basement stairwell.

Bianchi demonstrates his gift of tears as he pleads guilty to murder on October 19, 1979, in Bellingham's Whatcom County courthouse. Just minutes later, according to some witnesses, the confessed killer sat comfortably in another room, relaxed—and laughing.

what his reaction would be if he were shown incontrovertible proof of his guilt.

"Shock," he said.

The sanity hearing for Kenneth Bianchi took place on Friday, October 19, 1979, in Bellingham's Whatcom County courthouse, which was packed by the press and public. Despite the psychiatrists who believed Bianchi harbored multiple personalities, it seemed likely that Judge Jack Kurtz would order Bianchi to stand trial—and face the death penalty if he lost. There remained one way out, however. Prosecutors in Washington and California got together and came up with a plea-bargain offer that would cover the murder charges in both states. If he took the deal, Bianchi could plead guilty to some of the crimes and still escape the ultimate penalty by testifying against Angelo Buono. For turning state's evidence, Bianchi would get a life term on each murder count but avoid death row. And there was the possibility, remote to be sure, of parole at some time in the future.

On the night before the sanity hearing, lawyer Dean Brett went over all the evidence with Bianchi. At first the defendant continued to insist on his innocence, and his insanity. But eventually he agreed to the plea-bargain. The next day he listened with rising emotion to the litany of rape, torture, and strangulation to which he had confessed. Tears streaming down his face, he told the court: "I can't find the words to express the sorrow for what I have done. In no way can I take away the pain I have given to others, and in no way can I expect forgiveness from others."

Bianchi pleaded guilty to the murders of Karen Mandic and Diane Wilder and was sentenced to two life terms in Washington State. Within hours, he was escorted onto a chartered jet for Los Angeles. There he pleaded guilty to five of the 10 Hillside murders and received five life terms for murder, another life term for conspiracy to commit murder, and additional time on charges of sodomy. For his testimony against Buono, Bianchi would be spared the gas chamber and would have a chance of parole. Following California's practice at the time, the multiple sentences were merged into one life sentence with the possibility of parole in seven years and every three years thereafter. That meant he would spend up to 35 years in California prisons, then be moved to Washington's tough pen at Walla-Walla for at least 25 more years on his two life sentences in that state.

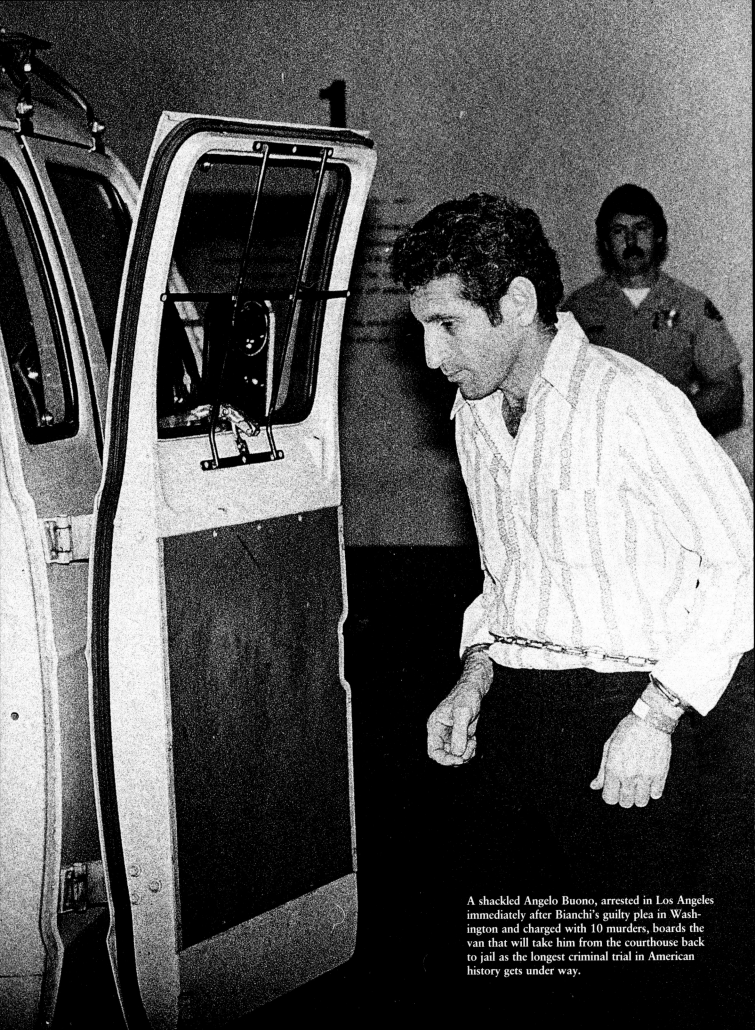

A shackled Angelo Buono, arrested in Los Angeles immediately after Bianchi's guilty plea in Washington and charged with 10 murders, boards the van that will take him from the courthouse back to jail as the longest criminal trial in American history gets under way.

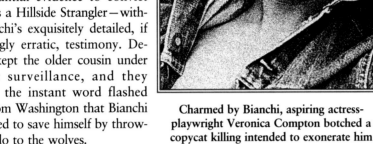

Charmed by Bianchi, aspiring actress-playwright Veronica Compton botched a copycat killing intended to exonerate him and got life for attempted murder.

Buono did not go to jail until Bianchi made his deal in Bellingham. For all his horrific personality and barbarous sexual behavior, for all the certainty of his involvement, the investigators had not uncovered enough circumstantial evidence to convict Buono as a Hillside Strangler—without Bianchi's exquisitely detailed, if increasingly erratic, testimony. Detectives kept the older cousin under 24-hour surveillance, and they pounced the instant word flashed down from Washington that Bianchi had agreed to save himself by throwing Angelo to the wolves.

In the Los Angeles County jail Buono was immediately assigned to the Highpower, a supersecurity section reserved mainly for prisoners at high risk from other inmates. For the most part, inmates in Highpower were informers or rapists whose victims were young—"baby-rapers" in jailhouse parlance. Buono made no friends there, and broke silence only once—but then fatally.

One day a prisoner named Steve Barnes asked him why he'd killed all those girls. "They were no good," Buono reportedly replied. "They deserved to die. It had to be done. But I only killed a couple of them. I ain't worried. My cousin's gonna go into his little nut bag."

That indiscretion would later be used against Buono during the trial. But he was right to trust that Bianchi would do whatever he could to undermine his own testimony, launching into his old act of trying to con and stymie the authorities with sudden contradictions, additions, retractions. Bianchi started a fevered correspondence with the psychiatrists who thought him insane, resurrected Steve, and fell back into his familiar amnesia. The grand liar was making a point: How could anyone believe a man who never told the truth about anything? Of course, Bianchi was trying to save not his cousin but himself, with the litany of his. And, in addition to the antitruth tactic, he kept a number of other salvaging irons in the fire.

Bianchi beseeched three women to go to bat for him. Soon after his arrest he sent his mother a hand-printed letter purporting to be a confession by an anonymous killer—the "real" Bellingham rapist-strangler. "Please forgive me I'm sorry I killed those girls," it began. "I was made to do it. Adams made me because I owed him. Binanch"—he carefully misspelled his own surname—"didn't have nothin to do with it." He pleaded with her to fly secretly from Rochester to Seattle and mail the letter to the Seattle *Times*. Perhaps for the first time, she refused to do what her son wanted. Instead, she told his lawyer about the letter.

Bianchi also pressed an old flame in Bellingham to give him an alibi for the Thursday evening interval when he'd been murdering Karen Mandic and Diane Wilder. The young woman eventually did as he wished, but then she recanted, leaving Bianchi back at square one. Finally, in 1980, he entered into a love-affair-by-mail with a 23-year-old Californian named Veronica Compton, a sometime actress and a budding writer at work on a play about people like Kenneth Bianchi: serial killers. Out of their impassioned exchange of notes and poetry came Compton's promise to help—but in a most bizarre fashion. At Bianchi's urging, Compton went to Bellingham and made a half-hearted attempt to garrote a larger woman she'd picked up in a bar. The idea was to demonstrate that the strangler was still at large—that the guy locked up in California was the wrong man. Veronica Compton failed in her mad mission and was arrested, tried, convicted, and sentenced to life imprisonment.

The preliminary hearing on Buono—Case No. A354231, People of the State of California, Plaintiff, versus Angelo Buono, Jr., Defendant—lasted 10 months. The prosecution's chief witness did his best to muddy matters; Bianchi repeatedly changed his testimony, messed up details, drew blanks on periods of time. On July 6, 1981, he told the court that he had "probably" faked multiple personalities and that he was "not sure" how truthful he had been in confessing his crimes to the psychiatrists; in fact, he said, he "probably" had been lying to them. One minute he said that he "probably" hadn't been present during the murders at all. Then he admitted witnessing the Los Angeles murders but denied all knowledge of those in Bellingham. It went on like that throughout the testimony as Bianchi skillfully tried to remove himself from play as a reliable witness.

A week later, it looked as if Bianchi had won. Buono's court-appointed defense attorney, Gerald L. Chaleff, and Katherine Mader, a skilled investigator brought in by Chaleff, had argued that the state had no case against their client beyond Bianchi's wild and unbelievable claims. Yet the motion to dismiss came not from them, but from Roger Kelly, the deputy district attorney who'd cut the original deal with Ken Bianchi. Kelly moved to dismiss all 10 murder indictments against Angelo Buono. With a pathological liar like Bianchi as a prime witness, he argued, the state could not hope for a successful prosecution. Besides, he noted, there were other holes in the case.

Buono's attorneys were jubilant, the police aghast. Judges routinely honored the prosecution's wishes in such instances, and there was no reason to think that this one—Superior Court Judge Ronald M. George—would behave differently. A product of Stanford Law School and a brilliant legal scholar, George had argued six cases before the U.S. Supreme Court as a deputy attorney general while in his thirties. Now a young 41, he mulled over what he'd seen and heard and said that on July 21 he would rule as to whether Buono should stand trial for murder—or go free.

When the day arrived, a cocky Angelo Buono strutted into the courtroom all set to walk out a free man. Attorney Katherine Mader put her arm around him and whispered in his ear. The defense team planned a celebratory dinner for that evening. Reporters and TV cameras were poised to record an amazing judicial event. Judge George did not disappoint them. In a 36-page opinion, he ripped into the D.A.'s office for suddenly concluding that it had no case after 22 months of proceedings, 10 of which had been consumed by pretrial hearings. He quoted Kelly as stating only two months earlier that the state had "more than sufficient evidence to show presumption of guilt."

The judge reviewed all the corroborating evidence that investigators had gathered to bolster Bianchi's confessions and his descriptions of life with Buono. There was a lot of it: Sabra would testify, as would others among Buono's legion of brutalized girls and women; Catherine Lorre would describe her narrow escape; a man who'd witnessed Yolanda Washington's abduction was slated to testify; lab analysis of fibers found on some of the dead bodies matched fibers from Angelo's Trim Shop.

Judge George focused not on Bianchi's contradictions, but on the underlying consistency of the confessions. However much Bianchi had tried to cloud his confessions, he and his cousin were always the protagonists. The judge said that it was the court's duty to dismiss the charges only if doing so would result "in furtherance of justice." That, he concluded, clearly was not the case. "The court's decision," he said, "is that our legal system should be permitted to run its normal course by appropriate submission of the issue of guilt or innocence to a jury selected from the community rather than leaving that issue to the disposition of the District Attorney." Motion denied.

The California attorney general's office scrambled to resume the case and was ready for trial on November 16, 1981. It took until the spring of 1982 to empanel a jury of seven women and five men. Those good citizens spent the ensuing two years—a total of 345 trial days—listening to a parade of 392 witnesses spewing forth more than 56,000 pages of testimony.

Kenneth Bianchi was witness No. 200 when he took the stand in June 1982 and remained there for 54 court days. He lied, as always. But the two deputy attorneys general prosecuting the case—Roger Boren and Michael Nash—skillfully sustained their star witness's credibility. Before Bianchi began, Boren warned the jury to expect some lies. But he noted that Bianchi had already confessed on tape, and the confession was played for the jury. The judge helped by reminding Bianchi that his verbal maneuvers endangered the plea bargain he'd struck with the state of California.

Again and again, the jury was shown the horror pictures of the murdered women's nude bodies. Maggots had eaten away part of Jane King's beautiful face by the time she was discovered. The prosecutors took the jurors on a series of excursions to the abduction and dumping sites. One dramatic night in December, the jury stood on the deserted mountain of trash where the Stranglers had disposed of the corpses of Dolores Cepeda and Sonja Johnson; a police helicopter circled overhead, illuminating other key locations with its searchlight. At last, on April 26, 1983, the prosecution rested its case.

Defense attorneys Chaleff and Mader—Chaleff drawing down $65 a hour from the state, Mader something less—counterattacked with skill and tenacity. Prosecution witnesses were subjected to merciless cross-examination, but mainly they stuck to their stories. At one stage, Chaleff

My morals and constitutional rights has been broken. I ain't taking any procedure in this trial.

ANGELO BUONO

moved for dismissal with charges of police misconduct; detectives, he said, had failed to inform him that a key prosecution witness had spent time in a mental hospital. Judge George denied the motion: The information had been available in police files since 1980. In her summation, Mader tried to minimize the issue of Buono's sexual vulgarity, his pimping and his mistreatment of females; nobody was perfect, she told the jury. As for what she delicately termed Angelo's "sexual preferences," why, President Warren Harding, Ernest Hemingway, and Charlie Chaplin had all liked young girls, she noted, adding that a magazine called *Kinky Contacts* had "a mailing list of 15,000 in the United States."

Gerald Chaleff spent the better part of nine days attacking Ken Bianchi's credibility, insisting that Bianchi had acted alone and had implicated his cousin Angelo only to avoid execution. The lifetime liar had duped everyone he'd ever met. How could a jury possibly believe such a man beyond a reasonable doubt? When the prosecution objected to this line, the judge warned Chaleff that "beyond reasonable doubt" pertained to the case as a whole, and not to any one individual's testimony.

The judge charged the jury on October 21, 1983. It took them nine days to reach a first verdict: The seven women and five men found Angelo Buono guilty as charged of murdering Lauren Wagner. The jurors then retired to consider the other nine murders. Three days later they returned a verdict of innocent in the murder of Yolanda Washington. (The jurors apparently concluded that Buono was guilty only of driving the car in which Bianchi strangled Washington.) The verdicts were now coming more quickly: Judy Miller, guilty, on Saturday, November 5; Dolores Cepeda and Sonja Johnson, guilty, on Monday morning, November 7; Kimberly Martin, guilty, that same afternoon; Kristina Weckler, Lissa Kastin, Jane King, guilty, guilty, guilty, on Wednesday, November 9; and finally, after a juror was taken ill for a few days, Cindy Hudspeth, guilty, on Monday, November 14.

Angelo Buono took the stand for the first time two days later. He'd remained silent and glowering throughout the trial, once flashing Bianchi an obscene gesture when the witness claimed to have had sex with one of Angelo's girls on the notorious waterbed.

Buono cut a sorry figure as he settled himself in the witness chair. His hair had gone gray, since in jail he could no longer dye it. He was thinner and looked wan. But he remained the total tough guy, contemptuous, thumbing his nose at everything and everybody. When Chaleff asked him what punishment he felt he should receive, he muttered, "My morals and constitutional rights has been broken." The judge asked him to speak up. "My morals and constitutional rights has been broken," Buono snarled. "I ain't taking any procedure in this trial." The gist of his message seemed to be that he felt his rights had been violated and that he didn't plan to be a party to the court proceedings. Chaleff asked him to clarify. "I stand mute," Buono said. "I am standing mute to anything further."

The prosecutors called for the death penalty, arguing that serial murders required nothing less. But the jurors, perhaps believing that Buono should not be punished more severely than Bianchi, settled on life imprisonment without possibility of parole.

On January 4, 1984, Judge George began the sentencing. First, because Bianchi had lied too much to have fulfilled his side of the plea-bargain, the judge ruled that he do the hardest possible time: The prisoner would be moved to the state of Washington's penitentiary at Walla-Walla. As of 1993 Bianchi was still there, having been denied parole twice. Most authorities on the case think it highly unlikely that he'll ever be released.

In sentencing Angelo Buono, Judge George made it clear that he personally favored execution. "There are some murders which demand the most emphatic denunciation of all, namely the death penalty."

The judge deplored the fact that the cousins had subjected their victims to lethal gas and hypodermic injections, to electrocution and strangulation, and yet were "destined to spend their lives in prison, housed, fed and clothed at taxpayer expense, better cared for than some of the destitute law-abiding members of our community." He concluded that neither society nor these "evil spirits" would benefit from imprisonment. "I am sure, Mr. Buono and Mr. Bianchi, that you will both probably only get your thrills reliving over and over again the torturing and murdering of your victims, being incapable, as I believe you to be, of ever feeling any remorse."

Angelo Buono stood impassively before the bench, staring at something only he could see. Bianchi just kept shaking his head, possibly wondering, as always, how such a mistake could have been made, how such a bad thing could have happened to a guy like him. ◆

A Breed Apart

Most people have seen, if only for a moment, the emotional cauldron that seethes behind the thin membrane of humanity. For some, a rip in this frail barrier may unleash enough demons to drive good people to murder. Mystery writers, after all, make their livings from the notion that nearly anyone, properly prodded, can be moved to kill.

The stories that follow, however, concern murderers of a special breed. These are men propelled by something terrible, perhaps unknowable, to murder—and beyond. Some inner twist—of rage, lust, impotence, or power, skewed intelligence or reptilian stupidity—renders them monstrous, and makes killing a mere adjunct to the further, unspeakable violations they perform. Thus, sampling this clutch of vampires, cannibals, necrophiles, and other oddities who murder again and again, one looks in vain for that cornerstone of ordinary crime: a motive that can be understood in human terms.

Charnel House

━ ━ ━ ━ ━ ━ ━ ━ ■ ■

A prudish, hypochondriac London clerk, John Reginald Halliday Christie strangled seven women, including his wife, and also murdered a victim's infant daughter. His tiny, three-room apartment at 10 Rillington Place in Notting Hill became a charnel house, with bodies buried in the walls, under the floorboards, and in the adjoining small garden. John Christie even used a human thighbone to prop up his garden fence and kept a small can filled with the body hair of his victims. So synonymous with horror did 10 Rillington Place become that the street name was later changed to Ruston Mews. But Christie was hardhearted even by the standards of his murderous trade. Having killed a mother and her baby, he coldly allowed the child's slow-witted father to be executed for the crime. All this from an unctuous, soft-voiced, balding man who'd served as a special police constable during World War II and bragged of having French film star Charles Boyer's sex appeal.

In reality, Christie was almost impotent and a necrophile, and he hated women, who often found him repulsive. Christie himself put his obsession more graphically. "They dress and paint up and give you the come-on," he said at the end of his career, "and you can't help thinking that they wouldn't look nearly so cheeky or so saucy if they were helpless or dead." In his distorted view, none of the murders had been

his fault. Four of the women he killed, he said, had made unwelcome sexual advances. The other three suffered from illness or depression, and Christie had been obliged to help them cut short their misery. To the end, he never admitted to killing the one victim he couldn't blame, 13-month-old Geraldine Evans.

Paradoxically, Christie seemed to be driven less by an evil design than by an enormously exaggerated and hypocritical morality that, while crippling him sexually, gave him license to do what he pleased to others. The seeds of that attitude were sown in his childhood in the Yorkshire mill town of Halifax, where he was born on April 8, 1898. His stern and upright father was a carpet designer for the local mills and a pillar of the community. A founder of the local Conservative party, he was also a leader in the Primrose League, an association aimed at promoting moral purity among the working classes.

One of seven children, young John was frequently beaten and humiliated by his father for the most trivial offenses. "He always made me feel so small," Christie later recalled. "He never really understood me." His sisters, Christie added, "were always bossing me around." Fastidious and fearful, the son had grown up a sickly child, remembered by some as "slightly morbid." If only they'd known. Christie later claimed that one of the great revelations of his early life came when he was eight, and his maternal grandfather died. Gazing at the corpse, he felt a sense of fascination and pleasure at the sight.

Outwardly, Christie was quite normal: good at school and mechanical handiwork, a choirboy, Boy Scout, and eventually assistant scoutmaster. But as his adolescence

wore on, he experienced sexual disaster. In his first attempt at intercourse, with an older teenage girl, he failed miserably and was quickly tagged with the cruel nickname of "Can't-Do-It Reggie," which stoked his surreptitious rage and shame. Among boys, he remained self-assured, but he began to keep his distance from women, preferring to stare longingly at them from afar. Still, he always claimed the interest was on their side. "I could hardly go anywhere but women would want to talk to me," he bragged. "It wasn't me who did the chasing. Girls were attracted to me."

Christie's mental kinks began showing in other ways. At the age of 17, while serving as a clerk with the local police, he was caught stealing. His father banned him from the house, and he became a vagrant, eventually enlisting in the army in September 1916. While he huddled in the trenches in France during the summer of 1918, he was blown off his feet by an artillery shell containing mustard gas. He said later that he'd lost his voice for months from shock, and ever afterward, when he grew fearful, he would retreat into a whisper.

Released from the army at the end of 1919, Christie regained enough sexual confidence to court and marry Ethel Waddington, a reticent, homely woman who was almost as passive as he was—definitely not the cheeky or saucy type that excited his lust and rage. Within a year, Christie, who'd found a job in the post office, was arrested for stealing money orders and sentenced to nine months in jail. About a year after emerging, he was charged with obtaining money by false pretenses and placed on parole. He and Ethel separated in 1924; that September he was jailed again for larceny. For the next five years,

Flanked by his dog and cat in this scene from about 1949, John Reginald Halliday Christie stands among towering hollyhocks in the London garden where he would bury four of his eight murder victims.

About two weeks before his 1953 arrest, Christie abandoned this grubby ground-floor flat in London's Notting Hill district, seen from the rear in this Scotland Yard photograph.

Still a smiling couple in this 1949 photo, third-floor neighbors Beryl and Timothy Evans got caught in Christie's web of death at 10 Rillington Place, along with their 13-month-old daughter, Geraldine.

Christie wandered aimlessly and anonymously through the seamy lower strata of British society.

The faceless drifting ended in 1929, when Christie was arrested for clubbing a prostitute with a cricket bat. He drew six months in prison. By now he'd become a marginal fixture in the underworld: a bespectacled habitué of lowlife bars. But in 1933, after another jail stint, for car theft, Christie made a renewed stab at respectability. He invited Ethel to return; she accepted. Christie found a ledger clerk's job to support them. In 1938 they moved into the ground floor of a tiny three-story house in the middle of a squalid slum: 10 Rillington Place.

Within a year, Christie's fortunes took a dramatic leap. Desperate for able-bodied candidates in the early days of World War II, the police were not closely checking applicants' records. Christie was able to find a new job as a special police constable, where his underworld contacts suddenly became valuable assets: He was twice commended for his police work. People on his beat nicknamed him the Doc for his habit of reading medical journals and giving impromptu diagnoses of his comrades' physical complaints.

During his fourth year on the force, Christie committed his first murder. The victim was a 21-year-old part-time prostitute named Ruth Fuerst, who worked in a local munitions factory. She met Christie while he was making his rounds. Waiting until his wife left to visit her parents in Sheffield, Christie invited Fuerst over. By his account, they had sex, during which he strangled her. He stowed her body under his flat's floorboards, then, the following night, carried it out to his tiny backyard and buried it.

At the end of 1943, Christie quit the police and went to work at a radio factory. There he met Muriel Eady, 31. Eady, who was no prostitute, suffered from a bronchial inflammation. Christie told her he had a remedy for her affliction and invited her home for tea. There he gave her a homemade inhaler filled with perfumed water—and something more. The handy host had modified the inhaler by running a tube in the device to a kitchen gas outlet. When Eady grew dazed, Christie tied her up, raped and strangled her, then buried her body in the tiny garden plot. "My second murder was a really clever murder," he later exulted. "Much, much cleverer than the first one." Perhaps this October 1944 slaying was sufficient; the killing ceased, for a time.

Christie's lethal impulse was revived in 1948 by the arrival at 10 Rillington Place of Timothy Evans, 23, an illiterate, mildly retarded laborer, and his pregnant wife, Beryl. Evans had the credulity and intellect of a 10-year-old, yet he was able to hold unskilled jobs. He'd been known since adolescence as a chronic liar who had difficulty telling fantasy from reality. The young family moved into the smallest apartment in the building, two floors above the reclusive Mr. Christie and his wife. Beryl proved a magnet for John Christie, however, and he showed up uninvited one afternoon when she was alone. He brought her a cup of tea and exuded neighborly interest.

Geraldine Evans was born in October, and in the following months her parents fell to bickering over everything from money to housekeeping. A more serious difference arose in the summer of 1949, when Beryl found herself pregnant again and said she would seek an abortion. Her husband was opposed, but she insisted. Downstairs, Christie stirred. He knew something of these matters, the Doc told Timothy Evans; he had once trained to be a physician. Perhaps he could be of assistance.

On November 8, 1949, after Evans had left the house, Christie performed an abortion on Beryl—or so he said. In reality, he beat, strangled, then raped her, and laid her out on a bed. He told the returning husband she had died during the illegal operation and, noting that they were now partners in a crime, got Evans to help move her body—carefully keeping him away from the woman's bruised neck and arms—to a vacant apartment on the second floor of the house. Christie told Evans he would later put Beryl's body down a nearby drain to conceal it. What of baby Geraldine, the desperate father wanted to know. Christie had friends in the suburbs, he assured Evans; they would look after her. Then, on November 10, when Evans was away from the house, Christie strangled the child and put her body with her mother's. The next evening he moved them into an outlying washhouse. Incredibly, workmen who had been in and out of the house got no inkling of the crime.

On November 14 Evans fled to his native Wales. Weeks later, tortured by guilt, he walked into the Merthyr Vale police station and confessed to murdering his wife. He did not mention Christie. While the admitted killer was detained there, Welsh police asked their big-city counterparts to check his story. Notting Hill constables duly inspected the drain outside 10 Rillington Place, where Evans believed his wife's body had been dumped, and found nothing. Then, under a more lengthy and intense interrogation, Evans made a much longer, detailed confession, outlining the abortion story and naming Christie as a partner in the affair. The police searched again, this time on the residential property, and again found nothing. They even managed to miss the thighbone—from the body of Muriel Eady—in plain view against a fence.

They did, however, question Christie, who immediately established a rapport as a fellow policeman. He told stories of the couple's quarreling and of Beryl's complaints that her husband sometimes grabbed her by the neck. When the police made yet another search on December 2, they found Beryl, as Evans had predicted—and Geraldine, whom the poor man believed was still alive. In the shock of discovering that his beloved daughter was dead, the weak-minded father confessed to both murders. He was charged only with killing his daughter—in police eyes, the crime that would take him most directly to the gallows.

Once the shock wore off, however, Evans realized that Christie must have murdered his child, and he said so. But his contradictory confessions had already caused police to discount his word, along with evidence that might have been in his favor. For his part, Christie put on a masterly performance as an ailing former police veteran who denied all knowledge of abortion, murder, or anything else. Besides, he asked rhetorically, what motive could he have for murdering an innocent child? Judge, jury, and prosecution responded as Christie had hoped they would. On March 9, 1950, steadfastly maintaining his innocence to the end, Timothy Evans was hanged at Pentonville Prison.

For more than three years after this narrow escape, Christie kept his murderous compulsions under control. When the tether snapped in 1952, the first person to die was his long-suffering, long-trusting Ethel, who'd become an inconvenient stay-at-home and a nag. Reaching over in bed early one morning, Christie strangled her with a stocking. He left her body in bed for two or three days, then buried her in the living room, under loose-fitting floorboards. He sent letters to her sister, saying she was ill.

Christie was now free to resume his foraging. Within a month he'd lured a 26-year-old prostitute named Kathleen Maloney to Rillington Place. He maneuvered her into what some writers have called a killing chair — a lawn chair in which he had replaced the seat with string and added an unobtrusive gas tube underneath. Maloney inhaled enough gas to be dazed, killed, and raped. The body sat there until morning, when Christie awoke and shaved nearby. Then he stuffed it into a small alcove behind a movable cupboard. A few days later another prostitute, Rita Nelson, met the same fate.

The killer's choice of his final victim showed how completely he had lost control. Hectorina Maclennan met Christie in early March 1953 at a café where she was making inquiries about rooms for rent. He offered to put her up at his place — but was shocked when she turned up there with an unemployed boyfriend. They stayed for three nights before Christie evicted them. But he was by no means through with Hectorina. He followed the couple and invited Maclennan back to 10 Rillington Place, an invitation the homeless woman gladly accepted. This time, his gas trap didn't work as planned, and his victim struggled before drifting into unconsciousness. Undeterred, Christie raped and strangled her and put her body with those of the two other women behind the cupboard. That evening

Christie told the troubled boyfriend that Hectorina wasn't there, and the man believed him. But it had been a close call.

Christie seems to have been aware that the end was close at hand. He'd sold off the furniture in his filthy apartment, and in the next few days he papered over his murder alcove, then illegally sublet the apartment to an Irish couple. He was leaving London, he told them, to join his wife in Birmingham. That night the building's owner

ETHEL CHRISTIE

Long-suffering Ethel Christie was strangled by her husband of 32 years and buried under the floorboards of their apartment's living room.

stopped by. When he discovered the new subtenants, he evicted them and put in a tenant of his own — a man who'd been living on the top floor occupied years earlier by the ill-fated Evans family. The new occupant began clearing out old clothes and rubbish that had piled up in Christie's former home. Then he decided to put up some wall brackets to hold a radio, but when he tapped one wall he heard a hollow sound. Peeling off a panel of wallpaper, he found himself looking at the body of Hectorina Maclennan.

Suddenly, police were swarming over the house they'd searched to so little effect before. A manhunt was launched for

Christie, who hadn't fled but wandered aimlessly around London, a man waiting to be captured. He was arrested while staring over a bridge on the Thames, watching the barges go by.

Once in Brixton Prison — the same one that had once held the unfortunate Evans — Christie bragged indirectly of killing women and claimed that he'd intended to murder a dozen. His trial for the murder of Ethel caused a sensation — not least because questions arose immediately about the guilt of Timothy Evans. Christie's sole defense was that he was insane during his crimes, including the murder of Beryl Evans, whom he'd gassed, he said, to relieve her misery. The jury rejected his defense in 80 minutes. On July 15, 1953, convicted of killing his wife, John Christie was led from the same Pentonville death cell Timothy Evans had occupied and hanged by the neck until dead.

But Christie's most heinous crime — letting Evans go to the gallows for the murder of his own wife and child — acquired a life of its own. Stung by public criticism, the British government ordered a rushed inquiry that in the space of eight days concluded that Evans had indeed killed Beryl and Geraldine. Christie's confession, the report said, was false. As outraged critics pointed out, this theory proposed that two murderers had lived in the same house and had hidden their victims around the place — while remaining ignorant of each other's actions. Determined to blur its inept handling of the case, the British government ignored such criticism — and stood pat for more than a decade.

In November of 1965, however, the clear miscarriage of justice in the Evans case was instrumental in swinging a parliamentary vote to abolish the death penalty. The remains of Timothy Evans were duly removed from a prison cemetery to a church graveyard, and a year later, the unfortunate man received a full, if posthumous, pardon. ◆

RICHARD CHASE
Bloodthirst

David and Teresa Wallin had moved into their modest single-story home at 2360 Tioga Way, in Sacramento's East Area, soon after their marriage in 1975. They were expecting their first child in about six months—a July baby. On this crisp winter Monday in 1978, 22-year-old Teresa had taken the day off work and was completing her morning chores. Now, as she carried a trash bag toward the front entrance, the unlocked door suddenly opened. A tall, scruffy young man stepped into her foyer, a .22-caliber pistol clutched in one hand. For an instant they stared at each other. Then the intruder fired twice, hitting Wallin in the head and arm. As she reeled from the attack, he moved quickly to her side and fired a third, fatal round into her left temple. He dragged her body to the master bedroom, then fetched a knife from the kitchen and picked up an empty yogurt container from debris scattered near the door. Returning to the corpse, he pulled back her clothing, sliced open the abdomen, and dipped the yogurt cup into the welling blood. The murderer began to drink, eagerly replacing his own blood supply, which he believed was dwindling. Like the vampire of evil myth, he was killing others to keep himself alive.

The twisted impulse that brought Richard Chase into the Wallin home on January 23, 1978, had been coalescing for at least a decade. Born in 1950 into a middle-class family in Sacramento, California, Chase had been a passive, well-mannered child, who got along with classmates and with his younger sister. But during his mid-teens Chase had begun to slide. After unsuccessful and troubling sexual encounters, he turned to alcohol and marijuana, neglected his studies, and only narrowly com-

"Sacramento Vampire" Richard Chase leaves a Palo Alto courtroom in 1979 after a jury found him guilty of six murders.

This Nevada police photograph of Chase was taken in August 1977 after authorities found him nude in the desert with a bucket of blood—drawn from cattle.

pleted high school. In 1970 he moved into a house with two female companions, and his behavior grew increasingly bizarre. He gave scant attention to personal hygiene, and his speech was often unintelligible. Finally his roommates moved out, and old friends avoided him. Isolation didn't bother Chase, however. He had become entirely focused on the inner workings of his body, especially his circulatory system: It seemed to him that his blood grew thinner, and his heart weaker, day by day.

Chase moved back to his parents' and, after they divorced in 1973, lived alternately with his father and his mother. He complained of physical impossibilities: His pulmonary artery had been stolen, he said, his heart periodically stopped beating, his body was falling apart. He even accused his mother of poisoning him. Physicians who examined him could find little wrong, but Chase was not reassured. Clearly, some further nutrition was needed. Soon he was

augmenting his diet with rabbits from a nearby farm. In April 1976 his father found him almost incapacitated by a mysterious kind of toxic shock. Taken to a Sacramento hospital, Chase explained that, in an effort to bolster his weak heart, he had been drinking rabbit blood—his condition, he later claimed, had been caused by eating a rabbit laced with acid. In June he was admitted to Beverly Manor, a psychiatric clinic.

As a patient, Chase brought a bizarre, Gothic note to Beverly Manor. One day he appeared with fresh blood splotched across his face; staff members found two dead birds outside his bedroom window, their necks broken and their bodies drained of blood. One nurse refused to allow another inmate to share a room with Chase, whom patients and staff alike nervously nicknamed Dracula. After Chase had been in the clinic about a year, his mother had him discharged, over the protests of some staff, but not Chase's doctor, who believed he had developed "good socialization" and a "realistic view" of his trouble.

Upon his release to his mother's care in July 1977, Chase moved into an apartment on Watt Avenue in Sacramento's densely populated East Area. Because he was

deemed dependent and unfit for employment, his mother received a monthly Social Security check of $246, which helped her to pay for his rent, utility bills, and groceries. At first, Chase continued to meet with physicians as an outpatient, but these visits soon stopped. To the few acquaintances he still had, Chase babbled about UFOs, attempts on his life, and Nazi plots, as his reality evaporated. He was rarely seen by neighbors, and when they did encounter him he hurried by without a word. Still, he seemed innocent enough, except for what some would consider a minor infraction of apartment-house rules: One woman who lived in his building noticed that Chase had brought home a quartet of forbidden animals—two Labrador puppies, a grown dog, and a cat. But, as she never saw the animals again, she let the matter go.

In fact, dogs and cats had been vanishing from the East Area for some time. Chase was answering pet-for-sale ads, buying the animals, and bringing them home for sustenance—he had embarked upon his restless quest for blood. On August 3, 1977, agents of the Bureau of Indian Affairs from Nevada's Walker River Reservation arrested Chase, who was found naked, covered with blood, and stranded in a remote part of the desert. His silver 1966 Ford Ranchero, stuck in the desert sands, yielded two red-smeared rifles and a bucket full of blood. Chase was released only when the bucket's contents were tested and turned out to be from cattle. What the agents could not have known was that Chase was in fact working his way up a bizarre food chain, from small pets to larger mammals. Early that December he added a .22-caliber handgun to his arsenal; on the 29th he shot and killed 51-year-old Ambrose Griffin, after surprising the man in his own driveway. A month later Chase killed Teresa Wallin—and coiled to strike again.

On the morning of January 27, Chase entered the home of 36-year-old Evelyn Miroth on Merrywood Drive, within two miles of his apartment. Inside the house were Miroth, her six-year-old son, Jason, her 22-month-old nephew, David Ferreira, and a friend, 52-year-old Daniel Meredith. When Chase emerged he left three corpses behind him, all shot in the head. Meredith lay on the living room floor. Jason's body sprawled on the floor of the master bedroom. On the bed was the naked body of his mother, her belly slashed. The toddler was also dead; Chase took his body with him when he drove off in Daniel Meredith's 1972 Ford station wagon.

But Dracula had been seen. Witnesses reported seeing a suspicious character in the neighborhoods of Tioga Way and Merrywood Drive on the days of the murders; a former acquaintance even gave police Chase's name after seeing a sketch of the suspect. On January 28, just five days after the Wallin murder, Sacramento police knocked on Chase's door. The killer didn't respond and ventured out only when he thought they had gone. But the police had waited for him, and Chase was arrested.

Even the seasoned investigators sent to inspect Chase's apartment were stunned by what they found. Floors, walls, bed, bathtub—everything—bore the stain and stench of blood. Three blenders in the kitchen bore traces of dried animal blood and tissue. Wall charts showed detailed cutaways of human anatomy, and strewn around the apartment were collars and

leashes, the sad paraphernalia of the pets Chase had adopted and killed. On a calendar he had written *Today* on Monday, January 23, and Friday, January 27, the days he'd gone to the Wallin and Miroth homes. *Today* had also been written on 44 other days in 1978—Chase had evidently just begun to kill when police found him.

On May 8, 1979, the Sacramento Vampire, as the press called Chase, was found guilty of first-degree murder for the slaying of Ambrose Griffin, Teresa Wallin, Evelyn Miroth, Jason Miroth, Daniel Meredith, and David Ferreira, whose small body had

been found, decapitated and stuffed into a cardboard box, in a dump area behind a Watt Avenue church. Chase was sentenced to death by lethal gas in San Quentin Penitentiary. But the vampire had other plans. While he waited on death row, his chronic depression was supposedly held at bay by a prescribed 150-milligram daily dose of a drug called Sinequan. At some point, though, Chase began hoarding the capsules. On December 26 he brought out his secret supply and gulped it down in a single, lethal dose. Then, his killing finally done, he curled up on his bunk and died. ◆

Hangman

That Saturday morning in July 1972 Gerard Schaefer, a big, friendly Martin County deputy sheriff, parked his new blue-green Datsun near the band shell on East Ocean Boulevard in Stuart, Florida. Waiting for him were blonde, 18-year-old Nancy Trotter, of Farmington, Michigan, and her brunette pal, 17-year-old Paula Sue Wells from Garland, Texas. The young women had met in Illinois, on what they later told police was their "vacation." They'd run into Schaefer the evening before when he picked them up for hitchhiking from Jensen Beach back into Stuart. He'd been in uniform then, and strict about hitchhiking laws in Martin County. But instead of taking them

Job applicant Gerard Schaefer smiles for the Wilton Manors, Florida, police camera in 1970.

in, he'd driven them back to the Palm View apartment they shared with a friend and offered to give them a lift to the beach the next day. His patrolling, he explained to them now, was plain-clothes, in his own car—an observance task, he said. They accepted his explanation. After all, the twice-married Schaefer was a polite, clean-cut 26, and a deputy sheriff besides. They climbed in and he headed out highway A1A toward Jensen Beach, on the Indian River side of Hutchinsons Island, a narrow, 20-mile-long sand bar that stretches from Stuart northward to Fort Pierce.

Schaefer chatted casually on the way and asked his passengers if they'd like to see an old Spanish fort on the island. They said yes—and quickly regretted it. Schaefer steered the Datsun onto a narrow dirt road and followed the track so far into the scrub that the girls became uneasy. At last he pulled up beside a small wooden storage shed, which he told them was the fort. The place was deserted except for clouds of mosquitoes, hemmed in by myrtle, wild grape, and low-growing palmettos. Trotter and Wells wanted to leave.

Perhaps encouraged by their nervousness, Schaefer began to torment them. He called them runaways and said he'd have to arrest them and send them home. Ordering the pair to get out, he searched them, then took two sets of handcuffs from the Datsun and cuffed the women's hands behind their backs before pushing them into the small sedan. His rhetorical threats grew more menacing. How would they like to be sold into white slavery? Would their parents pay a ransom for them? What if he buried them in this lonely place, made them vanish into the limbo of missing persons? After perhaps 45 minutes of such badgering, the powerful six-foot-one 200-pounder again hustled Trotter and Wells out of the car. Removing rope and rags from the trunk,

he bound and gagged his captives, then marched them separately to large banyan trees. Trotter's feet were bound with rope, and she was forced to stand on one of the tree's exposed, bonelike roots as Schaefer flipped a stout rope up and over a branch, secured it to the tree, and dropped a noose over Trotter's head. Leaving her precariously balanced on the narrow root, he put a noose around Wells's neck and looped it over a branch. He warned the girl not to run away, she reported later, advising her: "I'm just going down the road to meet that man that's going to buy you." With that final touch of terror, he walked away.

Ignoring Schaefer's warning, the desperate captives worked free of the ropes and rags he'd trussed them with. Then, still handcuffed, they fled for the main highway. Within the hour, Schaefer returned to the site and found them gone. He rushed home and called his boss. "I've done something foolish," he told Sheriff Robert Crowder. "You're going to be angry with me." He explained what had happened and claimed that he'd only wanted to show the girls the perils of hitchhiking. Crowder ordered Schaefer back to the station and set out to find the escapees.

Sheriff Crowder soon had ample cause to doubt Schaefer's tale. The sheriff and one of his deputies found Trotter and Wells on the highway, still fettered by Schaefer's handcuffs and draped in the rags and ropes with which he'd tied them up. Their story suggested an abduction, not a cautionary tease. By the end of the day Schaefer was off the force. Two weeks later he was charged with two counts of false imprisonment and two of aggravated assault—yet back on the street on bail until his trial, scheduled for August 14 but deferred to November. For Schaefer, the delay was a fatal opportunity.

On the night of September 27, in a

ranch-style home in Oakland Park, a northern suburb of Fort Lauderdale about 80 miles south of Stuart, Lucille Place fretted about her 17-year-old daughter, Susan. The girl was in the house with a new chum, 16-year-old Georgia Jessup, and a man introduced only as Jerry. Afraid Susan was again on the verge of running away—a year earlier she had run away to Rochester, New York—the mother pressed the girls for more information about their plans, but to no avail. When the trio prepared to leave, she later told police, "Jerry piped in then and said, 'Oh, we're just going down to the beach to play guitar.'" She was not much reassured and did not say good-bye when they drove off in Jerry's blue-green Datsun. But the worried parent had taken one precaution: She had copied down the license number: Florida 42D-1728.

Neither girl returned that night, or on the next three nights. Really worried now, Lucille Place reported her daughter missing. Her claim caused little excitement among local police—parents were always calling in runaways as missing persons, and usually the kids turned up. Still, the officer on duty duly copied down the license number and said he'd look into the matter. Incredibly, when she checked back a month later the police had still not found the car—in fact, they had copied one of the numbers wrong, and were searching for a license number that didn't exist.

The following March, a Sunday drive with her husband took Lucille Place to Stuart, where she noticed that all the local car tags began with the county designation 42—like the plate on the Datsun in which her daughter had been driven into oblivion six months earlier. She had also obtained Jerry's surname—Shepherd—and address from Georgia Jessup's mother. "When I saw those 42 tags all in Martin County and we were right there," she later told police,

Trussed to a banyan tree, Nancy Trotter re-creates for police the mock hanging Schaefer claimed was just an instructional prank to discourage her hitchhiking.

"I said, 'Let's go see where this house is' and it turned out to be Imperial Apartments." The manager said the man she was looking for "was in jail for molesting teen-age girls." The Places hurried to the sheriff's office, where they described Jerry Shepherd and gave police the tag number, which the mother always carried in her purse. This time it was traced immediately. The car, a blue-green Datsun, belonged to an ex-deputy who happened to be close at hand: Gerard Schaefer, currently resident in the county jail. At his trial he'd pleaded guilty to a lesser charge of aggravated assault and on January 15 had begun serving a one-year sentence.

Brought face to face with the prisoner, Lucille Place identified Schaefer as the man who had driven away with her daughter and Georgia Jessup. Schaefer denied it. Shown a photograph of Susan Place, he denied knowing her. For a few days, the matter seemed to be stalemated, a defrocked cop's word against a worried mother's. But on April 1 police suddenly took a closer interest in their former colleague.

In adjacent St. Lucie County, beachcombers searching for beer cans in the sands of Hutchinsons Island had stumbled upon two bodies that had been dismembered, decapitated, and buried side by side in a shallow grave. Uncovered by foraging animals, the corpses were badly decomposed; but teeth and several small pieces of jawbone soon verified that the remains were those of Susan Place and Georgia Jessup. Rope marks on the branch of a nearby 40-foot banyan tree suggested that they'd been hanged. Alerted to the find, the Martin County police quickly linked the

Trotter-Wells incident with Lucille Place's evidence and began to peel away the carefully cultivated facade of Gerard Schaefer.

As a boy Schaefer had frequently accompanied his father on hunting and fishing trips, but he appeared to have a passion for guns and a taste for killing that went beyond sport. "He enjoyed shooting things," recalled one neighbor, "things you can't eat—songbirds, land crabs." Schaefer himself later admitted decapitating cows and other farm animals. In 1968 he had been rejected by the Broward County sheriff's department when he failed a psychological test. When he tried to join the military in 1970, a psychiatrist noted "marked depressive and paranoid elation" and advised that he was a poor risk for service in any branch of the armed forces. But Schaefer persisted in his efforts to join the law enforcement fraternity. Graduated from the Broward County Police Academy in December 1971, he'd found a spot on a small police department in Wilton Manors, where he was fired seven months later for wandering away from his traffic-control post in search of a snack. Now, just 10 months after becoming a deputy sheriff in populous Martin County, he was serving time for assault—and was suspected of murder.

Days after the discovery of the bodies on Hutchinsons Island, Broward County sheriff's officers searched the Fort Lauderdale home of Schaefer's mother. He'd continued to store things there, including a desk and a locked trunk he'd warned both his mother and his wife never to touch. As police began tracing the contents of this secret hoard they understood Schaefer's need to keep it hidden. Among his souvenirs: two gold-filled teeth from the mouth of Carmen Hallock, 22, who had vanished from her house in Fort Lauderdale in December 1969; jewelry worn by Leigh Bonadies, 25, a Fort Lauderdale neighbor last seen in

September 1969; the passport of Collette Goodenough, 18, and the birth certificate of Barbara Ann Wilcox, 19, Iowa hitchhikers last seen on January 7, 1973, in Biloxi, Mississippi; jewelry belonging to Elsie Farmer and Mary Briscolina, both 14, whose bodies were found at a Plantation, Florida, construction site in early 1973. Also found were various items of women's clothing and photographs of nude, mutilated female corpses. But these chilling mementos barely scratched the surface of Schaefer's fascination with murder.

The big, friendly man had also left about 300 pages of what appeared at first glance to be fictional musings, some typewritten, some in Schaefer's neat, vertical hand. One tale describes, in gruesome detail, the hanging of one Mary Forman outside London in the summer of 1592. Another tells how hangman Stretch Harris came to Dodge City to string up the shapely Lola Erwin, leader of the all-woman Erwin gang. But the one that police found most compelling was a more contemporary narrative—a sketchy blueprint that evoked the mock hangings of Trotter and Wells, and the murders of Place and Jessup, on Hutchinsons Island.

Speaking in the first person, the narrator describes how he blindfolds and handcuffs an unidentified young woman, then leads her to the "place of execution," where he stands her on a ladder tied to his car's front bumper by a rope. He covers her face with a pillowcase as a makeshift hangman's hood, then fastens a noose

around her neck. She is "very ladylike in a black chiffon dress with her hair done up and black pantyhose and high heels," reports the protagonist, who returns to his car to finish a bottle of wine. Then he starts the engine and throws the vehicle into reverse, yanking away the victim's ladder. The woman drops against the taut rope, struggles for a time, then swings, inert. After 15 minutes, the killer walks back to inspect his work, then cuts down the corpse for a night of necrophilic lovemaking.

No one but Schaefer knows whether such accounts refer to actual murders or are the fantasies of a man who has killed, but less elaborately. Found guilty of the murders of Susan Place and Georgia Jessup, Schaefer drew two consecutive life terms. Some, believing Schaefer's writings are not fiction but the sick reflections of a score of other murders he has committed, wish he'd gone to the electric chair.◆

Detective Steve Williams of the St. Lucie County sheriff's office sifts sand on Hutchinsons Island in 1973, searching for the remains of missing teenagers Susan Place and Georgia Jessup.

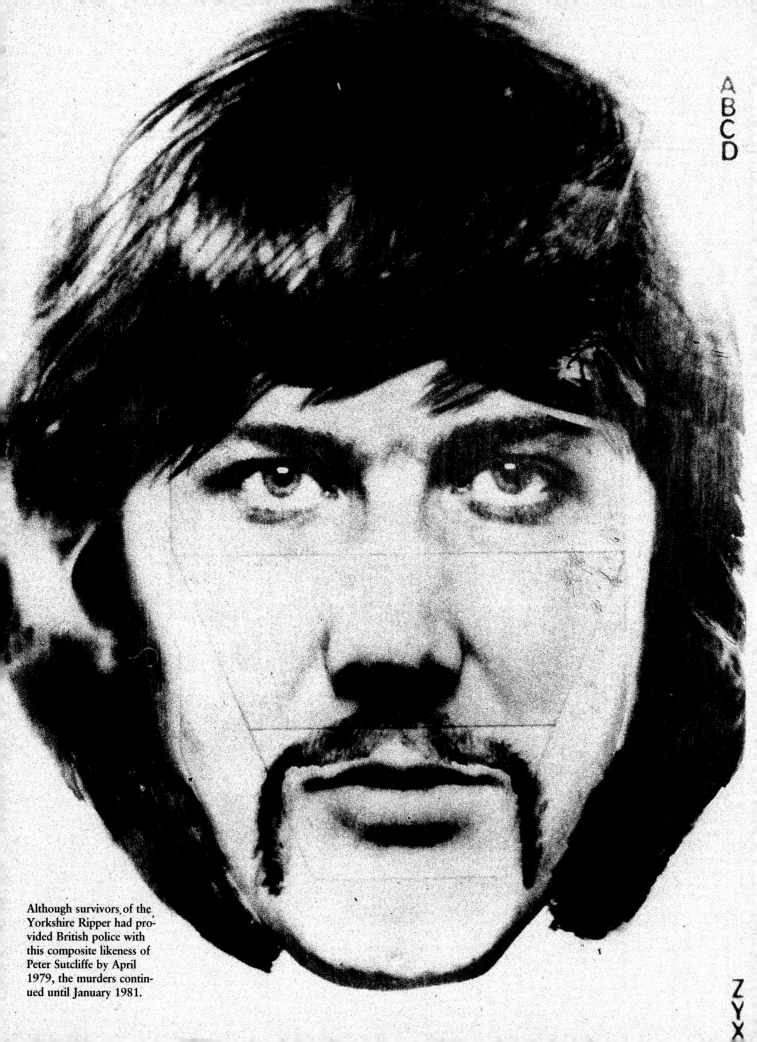

A
B
C
D

Although survivors of the Yorkshire Ripper had provided British police with this composite likeness of Peter Sutcliffe by April 1979, the murders continued until January 1981.

Z
Y
X

The Yorkshire Ripper

Peter Sutcliffe, a small, soft-spoken truck-driver who plied the motorways of northern England, seemed better suited for the role of victim than murderer. Shy, sensitive, and introverted, by day he lived out a tidy middle-class existence with his wife, Sonia, in a suburb of industrial Bradford, a sooty twin city to nearby Leeds. But by night he stalked the bars, deserted streets, and dark urban crannies where prostitutes loitered. Sutcliffe's victims were chosen virtually at random, but with few exceptions, he treated them with a gruesome sameness that conformed to the rigid mold of his obsession: He bashed in each victim's head with a hammer or similar tool, then slashed and stabbed her stomach and chest in a compulsive frenzy. The murders were so garish that the tabloids nicknamed him the Yorkshire Ripper, after Jack the Ripper, his 19th-century counterpart.

Withdrawn, reticent, and terribly sensitive to any real or perceived slight—that was how people in Sutcliffe's hometown of Bingley, about six miles north of Bradford, remembered him. Born in 1946, the frail child with wiry, jet-black hair and large, luminous black eyes was the eldest of seven children fathered by John Sutcliffe, a boisterous, gregarious ladies' man. Peter was closer to his quiet, devoutly Catholic mother, Kathleen, to whose saintly skirts he clung for years. At school, he was considered a bright but chronically unsuccessful student and was forever bullied. He had few friends. Personally, he was fastidious and reclusive, and he sometimes preened in the bathroom for hours on end.

Sutcliffe's seriousness and inability to communicate only deepened after he left school at the age of 15 for the working world. One of his first jobs was as a gravedigger, where coworkers remember him as having a bizarre sense of humor and occasionally stealing a corpse's private belongings. But the overall impression of friends was of a man whose idea of a good time was to sit rigid and immobile on a stool for hours at such local pubs as the Royal Standard—insular, alone—a time bomb of repression.

The Royal Standard was where the lonely Yorkshireman met his pretty 16-year-old wife-to-be, Sonia Szurma, the taciturn, introverted daughter of Czech émigrés. Sutcliffe courted her with agonizing propriety for seven years. Their painfully intense relationship nearly came to an end in August 1969 when Peter somehow found out that his beloved had been seeing another man. That night, Sutcliffe went out into Bradford's red-light district in bitter search of comfort and thought he'd found it with one of the city's prostitutes. But when, suddenly reluctant to consummate the purchased act, he asked her to return £5 of his £10, she refused; when he persisted, she had her pimp chase him away. Later, Sutcliffe would attribute his hatred of all prostitutes to that incident. Certainly, she triggered his latent violence. Within a month, Sutcliffe retaliated by whacking a Bradford prostitute—one he erroneously believed to be the one who had cheated him—on the head with a brick wrapped in a sock. Whatever his intention, the blow was not fatal. The dazed woman managed to note the license number of her assailant's getaway van, and the trail eventually led to its inarticulate passenger. Sutcliffe told police that he had only cuffed the woman with the flat of his hand. As she declined to press charges, he was let go with a warning.

Peter and Sonia weathered her infidelity, their own bond perhaps reinforced by another, more serious, fall from grace. In January 1970 his philandering father discovered that his long-suffering wife had been conducting a quiet affair with a local policeman and set up a devastating trap. He lured her to a hotel lounge where the unfortunate woman expected to meet her lover. Instead, she found her husband, two of her children, and Sonia waiting for her there. Not content with merely revealing the deception, John Sutcliffe forced his wife to display the newly purchased nightgown she had hoped to wear on her tryst. In later years, Peter's father felt that the shock of that domestic melodrama had helped shape his son's murderous career. "It shook him rigid," John Sutcliffe recalled. "He worshipped his mother and I think now that what I did turned his mind."

Although they had reconciled, Peter and Sonia led a life that was anything but calm. She entered teacher training in 1970 but, two years later, appeared to be experiencing a minor breakdown—she imagined, for example, the wounds of Christ on her hands. Vowing to pull her through, Sutcliffe remained at her side, at least spiritually. When left to his own devices, however, the young man began exploring the red-light districts of his region, feeding a secret curiosity about women—and, perhaps unwittingly, reconnoitering what would soon become his hunting ground, a shallow 100-square-mile triangle with Bradford-Leeds at the northern apex, and Manchester and Sheffield at the base. He and Sonia married in 1974 and began their highly charged, nervous life together. And, as interested in cars as he was secretly in females, Sutcliffe finished classes in June 1975 that licensed him as a long-haul truckdriver.

Barely a month later, the clamor of his hidden demons drove Sutcliffe into the July night, and this time there was no mistaking his intention: He was ready to kill. He walked up behind Anna Rogulskyj, an attractive divorcée often seen alone in Keigh-

Sonia Szurma and Peter Sutcliffe were married in the Bradford suburb of Clayton in 1974 after an intense and often stormy seven-year courtship.

ley, a northwest suburb of Bradford, and smashed her skull three times with a ball-peen hammer. When she fell to the ground, he repeatedly slashed her chest with a knife—then fled at the sound of an approaching voice. His victim survived after a lengthy brain operation. Six weeks later, Sutcliffe struck once more, at a 46-year-old cleaning lady, Olive Smelt. Ambushing her on a dark street in Halifax, southwest of Bradford, he bludgeoned her with his hammer, then pulled away her clothing to saw at the small of her back with a hacksaw blade. Again he was scared off before he could finish his murder, and surgeons were able to save Smelt.

Wilma McCann was not so lucky. The mother of four children, the 28-year-old prostitute left her house in Chapeltown, a red-light district in central Leeds, one autumn evening to go drinking and trolling for customers. She was found the next morning in a sports field about 100 yards from her home. She had been clubbed twice with a hammer, then stabbed 14 times in the chest and stomach.

Sutcliffe waited three months before striking again. In January 1976 Emily Jackson, 42, a part-time prostitute whose husband turned an understanding eye on her profitable sideline, climbed into a green Ford Capri outside a pub in the same red-light district where McCann had died. Jackson's body was discovered the next morning, the skull crushed by two blows, and the breasts, stomach, back, and neck stabbed 52 times with a sharpened Phillips screwdriver. The killer left one clue this time—the print of a petite, size-seven Wellington boot was stamped into Jackson's right thigh.

Public anxiety over the murders reached panic stage with Sutcliffe's next attack on a part-time prostitute, in February 1977. Irene Richardson, 28, had left her house to go dancing; she turned up cold and bloody on a Leeds soccer field, with her neck and chest savagely cut and stabbed. With this killing, the press began to speak of a Yorkshire Ripper.

The killer's next victim was discovered in April: Patricia Atkinson, 32, the mother of three, had gone to a local pub, where she'd drunk heavily and left, witnesses said, alone. On her way home, however, she had picked up a client—Peter Sutcliffe—and the pair had gone to her house together. There, he smashed her head four times with a hammer, then pushed her onto a bed, where he knifed her stomach. Police were sure the killer was the Ripper: He left a bloody size-seven boot print on the bottom bedsheet.

Two months later, in June, cruising the Chapeltown red-light district at 2 a.m., Sutcliffe spotted a young girl walking alone. He crept up behind her, hit her on the back of the head with his hammer, and then dragged her 20 yards into a playground before hitting her twice more and carrying out his stabbing ritual. Only 16, Jayne MacDonald was not a prostitute but a shoe clerk at a local Grandways superstore. With her murder, it seemed suddenly as if no woman in the region was safe from the hammer-wielding maniac.

But the net had begun to tighten. In October Sutcliffe had his first brush with capture. He had killed a prostitute, Jean Jordan, two miles from her Manchester home and was hiding her body in some bushes when the arrival of a car frightened him away. In his haste, he left behind another clue: a £5 note from his pay envelope that he'd given the woman as an advance for services never rendered. The note was brand-new, and therefore traceable. Worried about the fiver, Sutcliffe waited nervously for eight days, then returned to Manchester and found Jordan's body undiscovered. He searched her clothing but failed to find the incriminating note hidden in an inner pocket. Enraged, the thwarted

98

killer lashed at the body with a knife and a shard of glass, and he apparently tried to sever the head to conceal his trademark hammer blows. The body was discovered a day later—and so was Sutcliffe's money. The police quickly narrowed down to about 30 the number of firms that might have paid an employee with the bill, including T. and W. H. Clark, a Bradford haulage firm and Sutcliffe's employer since 1976. Sutcliffe was among the 8,000 men interviewed by police; they talked to him twice, and twice cleared him of suspicion.

Early in the new year, Sutcliffe killed 22-year-old Yvonne Pearson in Lumb Lane, Bradford's red-light district. Luring his victim to a littered vacant lot behind a mill, he smashed the prostitute's skull with several blows from a heavy framing hammer. When she began to moan, he tore clumps of horsehair from a discarded sofa and crammed it down Pearson's throat to silence her as she expired. Then he partially

undressed her and jumped up and down on her chest until the rib cage collapsed. Unnerved by passing cars, Sutcliffe then concealed the body under the sofa, where it lay for two months. When the body was finally found, a copy of the London *Daily Mirror* was found beneath one arm, evidently placed there by the killer four weeks after his victim's death.

By then Sutcliffe had murdered another streetwalker, in the nearby town of Huddersfield. He'd picked up 18-year-old Helen Rytka in the early evening, when there was still enough light for witnesses to think they could give a description: a

stocky, fair-haired man, they said—almost Sutcliffe's opposite.

And here the case took a bizarre turn. In March 1978 two letters were received in the area, one by the West Yorkshire police, the other by the Manchester office of the *Daily Mirror*. Postmarked in Sunderland, a North Sea port city about 75 miles north of Bradford, the cheerily derisive notes were from someone who signed the name Jack and claimed to be their Ripper. The letters were ignored as "the work of a crank."

On May 16 yet another Manchester prostitute, Vera Millward, was murdered and slashed. Police again came face to face

In 1977 the Sutcliffes bought Sonia's dream home on Garden Lane in Bradford, near the Ripper's hunting grounds.

99

Billboards urged citizens to help
police identify "Jack," who
claimed to be the Yorkshire Ripper but turned out to be a hoaxer.

HELP US STOP THE RIPPER
FROM KILLING AGAIN.

LOOK AT HIS HANDWRITING.

LISTEN TO HIS VOICE.
PHONE LEEDS
(0532) 464111.

IF YOU RECOGNISE EITHER, REPORT IT TO YOUR LOCAL POLICE

LONDON & PROVINCIAL

with the murderer just four months later. Detectives dropped by Sutcliffe's home to ask about his red Ford Corsair, which had been noticed at police checkpoints set up in the Leeds and Bradford area. For the third time, the unflappable Sutcliffe passed muster. Ten days later, he came unscathed through a fourth interview, when police were checking for tire treads that matched a set found near the scene of the Irene Richardson murder. This flurry of attention must have made Sutcliffe cautious: 11 months passed before the Yorkshire Ripper struck again.

Sutcliffe had reason to be careful. By now, he'd been on the rampage for four years and was the subject of the biggest criminal manhunt Britain had ever seen. Hundreds of police had been assigned to the case, and some 175,000 people had been questioned—Sutcliffe included. In late

March 1979, the West Yorkshire police received a third taunting letter. Still, they hesitated to pursue their mysterious correspondent in Sunderland.

Within days of the third letter, on April 4, the Ripper struck in Halifax. This time the victim was not a prostitute but 19-year-old Josephine Whitaker, a clerk in a local savings and loan. Once more, the Ripper's shadow fell over the women of Yorkshire—no one was safe.

Finally, in June, police believed they'd got their hoped-for break. From a Sunderland postal drop they received an envelope containing a cassette tape. "I'm Jack," the voice said. "I see you are having no luck catching me." It chided detectives, bragged of killings yet to come, and ended with a 1978 song, "Thank You for Being a Friend." This time police took the message seriously. Linguistic experts identified the

accent on the tape as a regional variant of Geordie, the working-class dialect of northeastern England—and very different from Sutcliffe's nasal, distinctive Yorkshire voice. Suspicion shifted away from Bradford even as Sutcliffe was being interviewed by police for the fifth time. In all, he was interviewed and released nine times—once, he talked to investigators wearing his telltale size-seven Wellingtons—and his car was spotted 36 times in the Bradford red-light district. He always had an explanation, which police always accepted, leaving him free to kill.

Sutcliffe murdered his next victim on September 2. The body of Barbara Leach, a 20-year-old Bradford University student, was found stuffed under a carpet in a Bradford trash bin, the skull shattered, the torso stabbed eight times. The Ripper task force realized, to its chagrin, that the Sun-

100

derland letters and tape had been a cruel hoax; attention shifted back to the Bradford-Leeds area.

But the Ripper had once more gone to ground. It was nearly a year before the body of 47-year-old Marguerite Walls, a Leeds civil servant, was found in August 1980. Police were uncertain that she was the Ripper's victim—she had been garroted, and not mutilated. In fact, Sutcliffe had merely declined to leave his signature. His stylistic change was temporary, however. On November 17 he bludgeoned and ripped Leeds University student Jacqueline Hill, 20, within sight of her residence hall.

Outrage over the Ripper's continued freedom to terrorize Yorkshire had been muted when his victims were prostitutes, who led notoriously dangerous lives; but the deaths of Jo Whitaker, Barbara Leach, Marguerite Walls, and Jacqueline Hill caused public anger to boil into the streets. Women demonstrated for better police protection, and the government launched a multimillion-dollar publicity campaign aimed at encouraging tips from the public. Despite the ensuing torrent of information, the killer remained at large.

When Sutcliffe next came into the hands of police, it was by happenstance. In January of 1981 two Sheffield police officers spotted a prostitute climbing into a brown Rover sedan. Her behavior suggested solicitation, which, unlike prostitution, is illegal in England. The constables decided to check it out.

The man behind the Rover's wheel identified himself as Peter Williams. The police checked his license plates and learned that they were stolen. When they informed the driver of this, he asked if he could relieve himself. The police said yes, and Peter Sutcliffe wandered into some roadside weeds, where he quietly disposed of a ball-peen hammer and a sharp knife. When he re-

turned to the car, he was taken in to the Sheffield station for questioning. Cool and collected, Sutcliffe went to the bathroom for a second time, at the police headquarters—and hid a second knife in the toilet tank. He admitted to stealing the license plates near Dewsbury, a village south of Bradford. Dewsbury police collected him and took him to their jurisdiction, where he informed investigators that he was a long-distance truckdriver and casually mentioned that he had already been interviewed in connection with the £5 note found near the body of Jean Jordan and for being seen in red-light areas. Until now police had evidently failed to notice their suspect's tiny feet. Sutcliffe was held for a second night. On the police grapevine, word got back to Sheffield that Peter Williams was still being questioned, but not about stolen plates: He was a Ripper suspect. One of the arresting officers suddenly remembered Williams's casual request for a bathroom trip to the bushes. The constable rushed back to the arrest scene—and turned up the hammer and knife.

The next day, Sutcliffe was asked where he was the night Jacqueline Hill was murdered. He'd been home, with Sonia, he said. The interrogator pressed him further. "I think you are in serious trouble," said the detective.

"I think you have been leading up to it," replied Sutcliffe.

"Leading up to what?"

"The Yorkshire Ripper."

"What about the Yorkshire Ripper?"

Said Sutcliffe, "Well, it's me."

Northern England broke out into celebration at word of Sutcliffe's capture—followed by bouts of rage. A mob of more than 2,000 gathered outside the Dewsbury town hall, demanding the long-banned death penalty. Incredibly, despite Sutcliffe's 16-hour-long confession of his crimes, his

lawyers arranged a plea-bargain, in which the killer would plead guilty to manslaughter by reason of diminished responsibility—the British equivalent of temporary insanity. But the presiding judge angrily threw out the deal and demanded that Sutcliffe be tried before a jury for murder.

Less forthcoming now than he had been initially, Peter Sutcliffe stuck to his insanity defense. He claimed that he had received his orders to kill from God, that he had been sweeping the streets of its prostitutes. "I would have gone on and on," he testified. "It was like some sort of drug." The jury was not impressed. He was found guilty of 13 murders—he had already pleaded guilty to seven attempted murders—and sentenced to life imprisonment with a minimum of 30 years. Sutcliffe was placed in a special wing of Parkhurst, a prison on the remote Isle of Wight.

Two years after his arrival there, the Yorkshire Ripper was himself savagely slashed by another inmate, who cut his face with a broken coffee jar. Sutcliffe began to suffer a mental breakdown. In March 1984 he was transferred to Broadmoor, Britain's renowned institution for the criminally insane. There he remains.

As an imprisoned madman, Sutcliffe exerts a strange gravitation upon visitors, especially females. A reporter who has interviewed him 21 times since he went to jail said in 1991 that Sutcliffe "has a placid quality that makes him almost like a child trying to please. He is calm, polite and matter of fact. He always seemed pleased to see me and enjoyed serving me tea and Jaffa-cake biscuits as we talked about the voices that urged him to do the things he did." Large numbers of women applied to visit the imprisoned celebrity who'd felt compelled to murder their sisters in such brutal fashion. Some have begun a campaign to set him free—so far, without success. ◆

Bloody Liar

To police in 26 states, Henry Lee Lucas seemed to be the all-time American nightmare: a coolly homicidal one-eyed fifth-grade dropout with a taste for necrophilia who, according to his epic series of confessions, raced across the country for nearly eight years on an anonymous rampage, murdering as casually as a man might order a burger at a roadside stand. "Killing someone is just like walking out of doors," he once said. "If I wanted a victim I'd just go get one."

By his own confession, Lucas felt the urge to go get a victim just about all the time. After he was charged with murder in 1983, Lucas evidently experienced a spiritual change and admitted murdering at least 360 people, about three-fourths of them women, using virtually any kind of weapon that came to hand. "We killed them every way there is except one. I haven't poisoned anyone," he explained to police. "We cut 'em up. We hanged 'em. We ran 'em down in cars. We stabbed 'em. We beat 'em, we drowned 'em. There's crucifixion—there's people we filleted like fish. There's people we burnt. There's people we shot in cars." He continued in his flat, emotionless twang: "We strangled them by hand. We strangled them by rope. We strangled them by telephone cord. We even stabbed them when we strangled them. We even tied them so they would strangle themselves."

The "we" in Lucas's open-ended confessions included a big bisexual pyromaniac named Ottis Toole, the smaller man's professed lover (although Lucas has claimed that they were just good friends) and sidekick. According to the tales told by both men, the two were partners in at least 65

murders. This dangerous version of Mutt and Jeff was accompanied by Toole's niece Frieda "Becky" Powell, a teenager who was, Lucas said, the love of his life—until he killed her too.

If Lucas told the truth, he is the most murderous individual of modern times. There's just one problem: A growing number of people, including former Texas attorney general Jim Mattox, believe his claims are a hoax. Although he has been convicted of 11 murders, many of Lucas's confessions involve feats of transport that defy the test of sense. Many of his confessions, skeptics say, were the result of coaching—some say inadvertent coaching—by police investigators. In their screening process, critics note, the Texas Rangers may have given Lucas enough knowledge of an unsolved murder for him to make a credible confession to having done it—or, as he puts it, to take the case.

A special Henry Lee Lucas task force in Texas eventually became a kind of bizarre booking agent for Lucas, making appointments with out-of-state authorities two or

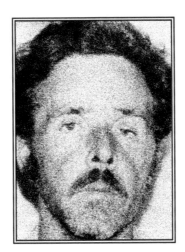

three weeks in advance to interview their talkative and cooperative prisoner. Lucas would listen to police explain an unsolved murder, look at photographs, sometimes visit the scene of the crime, and more often than not, take the case.

Those confessions, rendered more plausible by Toole's parallel admissions, eventually permitted police from 26 states to close more than 210 murder dossiers. But some observers suspected a pragmatic motive: As long as Lucas kept confessing, he was given special privileges and lived what was for him a life of luxury, with endless supplies of his favorite fast foods, airline travel to distant places, and lots of earnest attention. Confessing had made him a kind of celebrity. It also tended to weave his actual crimes, if any, into a vast tapestry of others, real and imagined. Finally—and more to the point—Lucas evidently understood that confessing was to him as swimming is to a man in mid-ocean: When he stopped, he was a goner. After his last confession, Lucas understod, he would be heading for death row.

This man who has alternately helped and mocked the law that holds him was born in August 1936 in Christiansburg, Virginia—and at the bottom of a social cesspool. "They ain't got, I don't think, a human being alive that can say he had the childhood I had," Lucas told one writer. He claims that his mother once pointed out his real father to him on a Christiansburg street, but the only male parent he knew was his stepfather, a drunken railway worker who had lost both legs in an accident, and who died of pneumonia after passing out in the winter snow when young Henry Lee, the ninth of nine children, was

A spruced-up Henry Lee Lucas *(left)* peers from a New Orleans police car in 1984, continuing in Louisiana the confessions begun in Texas, where the seedy, one-eyed drifter had been booked *(above)* the year before.

13. His mother, Viola Lucas, was a prostitute, and "mean as a rattlesnake" according to those who knew her. She beat and starved her children frequently, and singled Henry Lee out for special attention. She made him wear a dress and grow his hair long, girl-fashion—and once knocked him unconscious when he disobeyed. According to Lucas, she also forced him to watch her with clients.

A brother accidentally damaged Henry's left eye when he was 6; a year later, a teach-

Bisexual arsonist Ottis Toole claimed that he and his partner Lucas had murdered at least 65 people throughout the United States. Toole also boasted of barbecuing and eating some of his victims.

er striking at another student inadvertently hit Lucas, destroying all vision in the defective eye. But Henry Lee would not have been a prize student in any case: It took the boy three years to finish the first grade. He was also introduced to sexual perversion at an early age. By his own account he was exposed to necrophilia at the age of 10 by one of his mother's lovers, who killed a calf and invited the youngster to experi-

ment. "I would usually kill animals for sex," Lucas later related. "I had sex with them and eventually it got to where I went to human beings."

By the age of 14, Lucas had left school and already committed his first murder—or so he claimed. The victim, he later recalled, was a 17-year-old girl he met at a bus stop in Harrisonburg, Virginia, whom he kidnapped and raped. He said that he strangled her, although no record of such a victim was ever found. His earliest recorded brushes with the law were more mundane: A 1951 conviction for breaking and entering earned him a 21-month reform-school sentence. From then on, Lucas was in and out of jail for petty crimes.

But there's no lingering doubt about Lucas's next homicide: In 1960 he killed his mother at his sister's home in Tecumseh, Michigan, during an argument over his plans to marry. In his defense, Lucas claimed that his mother had died of a heart attack after he punched her and lightly cut her throat with a knife; in fact, an autopsy showed that the woman bled to death from the small puncture he'd inflicted. Lucas was sentenced to 20 to 40 years in prison.

He served just 10 years of his term. In August 1970 Lucas was paroled—and later claimed that he'd killed a woman within hours of leaving jail. The claim was never substantiated. His violent sexual compulsions were easier to verify, however. In 1971 he went back into a Michigan prison for four more years after trying futilely to force a girl at a school-bus stop into his car at gunpoint. "I have a sex problem," he

later admitted to detectives. "I just crave women all the time."

The problem only got worse. After he was again paroled in 1975, Lucas moved briefly to Pennsylvania, then to Maryland, where he married Betty Crawford, a nephew's widow, and took up residence with her and her three young children in a trailer park in Port Deposit, Maryland. The marriage exploded just two years later when his wife charged that he'd seduced the children—one of the few deviations that Lucas has ever denied. He then moved in with one of his half-sisters in Port Deposit but left after she accused him of molesting her young daughter.

Soon after, having drifted south to Florida, Lucas met his future sidekicks, Ottis Toole and Toole's niece Frieda, who preferred to go by the name of Becky Powell. The two men struck up a homosexual buddy relationship and, they claim, embarked on a spree of petty crime—and murder, as they put it, "for fun." They began moving back and forth across the South, robbing small stores and often killing the owners. In 1979 their trail, by Lucas's account, stretched from Nevada to Texas.

Among the early victims, Toole later confessed, were a young couple hitchhiking on Texas's I-35 after their car ran out of gas: Both were shot and killed. Almost a year later, near Georgetown on the same highway, Lucas claimed to have killed another young woman whose name was never discovered, but who became known as Orange Socks after the only articles of clothing found on her strangled body. Nothing was too low for the duo. Toole even claimed to have barbecued and eaten some victims. Lucas, asked if he'd participated, denied it, explaining that he didn't like barbecue sauce.

In 1981, back in Maryland, Lucas was sentenced to jail again—not for murder, but for stealing his brother-in-law's pickup truck. When he emerged that October, he made a beeline for Florida and Toole's niece Becky. She and her brother, Frank Powell, had been put into Florida juvenile homes in December. Lucas freed her, and the pair headed west. Ottis Toole remained in Florida, but he wasn't free for long. In January 1982 he burned down a rooming house, and one of the tenants was killed in the fire. Toole eventually received a life sentence for the crime.

The details of Lucas's run west with Becky are contested, but Lucas, in his early confessions, said that they made their way

Ottis Toole's 15-year-old niece Frieda "Becky" Powell became, according to Henry Lee Lucas, the only girl he had ever loved—and one of the hundreds of victims he claimed to have murdered.

across the continent by holding up convenience stores when they could and selling their blood when they couldn't. In January, when his run-down Ford sedan finally succumbed in Kerrville, Texas, Lucas and his underage lover began hitchhiking and were finally picked up by a California couple who hired him as casual labor. Lucas did the work well enough that, in May, the couple, who somehow survived the en-

counter, sent them to Ringgold, Texas, to work for the woman's mother, 80-year-old Kate "Granny" Rich.

Lucas lasted only a few days as a handyman at Granny Rich's rural home. The woman's daughters claimed that the seedy drifter and his girl were thieves and worse, and sent them on their way. Once again, a good Samaritan intervened. The Reverend Ruben Moore, head of a tiny fundamentalist sanctuary called the House of Prayer, picked up the hitchhikers and took them to his settlement, a converted chicken ranch. In August, Becky vanished. A tearful Lucas told the sad tale of how his beloved Becky had abandoned him to hitchhike back to Florida. She had ridden out of his life with a Red Arrow truckdriver, he said. Less than a month later, Granny Rich disappeared; and so, for a time, did Lucas himself, before returning to the House of Prayer.

By then, police had become concerned about the missing widow, and very suspicious of her one-time handyman. Although they'd taken Lucas to the Montague County jail for questioning, they were unable to make an arrest for more than six months, when they finally heard from the Reverend Moore that Lucas had given him a gun to keep. In Texas, gun possession by a convicted felon is illegal. Once again, Lucas found himself in the county jail—but this time, he apparently had a change of heart. Several days after being jailed, Lucas sent a note from his cell. "I have tried to get help for so long and no-one will believe me," he wrote. "I have killed for the past ten years and no-one will

believe me. I cannot go own doing this. I also killed the only Girl I ever loved."

The little drifter claimed to have had a revelation: that he would be forgiven all his sins if he confessed them. He soon admitted to stabbing his beloved Becky in an argument over her plans to return to Florida. He had cut her body into pieces and scattered them in the Texas woods near the town of Denton, he said. A few weeks later, he told police, he'd offered to drive the fragile Granny Rich to church one Sunday. Annoyed at her goading remarks about Becky's morals, Lucas said, he'd grabbed a knife from the car seat and stabbed her. He stored the old woman's body in a drainage pipe, then took it back to the House of Prayer—where he cremated it in a wood-burning stove.

"Is that all?" asked the investigating Texas Ranger.

"Not by a long way," Lucas responded. "I reckon I killed more'n a hundred." The confessions had begun.

In June 1983 Lucas created a sensation when he made the same claim in court. By then he had become famous in law enforcement circles, as more and more police officers made the trip to Montague County to question the compliant killer. By autumn, however, Lucas had begun to back away from fame—but too late. On September 30 he pleaded guilty to murdering Kate Rich, and he was given a 75-year sentence. Two months later he received a life sentence for killing Becky Powell. But the kicker came in April 1984: A jury found him guilty of killing the woman known as Orange Socks and sent him to death row. Seven other murder pleas earned Lucas five additional life sentences plus 135 years.

Soon after his arrest, Lucas had given intimations that all was not as it seemed. "They think I'm stupid," he'd warned a reporter in 1983, "but before all this is over, everyone will know who's really stupid." Now he said it had all been a hoax, a ploy to make fools of the police. Oh, he had "killed a few," he said, but nothing like what he had confessed to. His recantation came as no surprise to serial-killer experts, who always believed that Lucas was another breed of cat—he lacked the usual obsessive and highly focused hatreds, he killed in too many different ways, and he seemed not to care who or what his victims were. These experts set Lucas's murder toll at fewer than 10 people, and probably no more than three, including his mother.

In fact, by this time few serious observers believed Lucas's claims. His number of

Lucas killed scores, perhaps hundreds, and those who believe that he killed no more than three lies a no man's land of duplicity, in which the truth is nowhere to be found. "A big black hole of the law," one jurist called it.

Lucas's abrupt reversal found a sympathetic listener in a *Dallas Times Herald* reporter, who began to study the faint track laid down by the drifter and his companions. Comparing the trail with the confessions, he found that many described events were well-nigh impossible. While murder-

cas's alleged victims took his side, forcing Lubbock police to reopen the case given to Lucas. Other jurisdictions gradually followed suit.

Nonetheless, many police forces across the country, having removed scores of unsolved homicides from their books through Lucas's confessions, remain adamant that the semiliterate Virginia hobo was telling at least part of the truth when he admitted to his string of crimes. According to authorities, Lucas showed an extraordinary knowledge of dozens of murder scenes and other details that only the killer would have known, without, they say, undue coaching beforehand. Across the United States, as many as 170 murder cases remain closed by Lucas's confessions. In 1989

A celebrity on the national police circuit, Lucas was taken to murder sites across the United States, including this one in San Luis Obispo County, California, where he describes killing two little girls in May 1980 and burying them by a piling. Not convinced by his confession, officials still consider the case unsolved.

confessed crimes had grown astronomically—and in some cases the accounts were blatantly fanciful. At one point, he even confessed to the 1978 mass suicide known as the Jonestown Massacre—in which more than 900 people died by voluntarily drinking a cyanide-laced purple fruit drink called Flavour-Aide—in South America. Lucas claimed that he had driven down to the Guyanan rain forest with the poison. As an agent for a satanic cult called Hand of Death, he said, he and Toole had sent innumerable missing children into slavery in Mexico. He had snuffed labor leader Jimmy Hoffa. Henry Lee Lucas confessed to killings whenever and wherever they occurred, in Canada, overseas, he was guilty of them all—then, suddenly, he denied them all. Between those who believe that

ing the Texas hitchhiker called Orange Socks, for example, Lucas appeared to have been simultaneously receiving and cashing payroll checks in Florida. At the time of another confessed Texas murder, he was applying for food stamps in Illinois, and while allegedly committing a murder in Nevada, he was selling scrap metal in Florida. In the end, the Dallas newspaper claimed that Lucas had pulled off "the largest hoax in law enforcement annals," and that police had abetted the fraud in order to clear unsolved homicides from their books. Lucas himself said he had been warned that if he stopped confessing he would be sent directly to death row. A Texas attorney general's review essentially confirmed the newspaper's investigation. Eventually, even the parents of one of Lu-

three different Florida grand juries indicted Lucas and his friend Ottis Toole for four homicides to which both men confessed but now claim they did not commit. Because Lucas was already on death row in the Texas state prison at Huntsville, these charges were dropped. Five days before Lucas was scheduled to receive a lethal injection, however, Texas Governor William Clements stayed his execution pending further appeal.

But whatever the doubts may be, the case of Orange Socks is closed on Henry Lee Lucas as implacably as the steel jaws of a bear trap. And he still waits to be put to death for killing that anonymous woman—still the only man on earth who really knows how many times he wanted a victim—and went out and got one. ◆

River Rat

Rochester, New York, meant a fresh start for parolee Arthur Shawcross when he arrived there in June 1987. Indeed, the beefy 42-year-old adapted well to his new home. He married Rosemary Walley, a nurse who'd been his prison pen pal, and in time took her occasional coworker, Clara Neal, as a secret mistress. He worked nights, preparing salads for a food wholesaler, and lived quietly near the center of the city—he did not even own a car. During the day he was often seen on a brown Schwinn Suburban bicycle, a woman's model, as he pedaled to fishing spots along the deep, wooded gorge cut by the Genesee River on its way through Rochester to Lake Ontario.

Finding a new life hadn't been easy, for Shawcross was a man few people would have wanted for a neighbor. He'd spent a large fraction of his life in prison—two years of a five-year burglary conviction, and almost 15 years of a 25-year sentence for first-degree manslaughter. The technical term did not do justice to his crime. Back in 1972, while living in the upstate New York city of Watertown, Shawcross had murdered 10-year-old Jack Blake and raped and fatally strangled eight-year-old Karen

A tight-lipped Arthur Shawcross leaves a Rochester, New York, court after his 1990 arraignment for killing 10 women; another victim was found in a neighboring county. A much younger Shawcross *(inset)* had gone to prison 18 years earlier for murdering two children in Watertown, near Brownsville, his upstate New York hometown.

him him. To make the court proceedings simpler, authorities had indicted him only for the girl's slaying and called it manslaughter in exchange for a guilty plea. Labeled a psychosexual maniac by psychiatrists, Shawcross had been shipped off to the Wyoming Correctional Facility in Attica, New York, then to Green Haven Prison, where, after not quite 15 years of good behavior, he was released on parole at the end of April 1987.

Back on the outside, he'd tried to settle 30 miles south of Watertown, in Binghamton, but the local newspaper revealed his secret, and angry citizens forced him out. Then he tried Delhi and Fleischmanns, two Catskills hamlets, but the police there watched him so closely that he wanted to move on. Finally, parole officers steered him almost 200 miles northwest to the city of Rochester. They informed area police of Shawcross's presence and record and left them to supervise the parole of the apparently rehabilitated killer. Neighbors and work acquaintances found him friendly and mild mannered, and parole officers and mental health counselors who saw him on a regular basis felt that he was progressing well. And, after his fashion, he was.

In March 1988 the body of 27-year-old prostitute Dorothy Blackburn was discovered floating in Salmon Creek, which twists through Rochester's northwestern suburbs. In September another prostitute, Anna Marie Steffen, 28, was found dead in the Genesee gorge near downtown Hastings Street. More than a year later, on October 21, 1989, the remains of 59-year-old drifter Dorothy Keeler were found on Seth Green Island in the Genesee. A week later the body of Patty Ives, 25, was found stuffed under a pile of cardboard behind one of the city's YMCA branches. Postmortem examinations showed that Keeler had been beaten to death. The other three had been throttled by powerful hands. Beyond that, the badly decomposed corpses offered little forensic evidence.

In early November, a fourth prostitute,

Maria Welch, was reported missing. Then, on November 11, Genesee fishermen uncovered the remains of Frances Brown, 22, another Rochester prostitute. Police believed that the murders were too similar to be the work of different individuals—a serial killer was stalking through their city.

Arthur Shawcross followed news of the killings closely. He warned his wife and Neal to be careful and hung out at a local Dunkin' Donuts to discuss the latest news with the cops who gathered there. On November 23 a man walking his dog came upon the remains of June Stott, a slightly retarded 30-year-old, concealed by a piece of carpet in the gorge. Four days later, former beauty queen Elizabeth Gibson, 29, was found dead in Ontario, a small town to the east. Police patrols and surveillance were stepped up in the city's red-light district, and prostitutes armed themselves, but still the women disappeared. By year's end, June Cicero, 34, Darlene Trippi, 32, and Felicia Stephens, 20, had been added to the missing rolls.

The stymied Rochester police invited FBI serial-killer specialists in to help. As the feds studied the case, a profile of the murderer began to emerge: A white male in his thirties, mobile, and somehow trusted by the women who evidently stepped fearlessly into his car. Nevertheless, as the murderer continued to elude them, police began to hope they could catch him at the scene of his gruesome work. The break came with the new year.

Early on January 3, 1990, state troopers in a tan Bell Long Ranger helicopter flying at treetop height over Salmon Creek spotted a body in the icy water below, facedown, wearing only a white sweater and socks—they would identify it later as that of June Cicero. On a bridge overlooking the creek a man leaned out of the passenger door of a parked gray Chevrolet, apparently urinating into a pop bottle. The chopper alerted nearby patrol cars, which converged on the area.

Arthur Shawcross had just finished eat-

ing a salad when he saw the helicopter overhead. He climbed back into the Chevy he had borrowed from Clara Neal and set off for the nearby nursing home where his mistress worked. When he pulled into the parking lot, a police car drew up beside him. He was taken in for questioning.

The hefty parolee seemed very far from the FBI profile of Rochester's serial killer. He was not in his thirties but 44, gray haired, and paunchy. He had no car of his own, and his driver's license had expired. Moreover, he seemed too stupid to have eluded capture for so long—one lawman described the suspect's IQ as "room temperature." When police checked his background, however, their interest quickened. Unable to charge Shawcross, they impounded his borrowed car and released him—with a tail. His picture was circulated in the red-light district, where hookers knew him as Mitch or Gordo. A search of the Chevrolet turned up a pink earring that matched one found in the ear of June Cicero. The next morning police picked up Shawcross as he was cycling through downtown Rochester.

For hours the suspect denied involvement in the murders, claiming that he never went out with prostitutes for fear of catching AIDS. Then his interrogators decided to take a different tack. "I would hate to think that Clara's involved in this," one of them remarked. Shawcross lowered his head and replied, "No, Clara's not involved in this." His defenses breached, the murderer began to talk.

As Shawcross described the women he had killed, it became apparent that behind his mild exterior boiled a cauldron of terrible rage. Some perished when they ridiculed his sexual prowess. He'd strangled Cicero for calling him "no better than a faggot"—and for voicing her suspicions that he was the Genesee killer. He mashed Trippi's face into the car door after she called his performance "hopeless." But anything could trigger his explosive, deadly anger. June Stott was killed for claiming to be a virgin. Patty Ives was choked when she "got carried away" during sex. After Frances Brown accidentally snapped the gear knob in the car he was using, Shawcross "kept hitting her in the throat." Dorothy Keeler, whom Shawcross suspected of stealing from his apartment, threatened to reveal his fling with her to his wife. As he put it later, he took his victim on a fishing trip, on which "we didn't get no fishing done."

By the time of Shawcross's October trial the bodies of Welch, Trippi, and Stephens had been recovered. His confessions over, the killer's passion seemed spent. He refused to testify and sat motionless, shoulders hunched and head down during the 10-week trial. His lawyers argued unsuccessfully that his confessions had been obtained illegally, then switched to an insanity defense. To prove his mental instability they brought in psychiatrist Dorothy Lewis, who put the defendant under hypnosis. On a television screen in the center of the courtroom, a videotape showed Shawcross writhing and screaming as he relived events from his past. He became 11-year-old Artie, crying out as his mother sexually abused him. In another interview he adopted the high-pitched voice of his mother: "Nobody comes between me and him. . . . I hurt all them girls." Shawcross even spoke in the voice of a supposedly reincarnated medieval English cannibal.

In the end the jury agreed with the prosecution: Shawcross was acting. His earlier admissions to the police were far more convincing: His murders, he'd said, were "business as usual." On December 13, 1990, Shawcross was found guilty on 10 counts of murder and later pleaded guilty to an 11th. He was sentenced to 10 consecutive terms of 25 years to life to be served at the Sullivan Correctional Facility in Fallsburg, New York—this time with no possibility of parole.

Although the case had been broken, experts were still puzzled by the age difference between Arthur Shawcross and the

carefully assembled FBI profile. Some suggest that his years in prison must have put his murderous tendencies into a kind of suspended animation. The 1987 parole had broken the spell. Older but otherwise unchanged, Shawcross had stepped back into society to resume the killing begun by a much younger man 15 years before. ◆

A Rochester police officer photographs the remains of Frances Brown, Shawcross's fifth victim, discovered by fishermen near the Genesee River in November 1989.

When somebody put their hand on that doorknob, that's it, they're giving me their life.

EDMUND EMIL KEMPER III

3

Mother's Day

The young giant turned off U.S. 50 in Pueblo, Colorado, around midnight and searched the quiet streets until he found a pay telephone. He parked his rented Chevrolet Impala and made the call that had been on his mind off and on for two days now. Edmund Emil Kemper III wanted to tell the police in his hometown of Santa Cruz, California, what he'd done, and what he wanted to do now that his worst times seemed to be over. He got the number and shoveled change into the slots. When the duty officer answered, Kemper asked for Lieutenant Charles Scherer. He knew the lieutenant. Kemper had double-dated with Scherer's daughter, Susan, more than two years earlier, in February 1971. Besides, he thought that Scherer might be looking for him tonight.

The lieutenant wasn't there, the officer said.

Kemper told him to summon Scherer to the station. It was urgent. "The coeds. You know what I mean."

"Unless I have something to go on, I can't wake up the lieutenant."

"Tell him it's not a prank," said Kemper, "okay?" He told the man his name.

Ed Kemper. It rang a bell. The officer was vaguely acquainted with Ed, a friendly bear of a man. The bright, soft-spoken young man often drank beer with the Santa Cruz cops at the Jury Room, a bar across from the courthouse. It sounded as if Kemper had been drinking tonight.

Again, Kemper asked for Scherer. "I'm about two inches right now from doing a whole bunch of things. There's not really anything anybody can do about it unless I do something about it, you know. I want to talk to him."

The officer called Scherer and woke him up, but the lieutenant told the desk man that unless there was more to go on than some disjointed phone call, the matter could wait until morning.

Kemper drove around Pueblo for about an hour, then tried again. This time he called Santa Cruz collect. Another desk cop answered. He told Kemper that Lieutenant Scherer would be in the office at 9 a.m. and hung up.

Exhausted by two days' steady driving, jangled by a diet of soft drinks and No-Doz, Kemper drove a few miles out of town and slept fitfully in the Impala. Around 5 a.m. on Tuesday, April 24, 1973, he made a final call, this time from a phone booth on the outskirts of Pueblo. A third Santa Cruz police officer answered.

When Kemper asked for Scherer, this officer explained that the lieutenant wasn't available. Then: "What did you want to talk to him about last night?" At last, a voice in Santa Cruz expressed some interest.

"Coed killing!" Kemper shouted.

"What?"

"Coed killing!"

Everyone around Santa Cruz understood the term. It was tabloid shorthand for a rash of brutal murders that had swept the lower Bay Area the preceding year. Six female students attending various schools in the region had disappeared. Some of their body parts had turned up along the Pacific shore or in the coastal hills, and the media ran lurid stories about a killer preying on young women. "Where are you?" the cop asked Kemper.

"Pueblo, Colorado. I want the police over here!"

"What's your name?"

"Ed Kemper."

"Where are you exactly, Ed?"

Here Kemper lapsed into near-incoherence. "I've been driving for three days steady. I have almost a nervous breakdown. . . ."

"All right. Just tell me where you are and we'll have someone come and pick you up."

Kemper said he was about a block from Highway 50, at the intersection of 21st Street and Norwood Avenue, near a 7-Eleven and a Kentucky Fried Chicken outlet. He added that he was driving a Chevy Impala and read off the Nevada license number. He alluded obliquely to what he had in the car: the Winchester semiautomatic 12-gauge shotgun, the Remington bolt-action 30.06 rifle, the .30-caliber M-1 carbine, the 200 rounds of ammunition—and the knives.

By now, two Santa Cruz officers were on the line. While one kept Kemper going, the other used another phone to call the Pueblo police. Then the pair got back on the line with Kemper and began asking him about the women he'd killed. Kemper knew not only the victims' names but every detail of their physical appearance, what they wore, what he'd done to their remains. Finally one cop said to Kemper, "Give me a physical of what you look like, okay?"

"I'm six-nine and I weigh 280."

"How old?"

"Twenty-four." Kemper added that he'd been very upset for the last 48 hours. Early Saturday morning, he said, he'd killed his 52-year-old mother, Clarnell, and stashed the body, minus its head and right hand, in a closet. After a while he'd put her head with the rest of her. Then, a few hours later, he'd dumped the naked, raped body of his mother's best friend, 59-year-old Sara Hallett, in another closet. Kemper had left a cryptic note explaining the death of Clarnell. "Not sloppy and incomplete, gents, just a 'lack of time,'" he'd written. "Got things to do!!! Appx 5:15 a.m. Saturday. No need for her to suffer any more at the hands of this horrible 'murderous Butcher.' It was quick—asleep—no pain—the way I wanted it." Why had he killed the friend? Well, he'd done it as a kind of afterthought, as cover for his mother's sudden disappearance: She's off on a trip with Sally Hallett. In a way, she was. He gave the cop his mother's address in Aptos, a small town south of Santa Cruz, and said the apartment was locked but that a set of keys was hidden near a back wall. He added, "I don't know what's going to happen with all these damn guns lying around."

The officer asked about one of the student victims, Rosalind Thorpe. Kemper, always precise, replied that he'd murdered her with a .22 pistol—a Ruger automatic with a six-inch barrel.

"What else did you do to her?"

"Just cut off her head."

At that moment, a police cruiser swooped into the intersection. Patrolman David Martinez got out with his Smith & Wesson .357 magnum revolver drawn and approached the phone booth. "Whew!" Kemper exclaimed. "He's got a gun on me." Martinez kept the pistol on him until his back-up arrived minutes later. Then they took him in.

The Pueblo police knew little more than that they were dealing with a murder suspect. In size alone, their captive was formidable. "He just filled that phone booth completely up," said Officer Martinez; at first, he'd thought that two people were in the booth. Although soft, Kemper had the strength of the very large. When he'd worked on highway road crews his comrades had called him Fork Lift, because he could carry two 90-pound bags of cement on his outstretched arms. But the young man offered no resistance. He seemed to welcome handcuffs, and he had lots to say, rambling on about the coeds he'd killed. He also directed the Pueblo police search for incriminating evidence in his car, pointing out the wood-handled pocketknife that had given such good service. The arrest report written up later would note that "the principal was very cooperative at all times and seemed very calm."

Before dawn in California the Santa Cruz police, ignoring Kemper's instructions about hidden keys, broke into his mother's apartment in a drab little building in Aptos. "As soon as we broke the window we knew what he was saying was true," one sergeant said afterward. "If you've ever smelled death you never forget it." That same day, a contingent of policemen and public prosecutors set out for Colorado to get a statement from Kemper and bring him back to California. By the time they reached Pueblo, Kemper had already provided the local police with an account of his murderous career, summed up in a so-called offense report, a standard part of post-arrest procedure. The report listed eight victims, how each one died, and in some cases, how Kemper disposed of the body—or what was left of it.

But Kemper was still gathering confessional momentum. When the California contingent arrived he gladly agreed to describe all his deeds into a tape recorder, and he continued to expand on the narrative during the drive back to Santa Cruz—a drive that the police dragged out as long as possible in order to extract every detail. They marveled at his powers of observation and his memory; no one was much surprised to learn later that his IQ tested in the high 130s. He was not only mentally quick, he was also organized. His confession came out almost prepackaged for law-enforcement use, since he knew about police methods, a suspect's rights, rules of evidence, and even minor jurisdictional matters. A member of the prosecution team would later say, "He would be my all-time choice for most interesting criminal, and I've seen a lot of them in 20 years." Kemper, offered one Santa Cruz sergeant, was "the most personable dangerous person we'll ever see."

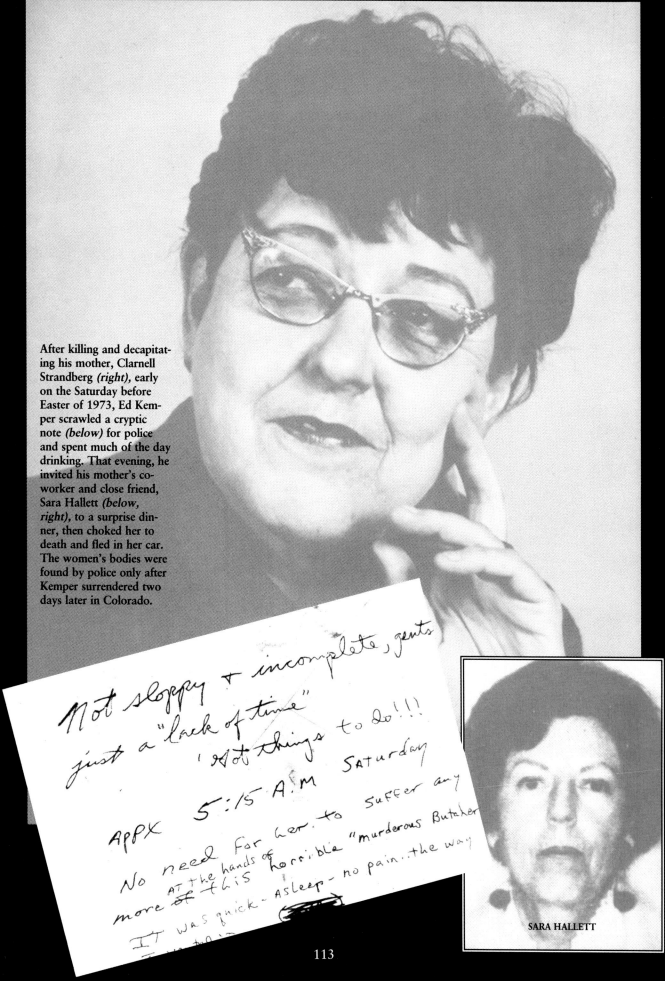

After killing and decapitating his mother, Clarnell Strandberg *(right),* early on the Saturday before Easter of 1973, Ed Kemper scrawled a cryptic note *(below)* for police and spent much of the day drinking. That evening, he invited his mother's co-worker and close friend, Sara Hallett *(below, right),* to a surprise dinner, then choked her to death and fled in her car. The women's bodies were found by police only after Kemper surrendered two days later in Colorado.

Not sloppy + incomplete, gents just a "lack of time" 'Not things to do!!!

APPX 5:15 A.M. Saturday

No need For her to suffer any more of this horrible "murderous Butcher" IT was quick - asleep - no pain..the way

SARA HALLETT

113

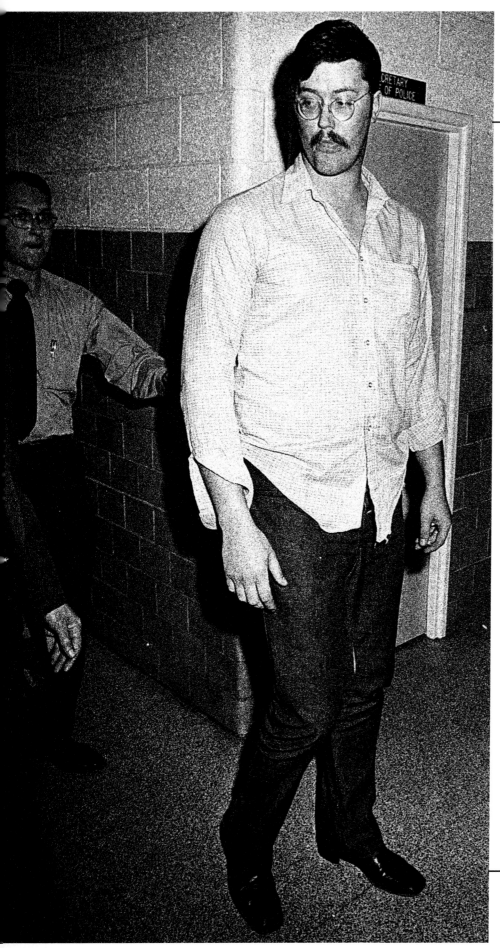

The six-foot-nine-inch 280-pound Kemper dwarfs his captors after his April 1973 surrender to Pueblo, Colorado, police.

Back in California the killer spent days helping the police find pieces of his victims' bodies and clothing, and in the months that followed, the stream of memories continued to flow almost unchecked. Among serial killers Ed Kemper was the supreme communicator, with a genuine intellectual interest in himself and his actions, which he described with the intelligent dispassion of a rocket engineer. To the many lawyers, psychiatrists, and journalists who interviewed him, he seemed remarkably, mesmerizingly open. But there were some things that neither he nor they would ever fully understand. At the core of Edmund Kemper, beneath the layers of recollection and self-observation and even a certain kind of charm, an unfathomable, monstrous void held sway — and always had.

The dark center of Ed Kemper evidently coalesced very early in the young man's increasingly tortured life. Kemper — called Guy by his family — was born in Burbank, California, on December 18, 1948, the second of three children of Edmund Emil Kemper II and his wife Clarnell, and the only son. In some ways, his parents were well matched. Both were heavyset and very tall — his father six-feet-eight, his mother six feet — and both were loud and argumentative. Kemper's sister Susan was six years older, and his sister Allyn was two years younger.

Much later Kemper would recall that, when he was four and his world of squabbling giants still seemed full of light, all of his fantasies centered on the wish that the family would be loving and that it would endure. But that same year, his father, who had served in Europe during World War II, went off to work on the atomic bomb tests in the South Pacific and stayed away for two years. When he returned, the clashes between the two parents grew louder and more violent. Clarnell constantly criticized her husband for not making more of himself; he drifted into a job as an electrician, which she considered menial and beneath his station. Sometimes they came to blows, with the children looking on. According to the father, Clarnell began to drink heavily.

Watching all this, the son fashioned an imaginary parent—a huge man with the courage and incorruptibility of he-man film star John Wayne. His dad was a fighter whose prowess was evidenced in the guns, bayonets, and machetes scattered around the house. But in that seething domestic arena, most of the fights were verbal, the kind of battle that Edmund Emil Kemper II never won. When Guy was seven years old his father left the household; when he returned briefly about a year later, everyone—even little Ed—could see that the marriage was over.

As the family storms raged, Ed developed strange ideas of play. He enlisted his little sister in a game featuring his own execution in a gas chamber. Her role was to tie him up, blindfold him, and tug on an imaginary lever that released imaginary cyanide gas; he would writhe and twist and finally slump over, dead. More often he was the executioner. His little victims included a doll Allyn had been given for Christmas; it disappeared, then turned up with the head and hands cut off. On another occasion the victim was a kitten. When the children quarreled over its ownership, Clarnell Kemper said that the kitten belonged to everyone. But Ed did not accept that. After killing the kitten by burying it alive in the backyard, he took the little body up to his room, decapitated it, then put the head on a spindle and prayed to it. One of his prayers, at home as in church, was that everyone in the world would die—except him. But

increasingly his death fantasies focused on specific people— his mother, his sisters—and became intertwined with sex.

In his skewed imaginings Kemper was powerfully drawn to older women, who exerted an attraction on him that may have evoked the strong maternal magnetism of his mother. When he was only eight years old he confided to his younger sister that he wanted to kiss his second-grade teacher. Allyn teased, "Why don't you do it?" He said, "If I kiss her, I would have to kill her first." Later in his childhood he crept from the house one night and took up a vigil outside the home of another admired teacher. He clutched a bayonet, he recounted later, and thought of killing her and

Guided by instructions from Kemper, Santa Cruz, California, detectives exhume his fourth coed victim's skull, which the killer had buried under a steppingstone behind the duplex apartment that he shared with his mother.

having sex with the body. Kemper had already struck the equation that would one day rule him: sex = love = death.

Perhaps aware of his dangerous confusion, Clarnell worried about her son's sexuality, especially after his father left forever in 1957, and she and her children moved from southern California to her hometown, Helena, Montana, where she found work as a bank teller. On the one hand, she hated any sign of weakness in him, fearing that he would turn out to be a homosexual—a condition brought on by overindulging a boy, in her opinion. Ed's subsequent contact with a homosexual cousin no doubt caused further concern. On the other hand, the mother took pains to repress the boy's strong, precocious sexuality. Some experts have speculated since that Kemper had been heterosexually overstimulated at an early age, perhaps by seeing his parents in bed together, and perhaps by some other familial contact as well. In any case, Clarnell seems to have regarded him as a sexual threat to his sisters.

When Ed was 10, Clarnell moved him out of the second-story bedroom near his sister Allyn's room and made him sleep in the basement, a windowless oblong of concrete walls and floors, topped by a creaky wooden ceiling. To go to bed Kemper had to walk down the stairs in the dark and cross half the basement to turn the light on. He later said that he'd begged to get out, that he'd been having nightmares and sleepwalking, that he'd believed the devil lived in the furnace, which burst into life sporadically during the night. The place terrified him. It also cauterized his dark center, at least in his view, for it was in that frightening coffin of a cellar that his fantasies of death and sex lurched toward the reality of murder.

By the time Kemper was 13 he'd begun killing neighborhood pets and other animals, including a second cat that seemed to prefer Allyn to him. He dispatched this one by slicing off the top of its skull with a machete to expose the brain, then, as the cat went into convulsions, stabbing it until it died. He buried most of the body, but kept some parts in his closet.

In fact, Kemper had embarked on the journey that would

If I kiss her, I would have to kill her first.

end on Easter weekend of 1973. Often, he recalled later, he would tiptoe into his mother's bedroom with a knife or hammer in his hand and hover there as she slept, savoring the picture of himself as executioner. He made a special mother-killing weapon, a spike on a stick, and let her see it. "She gave me a very strange look," he remembered. In the backyard he dug a series of graves—a hole for her head, a hole for her arms, a hole for her legs. Though some experts discount such tales as retrospective fantasy, few doubt that the mother was the one woman Kemper really wished to kill—the Mount Everest of death he would climb on a trail marked by dismembered female bodies.

Already alienated by his secret life of sex and murder, Ed was further distanced from his fellows by the gentle mask he wore in public. He was one of those big, soft, friendless kids whom other boys bully. His idea of impressing his playmates was to lie down on the road and make traffic stop for him. He didn't like sports. He was withdrawn and fearful, later remembering, "As I was growing up I shied away from loud noises and arguments." He'd been trained to avoid conflict by the warring giants of his childhood.

In Montana, Clarnell remarried twice. Neither match lasted very long, but one of Ed's stepfathers, Norman Turnquist, made an effort to be a good parent; he took the boy fishing and taught him about hunting and guns. Young Kemper wasn't interested. Ed fantasized about being reunited with his real father, who was then living in Van Nuys, outside Los Angeles. During one fishing trip near Helena, Kemper crept up behind Turnquist with an iron bar in his hand. He thought about smashing his stepfather's skull and stealing the car and driving south to be with his real father. That time he couldn't bring himself to do it.

Shortly afterward Kemper did run away from home to join his father, who quickly sent the boy back to his mother. He kept trying, however, and when he was 14 he seemed to succeed. On Thanksgiving Day, 1963, he took a bus to Los Angeles, presented himself to his father, and at long last, was told that he could stay. But the senior Kemper had remarried, and his wife was disturbed by the presence of the son—now almost six feet four inches tall, with a strange, brooding manner. At Christmastime, Ed was taken to visit his paternal grandparents, who lived on a farm near the remote town of North Fork, in the arid Sierra foothills about 50 miles northeast of Fresno. Only when they arrived did Ed discover that he'd be staying there permanently. The betrayed lad watched his father drive away, hoping—but perhaps not believing—that he would see him again after the holidays. The father never came back. Somehow Ed was not surprised.

Nor did it surprise Kemper that his lost father made no effort to keep in touch; instead, the man tried to shut his son out of his life altogether, obtaining an unlisted telephone number so that Ed couldn't call him. But the father stayed in contact with his ex-wife, Clarnell. One night she phoned to deliver a warning. "You're taking a chance leaving him with your parents," she said. "You might be surprised to wake up some morning to learn they've been killed." Clarnell must have been drinking, he decided, to say such a crazy thing.

Young Ed was miserable on the farm. His grandfather, a 72-year-old retired employee of the California Division of Highways, was vacant and passive. His grandmother, 66, was more of a presence, still working as an artist and writer of stories for juveniles, but Ed hated her. She was a strict disciplinarian and reminded him of his mother. She criticized him if he didn't do his assigned chores perfectly; she berated him for sullenness and for his tendency to stare blankly at people. Kemper later told a psychiatrist that his grandmother thought she was more than a match for any male "and was constantly emasculating me and my grandfather to prove it." By way of reinforcing this, perhaps, she made him do the indoor chores—the so-called women's work—while she chopped wood. And there wasn't much relief from misery away from the farm. The North Fork high school in which he started 1964 was as unfriendly as the Helena schools had been.

Hunting was the boy's one pleasure. His grandfather had given him a .22 rifle as a present, and Ed roamed the farm after school and on weekends, blazing away at almost anything that moved. Rabbits and gophers were approved targets: His grandfather paid a bounty for every one he shot. But his grandparents forbade him to shoot birds. "My grandmother loved her feathered friends," he remembered, noting with some satisfaction that he'd shot them wholesale. "You never saw so many birds disappear so fast."

In June 1964 Kemper returned to his mother's home in Montana, but he was sent back to North Fork in mid-August. His hatred of the farm, his life there, and the woman who seemed to hold him in her fist deepened. "My grandmother was riding me," he told a psychiatrist later. "She never rode me that bad before. I thought, 'I'll do it, not make one mistake,' but then she'd remind me two hours ahead of time, nagging before the fact. Then I thought of the ultimate weapon, getting her completely off my back. She wants the perfect boy? It would be perfect mechanization. I'll jump up and do it." But two weeks of playing the perfect boy had just the opposite effect. "One night she blew it, screamed at me, said I'd tried to scare her to get her to have a heart attack, kill her." All his death fantasies focused on the old woman.

On August 27, 1964, Kemper sat with his grandmother in the kitchen as she worked at a story she was writing for *Boy's Life,* the magazine of the Boy Scouts. She noticed him staring at her in that unsettling blank way of his and ordered him to stop it. He picked up his .22 rifle and went outside, saying that he was going hunting. As always, she warned him not to shoot the birds. That final nagging admonition stopped him in his tracks. Standing on the back porch, he turned and looked through the screened window at his grandmother, sitting just a few feet away, pondering her *Boy's Life* saga. Then Ed raised the rifle, aimed at the back of her head, and squeezed the trigger. The .22 made a flat *crack!* She slumped forward. He shot her twice more in the upper back. Then he ran inside to examine her. "There was blood from the right nostril like a faucet. One eye was open, one shut. I wrapped her head with a towel and put her down. I dragged her into the bedroom." He momentarily thought about undressing her but pushed the thought away. Instead, he stabbed the hated woman three times with a butcher knife until the blade was hopelessly bent.

Minutes later the boy heard his grandfather's pickup truck approach and stop beside the garage. Kemper stepped onto the porch and greeted the old man, who smiled and waved back. Then, as his grandfather started to unload groceries from the front seat of the truck, Kemper shot him once in the back of the head. Trying to explain his action to authorities, Kemper had—as he customarily had—a host of reasons, often conflicting ones. He was afraid his grandfather would beat him or kill him when he found out what had happened. He wanted to spare his grandfather the hor-

ror of seeing his wife's bloody body; he wanted to prevent him from having a heart attack. "I did it out of love," he said. Yet another reason was internal anarchy: "I was like a runaway plane, no control, such a rage."

Baffled as to what he should do next, Kemper briefly considered turning the rifle on himself, then reconsidered. Instead, he called his mother. "Grandma's dead," he told her. "And so is Grandpa." He tried to convince Clarnell that the shootings had been accidental, the result of a hair trigger on the .22, but she wasn't fooled. She instructed him to call the county sheriff. Soon he was in custody and, after some initial evasiveness, freely admitting the truth: "I just wondered how it would feel to shoot Grandma."

A psychiatrist examined the 15-year-old killer at length and submitted a report to the judicial authorities. His conclusions were unambiguous: He described Kemper as "psychotic at this time, confused and unable to function. Has paranoid ideation, growing more and more bizarre. It is noteworthy that he is more paranoid toward women, all except his mother, who is the real culprit. He is a psychotic and danger to himself and others. He may well be a long-term problem." Guided by that unequivocal prognosis, the California Youth Authority sent Ed Kemper away to Atascadero State Hospital for an indefinite stay.

Atascadero sits like a failed boarding school among the grassy coastal hills north of San Luis Obispo. Its mean stuccoed barracks enclosed by barbed wire and a broad no man's land, it is still the maximum-security mental hospital serving northern California, and still rather specialized. When Ed Kemper arrived there in December of 1964, the hospital's 1,500 patients were male sexual psychopaths — rapists, child molesters, sexual deviants of every stripe; many of them were violent, perhaps a tenth of them were murderers. But within what is called tough peripheral security, the atmosphere at Atascadero was very different from that of a prison. Here the emphasis was not on punishment but on cure, and only patients regarded as amenable to treatment were admitted. With a successful course of treatment, they could aspire to release in as short a time as two years. Inside the fence inmates were allowed considerable independence; they elected their own government

In 1963 Kemper went to live with his paternal grandparents in this remote farmhouse *(left)* near North Fork, California. Eight months later, the youth shot and killed his grandmother, then murdered his grandfather as he unloaded groceries from his pickup truck *(above).*

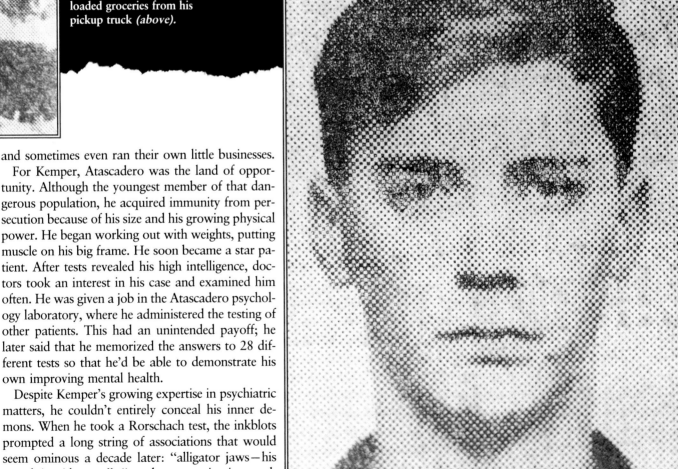

The Madera County newspaper ran this photograph of 15-year-old Edmund Emil Kemper III after the boy murdered his grandparents at their North Fork farm. One explanation he later gave authorities was: "I just wondered how it would feel to shoot Grandma."

and sometimes even ran their own little businesses.

For Kemper, Atascadero was the land of opportunity. Although the youngest member of that dangerous population, he acquired immunity from persecution because of his size and his growing physical power. He began working out with weights, putting muscle on his big frame. He soon became a star patient. After tests revealed his high intelligence, doctors took an interest in his case and examined him often. He was given a job in the Atascadero psychology laboratory, where he administered the testing of other patients. This had an unintended payoff; he later said that he memorized the answers to 28 different tests so that he'd be able to demonstrate his own improving mental health.

Despite Kemper's growing expertise in psychiatric matters, he couldn't entirely conceal his inner demons. When he took a Rorschach test, the inkblots prompted a long string of associations that would seem ominous a decade later: "alligator jaws—his mouth is wide open"; "two bears running into each

Patients are free to roam this
treed yard inside the barbed-wire
fence at California's Atascadero
State Hospital for men, where
Kemper spent five years.

other"; "a trapdoor with a spider at the bottom, sitting down in the hole waiting to snatch an insect." The doctor interpreting these descriptions found such clues equivocal. "There is evidence of a rather substantial amount of latent hostility," wrote one. "He gives the impression of a rather passive, dependent person rather than one who is overtly aggressive. The possibility of explosiveness is certainly evident, however."

In the opinion of most of the doctors who observed Kemper, that possibility was steadily receding. Even before his induction into Atascadero, one report noted that he showed "no flight of ideas, no interference with thought, no expression of delusions or hallucinations, and no evidence of bizarre thinking." At the hospital he was thought a good worker, exceptionally reliable and efficient. More important, he seemed to understand the roots of his disturbance. "I found out that I really killed my grandmother because I wanted to kill my mother," he was finally able to explain. "I had this love-hate complex with my mother that was very hard for me to handle, and I was very withdrawn—withdrawn from reality because of it. I couldn't handle the hate, and the love was actually forced upon me, you know. It was a very strong family-tie type of love." Such self-awareness, along with an outward appearance of stability, convinced doctors that he was a good candidate for release.

Kemper didn't entirely regret his stay there. For the first time, he'd been recognized as a special person—bright, capable, worthy of respect. He'd been given a measure of executive responsibility. He'd spent endless hours in group

therapy and had become something of an expert on mental illness; at the very least, he became fluent in its jargon. He'd even seen his father, who had dropped by to ask him not to write any more letters. Later, Kemper would say that he'd been "born" at Atascadero. But the birth carried a price: All that time in the exclusive company of male deviants had left him, he would comment later, unfit for normal relationships with women.

But there was much that Kemper didn't tell the psychiatrists. He neglected to mention that he'd spent hours discussing rape with expert practitioners, or that their most important lesson was that rapists were caught only if their victims lived. He didn't discuss the fact that the violent fantasies of his childhood had continued at Atascadero, intensifying around his new knowledge of what it was to kill, and what it might be to rape. In one fantasy he killed a girl, cut her body apart, and ate some of the flesh, then kept her head on a shelf as a sort of sacred object—a chilling foreshadowing of things to come. Long afterward he was asked—somewhat naively—why he'd kept this daydream to himself. "I never would have gotten out of there," replied Kemper. Atascadero had been, among many other things, a kind of vocational school, and he was ready to graduate.

Kemper remained behind the wire at Atascadero for five years, until November 1969. His star status, his probing self-knowledge, and his model behavior convinced his keepers that he was ready to return to the world. But there was a practical reason for his release as well. The state government, then headed by Ronald Reagan, wanted to halt the

During Kemper's stay, most of
Atascadero's 1,500 patients
were dangerous sexual offenders,
quartered in austere dormitory
rooms like this one.

"warehousing" of mental patients in California institutions and turn over as many of them as possible to the care of their communities. Atascadero stayed open, but its maximum-security facilities were now at a premium, and the hospital authorities felt pressure to send the more promising cases—Ed Kemper among them—back into society.

A month before he turned 21, Atascadero released Kemper to the California Youth Authority. He spent the next three months at a halfway house in California's Central Valley area, attending a community college where he earned straight As. The next step was to find him a permanent place to live. The Atascadero psychiatrists had em-

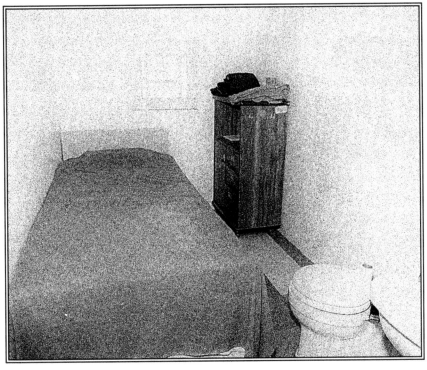

phasized that under no circumstances should he be returned to his mother. But the Youth Authority parole board, perhaps pressured by Clarnell, ignored those recommendations and—fatally, it turned out—discharged Kemper into her custody.

By then Clarnell had divorced her third husband and returned to California. She was using her last married name of Strandberg and had taken a job as an administrative assistant to one of the college provosts at the newly opened University of California campus in Santa Cruz.

Santa Cruz was a small, picturesque city poised on the northern lip of Monterey Bay about 75 miles southeast of San Francisco. Bordered by the Pacific on one side and the redwood-clad Santa Cruz mountains on the other, the city lived on tourism. But many of the visitors who saw the dramatic cliffs, submerged rocks, and cathedral-like forests

along that coast decided to stay. With its clean, soft air and abundant sunshine, Santa Cruz attracted a large retirement-age population—and legions of the young. Some of the latter opted for a flower-child existence in the hills; others used the cloak of the woods to concoct forbidden drugs. But most were drawn to Santa Cruz by the university, which occupied a lovely 2,000-acre hilltop site that had formerly been a ranch. At all hours students could be seen hitchhiking between the town itself and the UCSC campus or nearby Cabrillo Community College.

To Ed Kemper, emerging from the shadows of a mental institution, the setting and subcultures of Santa Cruz were blindingly novel. He'd spent half of the 1960s in the company of sexually twisted men, only to step into a new world where sex and pretty girls were everywhere, and Love was a kind of cultural password among strangers. An outsider all his life, Kemper could haunt only the fringes of this brave new society, disturbed, jittery, and, as always, alone.

After moving into his mother's duplex apartment in the suburb of Aptos in February 1970, Kemper worked as a laborer in a local Green Giant canning factory for a while, then found a job pumping gas. But what he really wanted was to be a cop. The problem was that local jurisdictions had a height restriction, and, as it turned out, so did the California Highway Patrol.

If the peaceful giant couldn't actually be a policeman, he could at least hang out with them. His favorite drinking place was the Jury Room, a bar near the Santa Cruz court-

Popular with off-duty police officers and workers from the nearby courthouse, Mandella's Jury Room was Big Ed Kemper's favorite Santa Cruz hangout.

house, filled with off-duty officers and an entourage of law-enforcement groupies. Kemper hoisted beers with them and passed the evening hours discussing guns and other matters of mutual interest. One acquaintance gave him a badge from police training school. Another made him a present of a pair of handcuffs.

Kemper spent part of his salary on a motorcycle and roared around the San Francisco Bay area on it—between crashes. His first accident occurred in November of 1970, when another driver made an illegal left turn and hit him. He was unconscious for 15 minutes and sustained facial fractures and a separation of his left shoulder. Kemper sued the driver for $45,000 but later settled for $15,000. He also picked up a banana-colored 1969 Ford Galaxie 500 two-door and had it fitted with a two-way radio and a whip antenna of the kind used on police vehicles.

When his mother's 18-month custody of him ended in July 1971, Kemper rented an apartment of his own on Union Street in Alameda, a bayside suburb of Oakland. Not long afterward, he found a job as a laborer for the California Division of Highways—a position that taught him much about the roads in the region, including byways where a person was unlikely to be observed. He passed much of his free time driving around, drinking, and reading pornographic literature and crime magazines for stimulation. He also bought a couple of knives.

Yet this newfound independence was not all Kemper had expected it to be. He continued to spend a good deal of time with his mother, even though the two of them fought constantly. She ragged him for laziness, passivity, slovenliness; she also told him that his strange, brooding air scared people away and was wrecking her social life. She once blamed "you, my murderous son," for the fact that she hadn't slept with a man for five years.

The mother also took pains to make Kemper see that he was far beneath the UCSC coeds with whom she passed her days. "She's holding up these girls as being too good for me even to get to know," he complained later. "I'm saying, 'Well, why don't you introduce me to some of these girls and quit telling me about them?' She says, 'You're just like your father, you don't deserve to know girls like that.' She's foisting off on me these ugly turkeys." Then, almost as an afterthought: "We didn't even have enough class to keep the arguments quiet where the neighbors wouldn't hear it."

Despite all the bitterness, however, the mother-son tie held fast. Clarnell encouraged his stays in Aptos and got him a car sticker that would enable him to visit her on campus—a sticker that hitchhikers took as a sign of university affiliation, and thus of drivers who could be trusted.

Within this turbulent cocoon of normality, however, Kemper's inner darkness continued to evolve, possibly fostered by a significant event in the summer of 1971. Following his yearning to see his father, he'd traced Edmund II through the Los Angeles Electricians' Union and got in touch. Unwilling to admit his son to his home, the father

had agreed to meet Ed on some neutral site. The two big men spent an evening at a restaurant, drinking, having clamorous mock arguments over who'd pick up each tab— Ed did, for he knew his father never had money—during their four-hour eating and drinking contest. Other patrons cringed at the pair, who seemed like giants ready to fight. "We resolved all the psychic goodies," Kemper quipped later, "about the grandparents and how he had forgiven me and everything."

On the way back to the Bay Area from Los Angeles, Kemper stopped for two women hitchhikers. Driving north, chatting amiably with his passengers, he wondered what they'd look like with no heads. Back in Alameda, such images began to flood his conscious moments. In the months that followed, knowing where such fantasies now must take him, he began a lengthy rehearsal, picking up female hitchhikers all over the Bay Area and beyond—more than a hundred of them, he estimated. None of these riders was harmed; indeed, throughout his brief reign of terror, Kemper would continue to give scores of riders safe passage. For now, he wanted to see how these trusting women behaved, how wary they were, how they reacted when he made a wrong turn. He practiced putting them at their ease.

Kemper also made some material preparations for the inevitable encounter. He removed the whip antenna from his car; it was too conspicuous. He put a blanket in the car,

and some knives, and some heavy plastic bags. He adjusted the door lock on the passenger side so that he could reach across, pretending to lock it, and slip in a piece of plastic that would prevent the door from being opened from the inside. By spring he was ready to hunt.

Sunday, May 7, 1972, was the kind of day that Californians boast about, the air scrubbed and gleaming, bearing a touch of the sea. At about 4 p.m. Ed Kemper, in dark western-style denim jeans and a tan checkered shirt, steered the yellow Galaxie down Berkeley's Ashby Avenue, near the San Francisco-Oakland Bay Bridge. He'd been cruising, looking for the right people, time, and place. Under the seat was a 9-mm. Browning semiautomatic pistol that he'd borrowed from his former boss at the gas station. Approaching a ramp that directed cars onto the Eastshore Freeway, he saw what he wanted—a twosome.

Mary Ann Pesce and Anita Luchessa were both 18, both petite and pretty. Pesce was wearing blue jeans, a purple sweater, and a purple felt hiking hat. Luchessa was dressed in striped bib overalls, a red T-shirt, and a red nylon jacket and wore round, gold-rimmed granny glasses. As roommates at Fresno State College they'd discovered a strong mutual interest in skiing. Of the two, Pesce was the better skier—an Olympic aspirant—and also much more worldly than her friend: She'd spent her teenage years in Germany and Switzerland because of her father's job as director of the international operations of an aerospace business. Luchessa's background was simpler. She'd grown up on a farm near Modesto, California. Seeking a break from their studies, they'd hitched over to visit friends in Berkeley and were now on their way to see someone Luchessa knew at Stanford University in Palo Alto, about 35 miles south of San Francisco.

The two hitchhikers slid onto the front seat of Kemper's car without hesitation. Kemper told them that he happened to be going toward Stanford. Then he made some random turns to see if they were familiar with the roads in the area. They were not. He headed east on Highway 580, directly away from their destination. He was talking, telling them that he worked for the highway department, chatting about his CB radio. "They thought I was a secret agent or something," he later said.

Out in the dry hills near Livermore, Kemper turned off 580 and drove south on a series of progressively smaller roads. Beyond a housing development he spotted a dirt track leading into an orchard. He pulled in, drove to the end, and put the gearshift in park. Then he brought up the pistol. "What do you want?" asked Pesce.

"You know what I want."

As Anita Luchessa sagged back in silent terror, Pesce took charge. She reasoned with him in a calm voice, saying that he could tell her about his problems, wisecracking a bit and showing no signs of being intimidated by the gun. "I was really quite struck by her personality and her looks," Kemper would recall. "There was just almost a reverence there," he added, referring to his admiration of the young woman. He said that he'd take the pair back to his apartment in Alameda. "I made it sound like I was gonna play a few games, and they knew what I meant by that." Luchessa would have to ride in the trunk, he said.

He handcuffed Pesce to the seat-belt mechanism and led her friend to the rear of the Galaxie. "Please don't do this," Luchessa begged, but she obeyed and got into the trunk. Back in the car he switched the handcuffs to a position behind Mary Ann Pesce's back, then put a plastic bag over her head. Until that moment, she'd been calm, but the suffocating bag unnerved her. She said she couldn't breathe. He told her he'd tear a hole in it, but instead he looped a cloth bathrobe tie around her neck and yanked it tight. The cloth caught in her mouth and broke. "I just got mad and reached in my pocket and pulled out a knife and flipped the blade open," Kemper remembered.

Pesce asked Kemper what he was doing. Her back was to him. "I poised the blade over her back, trying to decide where her heart was, and struck and hit her in the middle of the back, and it stuck a little bit, and she said something like 'Ow' or 'Oh,' and I pulled it back out and I did it again," Kemper recalled. "She was struggling around a little bit. Then I started thrusting hard, but apparently the blade wasn't long enough. I struck in several places in both sides of the back and noticed as I went farther down the back that she was a little louder and more painful in her cries, but none got really loud. That always bothered me. It was almost like she didn't want to blow up and start screaming or something, she was maintaining control."

Mary Ann Pesce was also fighting for her life. She twisted under him and he stabbed her in the stomach, but she spun away from the knife. He continued to stab, and she continued to cry out. One cry seemed to come from her back.

"There were several holes in the lung area and bubbles and things coming out," he said. "She turned her head and called out her friend's name, her first name. It was slow and it was not loud. That was the last thing that she said." Kemper yanked her head back and cut her throat. "There was absolutely no contact with improper areas," he later insisted, as if it made a difference. At one point he had apologized to her when his hand brushed her breast.

Then it was Anita Luchessa's turn. When he opened the trunk, her eyes fastened on his bloody hands. He told her that he'd broken her friend's nose and that she needed help. As he spoke he picked up a bone-handled Bowie knife that he kept in the trunk. When Luchessa tried to climb out, he

stabbed her hard, but the blade didn't penetrate her stiff new denim overalls. He stabbed her again, and she flung herself back into the trunk, crying, "Oh God, God!" He tried to slash her throat and gashed his own hand in the process. She covered her throat with her hands, and he swept the blade across her fingers, then thrust the knife deep into her left side several times.

Luchessa kept fighting, and Kemper cut her forearms so badly that the bones were exposed. "She looked at it, and I could see the expression on her face of shock," he remembered. "When she saw that wound on her arm, she just starting screaming, very loud and piercing, and that shocked me, and I stood back and I didn't know what to do." He

Below a ruined taillight, Kemper's yellow 1969 Ford Galaxie bears an *A* parking sticker from the University of California at Santa Cruz.

ANITA LUCHESSA

Fresno State College roommates Anita Luchessa *(left)* and Mary Ann Pesce, both 18, were thumbing to Stanford University when Kemper picked them up in May 1972, drove them to a deserted orchard, and killed them.

MARY ANN PESCE

struck at one eye, trying to go through the socket, then, "grabbing at the sound," he shoved his fingers in her mouth to silence her. "I think at that point, she started dying," he said. "She went semiconscious or delirious, moaning and waving her arms around, fending off an imaginary assailant that wasn't there any more." He dropped the knife into the trunk and shut the lid. For an instant he thought he might have put the car keys in the trunk when he opened it, but he found them in his back pocket.

Kemper drove back to his apartment in Alameda, parked in the garage, and later that night moved the bodies upstairs. Once they were safely transferred, he put them in the bathtub and cut their heads off.

With later victims, his postmortem surgery would often involve cutting off the victim's hands. He claimed that he separated the body and hands to delay identification—no hands, no fingerprints. He gave the same sort of reason for his removal of heads; decapitation eliminated any identifying dental clues. But the cutting off of heads was more than a mere precaution—it was one of Kemper's favorite aberrations. The beheading gave him a sexual thrill, and more: "There was almost a climax to it," he said. "It was kind of an exalted, triumphant-type thing, like taking the head of a deer or an elk or something would be to a hunter." He spoke to the heads and used them sexually. In some cases he kept them until decay became a problem.

Even when he was in full confessional flow, Kemper didn't like talking about these post-death rituals—still, he did talk about them. He admitted taking Polaroid shots of what he did to the bodies. He admitted, more grudgingly, to a variety of necrophilic sex acts. He admitted to disfiguring the heads and to preserving some of the hair and pieces of skin. But only when a psychiatrist questioned him under sodium amytal—sometimes called truth serum—did he reveal that he'd kept and eaten parts of some victims.

Destruction, possession, humiliation of the corpse—all were bound up together, inextricable and in many ways inexplicable, although Kemper doggedly tried to find an explanation. "I needed to have a particular experience with a person and to possess them in the way I wanted to," he said at one point. "I had to evict them from their human bodies." On another occasion he observed that "if I killed them they couldn't reject me as a man. It was more or less making a doll out of a human being, carrying out my fantasies with a doll, a living human doll."

The spilling of blood was not the point. "Blood was an actual pain in the ass," Kemper explained. "What I wanted to see was the death, and I wanted to see the triumph, the exultation over the death. It was like eating, or a narcotic, something that drove me more and more and more."

The day after those first murders Kemper drove into the Santa Cruz mountains to get rid of the remains. Although he chose a rugged and remote location for disposal, he was interrupted in his work by the appearance of a couple and their dog. Watching Kemper digging a shallow trench at the base of an embankment, the dog started barking. Kemper could hear its owners urging it to be quiet and to come away, in voices that he took to mean that they'd seen a very incriminating piece of evidence. On the ground beside Kemper's car lay a white plastic bag that held some of the victims' clothes. It was the same bag that had covered Mary Ann Pesce's head while he stabbed her, and it was spattered with blood. But the couple called their dog and hurried off, and he heard no more of them.

Although rattled by the encounter, Kemper labored on, trying to be as inconspicuous as possible. He dug separate graves for each body, threw their heads into a deep ravine, and disposed of their wallets and few possessions elsewhere. But in his imagination he was not quite finished with them. About a month afterward, he drove his motorcycle back to the place where he'd murdered the young women, reliving those moments in his mind—a compulsion that one serial-killer expert calls "rolling in it." Mary Ann Pesce never ceased to fascinate Kemper, who still had that "reverence." He returned to her grave several times. "I visited there to be near her," he explained; "I loved her and wanted her."

In August, Mary Ann Pesce's head was found by hikers and—as Kemper had foreseen—was identified from dental records. He learned from newspaper articles that her parents were affluent and lived in Camarillo, just north of Los Angeles. He drove down to take a look at the neighborhood. "It was in the country club property area, very upper class, and I was right about her," he reported later. "Because she had things like an address book with names and addresses from all over Europe." She was, he said, just the sort of person his mother most admired—the sort, as Clarnell Strandberg had made cruelly clear, that Ed Kemper could never hope to marry.

Not that marriage was out of the question for the young murderer. About a month after he killed Mary Ann Pesce

If I killed them they couldn't reject me as a man.

and Anita Luchessa, Kemper met a 17-year-old girl named Carla. She lived in the farming town of Turlock, about 100 miles east of San Francisco, but she sometimes visited her sister, who lived in Santa Cruz. Kemper began seeing Carla on weekends. Almost a year later they became engaged—and indeed would remain engaged up until the moment of Kemper's arrest. But the relationship was entirely platonic; Ed Kemper preferred sex with the dead. Carla described him as the perfect gentleman. They saw each other every few weekends in Turlock, where he slept in a separate room in her family home, and where they went to a shooting range to practice firing his guns. Sometimes she would visit him in Santa Cruz.

That June, Kemper had his second serious motorcycle accident. Booming through Oakland, he lost control of the bike and crashed, breaking his left forearm so badly that the doctors had to insert a steel plate and six screws, and he remained in a cast for the next nine months. Now work was impossible, and maybe even undesirable: He drew a modest disability stipend. But even hobbled, the powerful young giant could kill; with one arm in a cast he handled women's bodies as if they were broken dolls.

Kemper next surrendered to the urge to cruise on September 14, 1972. He went out hunting in the Ford, again dressed in what he later called his murder clothes—the tan shirt and dark jeans he'd worn when he killed Pesce and Luchessa. At about 7 p.m. 15-year-old Aiko Koo was on her way from her family's apartment in Berkeley to an advanced dance class in San Francisco. She'd been given money to take a bus, but—in defiance of parental instructions—she chose to hitchhike.

Aiko Koo was small and lithe, with long dark hair. Her father was a Korean national, her mother a Latvian immigrant. The parents had met at New York's Columbia University, but their liaison was brief: The father had disappeared at the first sign of pregnancy. Later the mother moved to Berkeley, got a job with the university library there, and for the child's sake, studied Korean culture. Much of her salary went toward advancing Aiko's career as

AIKO KOO

a performer of Korean dance. The girl was very good, already a professional. But in other ways, she was still quite naive, and she hopped right into the banana-colored Galaxie driven by the huge, friendly man.

Even when he began driving on and off the highway ramps in an erratic, confusing way, Aiko detected no danger. Not until they were well down the coast, heading toward Santa Cruz, did she recognize that she was in terrible trouble. Her first response was to say pleadingly that she would be late for her class.

"I'm afraid you're not going to make that ballet class tonight," Kemper replied. At once Aiko began begging him not to kill her. He pulled out a borrowed .357 magnum revolver and pressed the big muzzle against her ribs. He intended to kill himself, he said reassuringly. The girl began whimpering.

When he neared the Santa Cruz area he turned off into the mountains and followed a side road to a secluded spot among the ferns and towering redwoods. He stopped, got out, and ordered Aiko into the backseat. She quickly obeyed. Kemper then discovered to his horror that he'd locked her in the car with the keys and his pistol. He knocked on the door and the girl let him back in. It was her death warrant.

Kemper had decided to kill in a different way this time. First he sealed her mouth shut with a three-inch-wide strip of medical tape. Then, keeping his right hand over her mouth, he cut off all air by pinching her nostrils shut. Her arms were free, and she fought with desperate strength, kicking at the car window, grabbing at his testicles, thrashing beneath his big body. But darkness soon engulfed her. When her breathing had stopped he hauled her out of the car, put her on the ground, and raped her.

Then, to his astonishment, the girl began to breathe again. He choked her with the muffler she was wearing until he was sure she was dead. By that time, he later said, "I was hot, tired, and thirsty," so he put her body in the trunk and drove to a nearby mountain bar for a few beers before continuing on to his mother's apartment. Clarnell and her

Hitchhiking to an evening dance class in San Francisco, 15-year-old Aiko Koo became Kemper's third Bay Area victim.

son talked idly for a while, "just passing the time," he recalled. When he left the apartment to go back to Alameda, he took a peek into the trunk, "admiring my catch."

Back at his own place around 11 p.m., Kemper carefully went through the bag Aiko Koo had carried, studying her meager possessions: crocheting materials, a few coins in a leather purse, some corrected school papers. He took her body to bed. The next morning he dismembered her, put most of the body parts into garbage bags, and drove back to the Santa Cruz mountains to bury them — all but the girl's severed head.

As Kemper continued to kill, he was also busy on another front. Some weeks earlier he'd hired an attorney to help him get his juvenile record "expunged," a common practice intended to keep the mistakes of childhood from haunting the reformed adult. He wanted a clean record so that he could enlist in the military, he said. In fact, although he'd assembled $800 worth of rifles and shotguns, he wanted to be able to buy handguns without lying about his past and thus exposing himself to criminal charges. The key step — arranged by the attorney — was to supply the court with two expert evaluations of Ed Kemper's mental health. Accordingly, Kemper drove to Fresno on September 16 — two days after killing Aiko Koo — and submitted to examinations by two "courthouse psychiatrists," as he contemptuously called them.

They looked back at his childhood and questioned him at length about his life since leaving Atascadero. He told them how he was playing such social sports as Ping-Pong and tennis, how he pursued computer courses at a community college. He described the quiet amity of his life with Clarnell and his younger sister in Aptos. His entirely spurious account was accepted uncritically. "He showed no evidence of any tendency toward any anti-social behavior, and there was a total absence of any stored-up anger, bitterness or resentment that one would expect if some anti-social behavior pattern were manifest," concluded one psychiatrist. "In effect, we are dealing with two different people when we talk of the 15-year-old boy who committed the murder and the 23-year-old man before us now."

The other expert, ascribing Kemper's killing of his grandparents to a "split" between his rational mind and his feelings, wrote, "He appears to be functioning in one piece now, directing his feelings toward verbalization, work, sports, and not allowing neurotic buildup within himself."

Kemper got what he wanted: The record of his juvenile past was sealed, even though the district attorney and judge were uneasy about the erasure; the psychiatric reports gave them little choice. Only later would the two doctors learn that on the day he'd spoken to them, their thoroughly rehabilitated interviewee had wrapped Aiko Koo's head in what he would jokingly call a "plain brown wrapper" and stashed it behind his sofa at home. He would keep it for several more days.

In January 1973 Kemper moved out of his Alameda apartment and back into his mother's place in Aptos. That same month he bought the first pistol of his very own — a .22 Ruger automatic — and from the moment he walked out of the store, he had an overwhelming urge to go hunting. He began driving around Santa Cruz, picking up hitchhiking women. The first three escaped "execution," as he phrased it, because he felt that too many people had seen them getting into his car.

Around 5 p.m. a hard rain was falling and the streets were mostly deserted. Kemper cruised along Mission Street in downtown Santa Cruz. A young woman wearing brown bell-bottom pants and a blue waterproof jacket stood in the downpour with her thumb out. Her name was Cynthia Ann Schall, and she was looking for a ride to a class at Cabrillo College. Kemper later described the 18-year-old as "a large girl. She was, I think, five-foot-four inches, maybe 160 pounds, straight, medium-long blonde hair, and very large chested — uh, breasted, I should say."

Feigning a need to talk to someone about his own girl trouble, Kemper drove up into the hills. But when he stopped the car, he had little to say. Instead, he showed Schall his new gun, handling it nonchalantly. Terrified, she begged him not to kill her. Kemper maintained his casual manner, toying with her, pretending to be persuaded when she said she mustn't miss her class because she'd fail the course and her parents would stop paying for her education. He told her that he wanted to take her to his mother's apartment. They would talk, he said. But on the way she would have to ride in the trunk so that inquisitive neighbors wouldn't see her.

The frightened young woman refused; they could talk in a parking lot on the college campus, she said. But in the end Cindy Schall did as she was told. As she was settling herself in the open trunk, rearranging the articles there, she heard a sharp click and glanced toward Kemper — and into the small eye of the .22's muzzle. She'd heard the hammer come back. Unable to watch what she knew must follow, she flinched down as he pulled the trigger through. There was a snap of sound and a single hollow-point long-rifle round burrowed fatally into the top left quadrant of her brain. "Her eyes didn't even shut," Kemper would recall with a kind of technical wonder. "Nothing flexed or moved. It amazed me so much because one second she's animated and the next second she's not, and there was absolutely nothing in between, just a noise and absolute, absolute stillness."

Kemper went to his mother's apartment and, finding no one there, put Cynthia Schall's body into a closet. When Clarnell came home he chatted with her for a while, then went to bed. The next day, after his mother left for work, he used the body for sex, then cut it into pieces, using an ax for some of the tougher parts. The remains were divided up among several plastic bags and heaved off a 400-foot coastal cliff about 20 miles south of Monterey. Schall's legs were discovered the next day; they had come to rest near the road. Other parts of the corpse floated ashore over the next few weeks— a hand found by a surfer, part of a torso washed up on Santa Cruz beach. "Wouldn't it be weird," Kemper ventured to his fiancée, "to be swimming along and have it touch you?" In fact, as he and Carla drove around the area, Kemper would now and then throw in some comment about the mountains where those coeds were found, or about the hitchhiker killings.

Cynthia Schall's head didn't turn up for a long time. Kemper kept it in a box in a closet in his mother's apartment, then buried it beneath a steppingstone just outside the back door—facing his bedroom window.

CYNTHIA SCHALL

Cynthia Schall, 18, met Kemper as she hitched to school on January 8, 1973, the day he bought his first handgun.

It amazed me so much because one second she's animated and the next second she's not, and there was absolutely nothing in between, just a noise and absolute, absolute stillness.

"I talked to it, I said affectionate things," he told police, "like you would say to a girlfriend or wife."

The murder and disposal of Cynthia Ann Schall was problematic for Kemper on purely technical grounds. The precise killer had strict parameters for his hunting expeditions. One was to observe his surroundings very carefully before acting. "If I knew I was going to commit a crime on a certain day," he said, "I watched very carefully the situation—the flow of traffic, how heavy the police traffic was, how observant they were being of me in particular and the people around me, the mood of the hitchhikers." Another rule was never to circle back for a likely-looking candidate, since a second go-round would increase the chances of being noticed—and might stampede the prey. The most important rule, however, was not to work too close to home. That was the rule he'd broken with Schall, and while it troubled him, he would break it again on February 5.

That evening Kemper and his mother had a savage argument. He couldn't remember what it was about, because they argued perpetually, about everything. Kemper stormed out of the house, determined to kill immediately. To himself, he said, "the first girl that's halfway decent that I pick up, I'm gonna blow her brains out." He got into his car and headed for the UCSC campus. The university sticker that his mother had given him ensured easy access and camouflage; besides, there seemed a certain rightness in looking for a victim where his mother worked.

Once again, rain offered a measure of concealment. He passed a tall young woman walking along a glistening campus road. Perfect. He stopped. She approached and opened the door. Later he would tell

Grisly Fremont F

2 HEADLESS

a reporter, "When somebody put their hand on that doorknob, that's it, they're giving me their life."

They continued on a little way, engaged in small talk. Then Kemper saw another prospect—"very good looking, nicely built and everything, and intelligent and moderate in her dress and everything, nothing outlandish." She smiled in the headlights, stuck out her thumb, and when Kemper pulled up, slipped into the backseat. The first hitchhiker was 23-year-old Rosalind Thorpe; the second was 20-year-old Alice Liu.

Kemper drove past a kiosk where a campus guard was stationed, following Coolidge Drive where it descended a wooded hill overlooking the lights of Santa Cruz, and the sea. He slowed, commenting on the beauty of the scene. But his mind was on death, and he found suddenly that he couldn't wait a moment longer. As the car continued to roll forward, he brought out the pistol that had been hidden beneath his leg. He aimed it at Thorpe and fired, hitting her above the left ear. "She had a rather large forehead, and I was imagining what her brain looked like inside, and I just wanted to put it right in the middle of that." He turned to see Alice Liu cringing into a corner of the backseat, her

hands covering her face. He fired at the hands, missed twice, then hit her near the temple on the third try. She began to moan.

The car glided slowly down the hill, approaching a four-way stop manned by two campus police. Kemper considered blowing through, then thought better of it. Instead, he turned up the car radio to muffle Liu's steady groan of pain and terror, then threw a coat over her; he placed a blanket over Thorpe's body. As he passed the cops, Alice Liu resumed her sad song in the backseat—"a very strange sigh," as Kemper described it. "It would start out very sharp, almost like a sniffle, and then it would taper off and become a little bit more like a masculine sigh than a fine girl, a petite-type girl like she was." The sounds were "very disconcerting," but Kemper resisted further action until he'd driven through Santa Cruz and on to an unpopulated area. When no cars were in sight, he turned around and shot Liu in the side of the head.

In a parking area near a beach, Kemper transferred the two bodies to the trunk. Then, after cleaning himself up at a gas station, he drove home and chatted with his mother; the quarrel that had sent him out to murder was now behind them. A little after 10 p.m. he told her that he was going out to get some cigarettes. He did feel a craving just then—but not for tobacco. He went to the car, opened the

d CORPSES

Banner headlines such as this one from a Bay Area newspaper fed rumors that the coed killings were the work of a satanic cult or vampires.

San Francisco Bay area was in an uproar. Authorities in four counties launched a massive investigative effort, universities initiated rigid security procedures, and newspapers filled their front pages with stories about the grisly discoveries. One San Francisco television reporter speculated that the killings were the work of a satanic cult; the reporter offered some imaginative specifics, making much of "a rumor that the butcher killer always strikes during the phase of the new moon." The picture was further complicated by coincidence: Improbably, another serial killer—Herbert Mullin—was also at large in Santa Cruz *(pages 134-135).*

Despite the publicity, hitchhiking continued to be a popular mode of transportation among Bay Area youth, and Kemper continued to be a generous provider of rides. He gave lifts to dozens of college women who were delivered safely to their destinations. "You know what we were talking about as we were driving around, almost as often as not?" mused Kemper after his arrest. "This guy that's going around doing this stuff. They'd be telling me all about this guy, comparing notes, speculating on what he looks like, how he carries himself, why he's doing this stuff. Telling *me* about it. The second they started talking about that, they didn't realize it, but they were getting a free ride." Curiously, he was unable to kill riders who talked about his killing. In fact, Kemper had murdered his last hitchhiker.

Now the killer's fantasies veered toward a higher stratum of destruction. He envisioned his stalking door to door in his Aptos neighborhood, killing everybody on the block. He thought that he might have to move his operations elsewhere "as soon as this area dried up." He fantasized about depositing heads in front of the police station. The people who knew him best had begun to suspect him—he was sure of that: One day his mother asked him if he was connected to the killings; he denied it. His sister Allyn, by then married and living in Santa Cruz, asked the same question and received the same answer. The murders had reminded her of the mutilated dolls and cats of their childhood.

Although Kemper finally was able to take the cast—repeatedly bleached to remove bloodstains—off his left arm, his huge body began to betray him in other ways. One day in early April 1973 he and his fiancée, along with his

trunk, and severed each victim's head with a butcher knife. The excitement of decapitation was heightened, Kemper admitted later, by the fact that his mother could have seen him if she'd bothered to come to the window. But she didn't; Clarnell had never shown much interest in what her son was up to.

Left alone in the apartment the next morning, Kemper brought Alice Liu's body in for sex. Afterward, he washed the body to remove traces of his semen. Then he removed the hands. Next he worked on the other woman's head to dig out the bullet, thinking that the flattened wad of lead might somehow be used as ballistic evidence against him. Late that night he drove north and threw the remains off the side of a road in Alameda County. The heads and hands, which he'd been carrying in a plastic dishpan, he took up the coast to a precipice called Devil's Slide and tossed them over—onto a beach.

Such sloppy disposal hardly jibed with his operational rules, but Kemper didn't care. He was hampered by the cast that still covered his left forearm, and he was nervous about the possibility of capture; the police had found Schall's remains so quickly. Untroubled by murder, he urgently needed to get rid of the bodies. The process of disposal, he said later, was giving him ulcers, and he began to get careless.

The public now knew all too well that a mutilation-minded killer was at work in the region. Cynthia Ann Schall's remains had been identified in late January. The bodies of Rosalind Thorpe and Alice Liu were found on February 15, just 10 days after their deaths. Now the entire

131

After hiding their bodies in the mountains to the east, Kemper threw the heads and hands of Alice Liu *(inset left)* and Rosalind Thorpe *(inset right)* off Devil's Slide, as this lonely stretch south of San Francisco is called.

ALICE LIU

ROSALIND THORPE

mother and his sister Allyn, traveled to Fisherman's Wharf in San Francisco and visited the Wax Museum there. One of the attractions was a guillotine with a beheaded manne-quin. Kemper became ill at the sight and insisted on leaving. Carla later remembered that she felt her relationship with Kemper cooling and nearing a breakup. Kemper had been acting weirder and weirder, and she thought he must be dating someone else.

That same weekend, Kemper had an unnervingly close call. A few days earlier, he'd bought a .44 magnum revolver in a town near Santa Cruz. The purchase forms required him to state whether he'd been in prison or a mental hos-pital. Since his juvenile record had been sealed, he chose not to mention his time in Atascadero. As it happened, while the details of his early murders had indeed been sealed, his file at the Santa Cruz sheriff's department, though coded as a juvenile record, bore the notation: "Double homicide, record sealed." When the handgun registration apparatus duly reported Kemper's purchase, the sheriff's office real-ized that Kemper had lied about his past. As a convicted felon, he could not own a handgun. They went out to Aptos to confiscate the gun, intending to explore the matter further in court.

Kemper drove up just as Sergeant Michael Aluffi of the Santa Cruz sheriff's office was looking for the apartment. When the sergeant asked for the pistol, Kemper started to let him in, then remembered that the gun was in the trunk of his car. Aluffi and his partner, Sergeant Don Smythe, stood bracketing the Galaxie as Kemper retrieved the weap-on. The pair saw nothing unusual about the trunk, took the pistol, and drove away.

But, to the jittery killer, the visit only verified his worst suspicions: The police were quietly closing in on him. They hadn't asked him about the .22 pistol, but now they'd come out for the .44. Why had they suddenly become interested in him? For Kemper, this behavior of the Santa Cruz au-thorities was ominous and unnerving.

Ed Kemper felt time draining away—but his work was still unfinished. There was something else he had to do, something he'd been contemplating secretly since child-hood. "I felt that I was going to be caught pretty soon for the killing of these girls," he said after his arrest, "or I was going to blow up and do something very open and get myself caught, and so I did not want my mother. . . " At this point, words briefly failed him; then he resumed: "A long

Unnatural Disaster

As Edmund Kemper preyed on Bay Area co-eds, a second serial killer—like Kemper, an alumnus of California's mental institutions—created a terrifying counterpoint. But Herbert Mullin had a motive far different from Kemper's twisted lust: In Mullin's psychotic view, his murders were the only way to prevent another catastrophic California earthquake.

The son of an itinerant furniture salesman and postal clerk, Mullin was born in Salinas, California, on April 18, 1947, the 41st anniversary of the San Francisco earthquake of 1906—a fact that loomed steadily more significant to his troubled mind. By the time he was 20, Mullin had become a moody, hostile dabbler in Eastern religions and the drug culture and was prone to violent outbursts. In 1969 he terrified his parents when he began to imitate every movement of his brother-in-law, behavior known as echopraxia, a strong symptom of schizophrenia. A day after he began his compulsive mimicry, Mullin checked into a mental hospital, where he was, in fact, diagnosed as a schizophrenic. A voluntary patient, he checked out six weeks later.

Mullin shaved his head, and once declared mysteriously that "Murder is an act of love." By October his behavior had become so alarming that he entered another mental hospital. Late that same year, however, he was again discharged as a voluntary outpatient, though his prospects were considered "grave" by his doctors.

In 1972 the disturbed 24-year-old arrived in Santa Cruz to visit his parents. Soon he was receiving "telepathic" messages from his father. "Herb," the voice would say, "I want you to kill me somebody." On October 13 Herb obliged. He clubbed an old man to death on a road in the Santa Cruz mountains. Not two weeks later, Mullin picked up a young woman hitchhiker in his beat-up 1958 Chevy station wagon. He stabbed her to death and hid her body in the hills. On November 2—All Souls' Day—Mullin stabbed a Roman Catholic priest to death in his confessional.

By this time Mullin believed he'd been chosen by Albert Einstein as the "designated leader" of his generation, intended to save California from a severe earthquake by offering up human sacrifices. And his telepathic voices changed; now they were those of his victims, giving their permission to be killed.

In January 1973 Mullin took five more sacrifices. Using a newly purchased .22 revolver, he shot and killed a small-time drug dealer he'd once known, along with the man's wife. Then he murdered a woman and two children whose house he'd called on earlier by mistake.

Early in February he came across four teenagers camping illegally in Santa Cruz State Park. Walking into their tent, he told them to leave, then shot them, and left their bodies where they fell.

On February 13 Mullin was loading firewood for his parents into his car when his inner voices spoke again. "Don't deliver a stick," they said, "until you kill somebody." As he drove through Santa Cruz, Mullin spotted a 72-year-old man working in a yard, leaned out the car window, and shot him. Armed with a neighbor's description of the car, police had the killer within minutes. He quietly accepted his arrest.

During his three-week trial Mullin offered only rambling discussions of his earthquake theory, and a chilling rationale for his crimes: "A rock doesn't make a decision while it's falling," he said, "it just falls." Mullin showed little interest when the jury decided that he was sane, found him guilty on 10 counts of murder, and sent him to California Men's Colony at San Luis Obispo, where he is serving a life sentence.

Serial killer Herbert Mullin leaves Santa Cruz courthouse after being arraigned for six murders in February 1973.

time ago, I had thought about what I was going to do in the event of being caught for other crimes, and the only choices I saw were just accept it and go to jail, and let my mother carry the load and let the whole thing fall in her hands, like happened the last time with my grandparents, or I could take her life."

Another incident may have also propelled him. A week after the officers' visit, Kemper had picked up two hitch-hikers, and their route took them close to the orchard where he'd killed Mary Ann Pesce and Anita Luchessa, his first coed victims. Again he'd felt the urge to murder but sup-pressed it and took them safely to their destination. "I said she's gotta die and I've gotta die, or girls like that are gonna die. And that's when I decided to murder my mother."

On Good Friday, April 20, 1973, Kemper arrived at the Aptos apartment, watched television, drank beer, and wait-ed for his mother to come home from a university function. He slept for a time, then woke at 4 a.m. He went to his mother's bedroom and found her there, just turning out the light after reading a book.

"What are you doing up?" she said.

"Oh nothing. Just wanted to make sure you were home."

"Oh, I suppose you're going to want to sit up all night and talk now." Recounting this, Ed Kemper's eyes gleamed with tears. "I looked at her and said, 'No, good night,' and I knew I was going to kill her, and I was so cold and so hard." He bade Clarnell Strandberg good night and went back to his bed, thinking about what he would do. "I cer-tainly wanted for my mother a nice, quiet, easy death like I guess everyone wants."

At 5:15 Kemper returned to her bedroom. He had a ham-mer in his left hand and his pocketknife—blade open—in his right. He stood over her for a few minutes. Then he swung the hammer hard and hit her behind the temple. Blood poured down her face. She was still breathing. He listened to familiar sounds. "I heard blood running into her. I guess it was her windpipe. It was obvious I had done severe damage to her, because in other cases where I had shot people in the head, I heard the same—or it had the same effect—blood running into the breathing passages."

Then it was time for the knife. As he later remembered that moment, "I decided that what was good for my victims was good for my mother, so I lifted up her head, took the knife and cut her throat first. Then I removed her head." This made him feel ill, but he soon recovered and continued with his surgery. He cut off her right hand. Then he cut out her larynx—that hated instrument of verbal abuse—and put it in the garbage disposal to be chewed up.

Clarnell Strandberg's "nice, quiet, easy death" went on for a long time, as Kemper worked his way through the labyrinth of fantasies he had taken a lifetime to build. He was "not a lizard, not a rock. I came out of her vagina, you see, I came out of my mother, and in a rage, I went back in," he explained. "I cut off her head and I humiliated her corpse and said, there, you know, six young women died because of the way she raises her son, and the way he grows up. And what are her closing words? 'I suppose you want to sit up all night and talk.' God, I wish I had."

In a later psychiatric examination, Kemper said he'd put his mother's head on the mantel and then thrown darts at it, screamed at it, and smashed its nose with his fist, splash-ing blood across the wall. The details are uncertain. Some-

I *said she's gotta die and I've gotta die, or girls like that are gonna die. And that's when I decided to murder my mother.*

time after sunrise, his long-suppressed wrath—and deformed love—were spent. He put the body in the closet and did his best to clean up the apartment.

Sleep was out of the question. He spent much of Saturday morning drinking beer with an acquaintance. Then he began to worry that his mother would be missed if she wasn't seen on Easter Sunday or failed to report for work on Monday. An idea came to him: He would make it look as if she'd left on a trip. She sometimes did go away on weekends, often with a close friend and fellow university employee, Sally Hallett. In that confused moment his logic decreed that the friend would also have to die.

Kemper spoke to Hallett on the telephone late that afternoon and asked her to come over for dinner. It was to be a surprise for his mother, he said. Hallett seemed delighted at the prospect. Preparing for her, Kemper closed all the windows and put a length of nylon rope in the living room, along with a broken drill shank that could serve as a club. He also placed a carbine in the adjacent room, brought some plastic bags in from his car, and put handcuffs in his pocket. He waited.

At 8 o'clock Sally Hallett breezed in. He greeted her warmly, and she headed toward the living-room sofa, saying with a weary sigh, "Let's sit down. I'm dead."

Her host agreed. He hit her in the stomach. She staggered back, gasping, "Guy, stop that." He hit her again, then yanked her backward against him with his left arm—the arm weakened by months in a cast—around her neck. Kemper lifted the woman off the floor and held her there, the arm tight on her throat. Her struggles subsided sooner than he expected. Her eyes bulged out and her face darkened. Only later did Kemper realize that his choke hold had crushed her larynx.

Then came the necessary conclusion. Kemper undressed her, dragged her to his bed, and heaved himself onto her body. His next step was to put all his guns into Hallett's car. That done, he went into town and spent a couple of hours drinking with the off-duty policemen who hung out at the Jury Room. When he returned home he went to sleep in his mother's bed.

At 10:15 on Easter morning, confused and panicky, Ed Kemper began his last cruise, one that, unlike his customary ones, had no discernible plan. His arsenal loaded into the trunk of Hallett's car, he set out toward the northeast, expecting, he said afterward, to die in a hail of police bullets.

Driving up toward Sacramento, he tuned the radio for bulletins about a double murder or the search for him or his stolen car, but he heard none. He stopped for gas in Sacramento, then drove on to Reno, Nevada. There, some inner compass led him to the campus of the University of Nevada. But he ignored the opportunities the campus presented. "I didn't really want to go out and kill all the young coeds in the world," he later told police. "It was starting to weigh kind of heavy. Let's say I wore out of it, and the original purpose was gone." Clarnell, the "original purpose," lay dead in her Aptos apartment.

Figuring that the police would be on the lookout for the Hallett car, Kemper drove to a Reno gas station and told the mechanic to check it for electrical problems. That would keep it out of sight for a while. He rented a Chevrolet Impala from Hertz and kept going, crossing the Nevada desert into Utah, with brief stops for gas and soft drinks and No-Doz. Winding through the Rockies across the Utah line, he was pulled over for speeding in Cimarron, Colorado. Watching the highway patrolman approach, Kemper must have feared the worst: Maybe the anticipated shootout with the law was finally at hand. But the trooper let him go on his way after he put the cash payment for the $25 fine in a nearby mailbox.

As the hours and miles passed, the fugitive sank deeper into exhaustion, literally quivering with fatigue, feeling as though he were about to fly apart. Thoughts of shootouts and mass killings grew so vivid that they seemed hallucinatory. He could see his awesome finish. "My mind was starting to go," he said later. "I was afraid that anything could cause me to go off the deep end, and I don't know what would happen then. I had never been out of control in my life." He drove as far as Holly, in the southeast corner of Colorado, almost on the Kansas line. There, for reasons known only to him, the young man turned back toward the black serration of the Rockies—and the host of imaginary lawmen and other specters that pursued him.

Kemper began to think about Charles Scherer. He'd known Susan Scherer and met her dad briefly; the big police lieutenant had evoked Kemper's lost father, a John Wayne kind of man. The bond also had a menacing flip side: As he'd neared the end of his tether, Kemper had thought about murdering Susan, or Scherer, or perhaps the Santa Cruz district attorney, Peter Chang. "So I came upon the idea of calling up Lieutenant Charles Scherer at the Santa

As investigators watch, undertakers remove the headless body of Clarnell Strandberg from her Aptos apartment on April 24, 1973, three days after Kemper bludgeoned his sleeping mother with a hammer and methodically savaged her remains.

Santa Cruz sheriff's deputy Bruce
Colomy removes Kemper's mana-
cles before the verdict is read at
his 1973 trial.

Cruz Police Department, long distance, knowing I couldn't wait until morning," he said. "I just wanted to say where I was and see what I could arrange as far as surrender, and if it was not satisfactory, then I would continue on." To the end—the shootout, the killing spree, whatever.

With that decision, however, Kemper had come to the close of his short, murderous career, one that had cost 10 lives in all, eight over the past 11 months. The ultimate victim, for him, was Clarnell Strandberg. "I had always considered my mother very formidable, very fierce, and very forbidding," confided Kemper. "She had always been a big influence on my life, and whether I hated her or loved her, it was very dynamic." Then: "It was amazing to me how much like every other victim of mine she had died; how vulnerable and how human she was. It shocked me quite some time."

On April 30, 1973, Kemper was taken to the Santa Cruz courthouse, where he stood quietly as multiple charges of murder were read against him. He had no objections; he wanted to help the police in every way he could. They, in turn, were happy to let him play the role of chief investigator; when he led them to places where he'd buried or thrown the remains of his victims, his hands were free, and his cuffs were slung, police-style, on his belt.

The only real question was his sanity—or, more particularly, whether he would be locked away in prison or sent back to a place similar to Atascadero. If he went to prison, he would be eligible for parole at intervals in the future, but the likelihood of Ed Kemper's ever being released was slender indeed. If he was placed in an institution for the criminally insane, psychiatrists might one day decide that he had regained his mental health and release him. As Kemper himself has pointed out, he is horrific proof of that possibility.

The public defender appointed to represent him entered a plea of "not guilty by reason of insanity." Kemper, of course, had been declared insane when he was 15, but now the stakes seemed very much higher. The legal hurdles for a successful defense were also high. Under California law, Kemper would be considered sane and competent to stand trial for murder if he had understood his acts and been able to discriminate between right and wrong at the time of their commission.

Between his arrest and conviction Kemper tried to slash his wrists four times—feeble efforts for one with his skills—using such tools as a clip from a ballpoint pen and a sharpened pen cartridge. But as the trial proceeded he appeared to calm, to soften. He broke into tears when he took the witness stand and talked about a childhood of domestic fighting, rejections by schoolmates, and his repressed hatred of his mother.

The families and friends of the victims and the jury of six men and six women found the trial heavy going. One afternoon was devoted to a description by pathologists of exactly how each victim had died and what was done to each body. Over a period of two days the courtroom listened to seven hours of taped confession by Kemper, excruciating in its matter-of-fact, technical detail. Later the jury and spectators were invited to leave the courtroom to inspect the killer's banana-colored Ford Galaxie and its splotches of old blood.

A series of psychiatrists testified that, under the California definition, Kemper was sane. He'd known what he was doing, they said. The jury agreed. Although the trial lasted three weeks, the jurors needed only five hours to reach a decision: On November 7, 1973, Kemper was declared sane and deemed guilty on eight counts of first-degree murder. The next day Judge Harry F. Brauer sentenced him to life imprisonment (California did not reinstate capital punishment until 1974). The judge added that he would inform the proper authorities "in the most persuasive language I know that you must never be released at any time in your natural life. May God have mercy on your soul, but I must protect the rest of the people from people like you."

Kemper listened without emotion. Then he said, "Yes, sir, I understand."

He was sent immediately to the California Medical Facility, a prison in Vacaville, and there he remains. As at Atascadero, he is a model inmate, although he knows now that, no matter how well he behaves, the road back to normal society is probably closed forever. But Ed Kemper had known that when he made the first call from Colorado. In his 20 years in prison, he has dabbled with the idea of a lobotomy, perhaps hoping to release inner demons that only he can hear. He reads and, in his pleasant, well-modulated voice, records books for the blind. And he is never entirely alone. His victims, he believes, are with him always. As he said at his trial, "I wanted the girls for myself as possessions. They were going to be mine. They are mine." ◆

Ed Kemper secretly retained these student ID cards and other personal effects of his last two coed victims, Rosalind Thorpe and Alice Liu. He often kept and pored over such souvenirs, trying to get to know the women he'd killed.

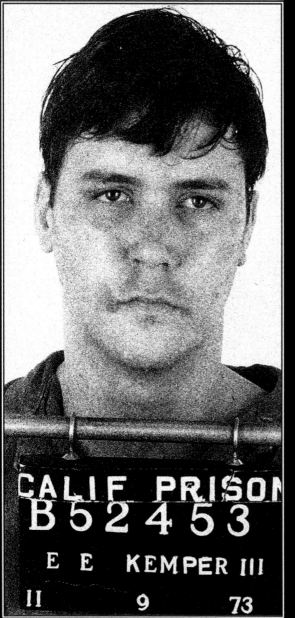

His mustache shaved off, a youthful Edmund Kemper poses for the Vacaville prison camera on November 9, 1973, the first day of his life sentence. Although still behind bars, he's been eligible for parole every three years since 1982.

I am a mistake of nature. I deserve to be done away with.
ANDREI CHIKATILO

4

Stalin's Child

Inside the dense forest, the low September sun flickered through the still-green leaves, creating a world that trembled and altered like the man's fantasies. Now he was a lonely Soviet guerrilla warrior, surrounded by German soldiers, ready to kill the invader. Now he was a gray wolf, stalking among the shafts of light and beams of shadow, poised to turn and tear at his prey. Now he was an angry, middle-aged loser, teased and bullied and thwarted by God, family, and country almost from birth. Now he was an impotent man about to find a moment's contentment from the 17-year-old girl who walked, oblivious to his churning imagination, at his side. His personas might be as evanescent as figures on a screen, but, on this third day of September 1981, Andrei Romanovich Chikatilo was about to discover who and what he really was: A horrible reality waited in the forest for him, and for the girl.

Fear and excitement sent adrenaline coursing through the powerfully built 44-year-old as he steered the teenager past a string of summer huts and cafés set down along the water, past the crowd of families and lovers celebrating the final days of another brief Russian summer. Across the Don River lay the grimy, sprawling historic city of Rostov-on-Don. The gold dome of the cathedral, the pale flanks of cruise ships in port, and the white high-rise apartment towers ringing the old town glowed in the late-afternoon light. Passersby took little note of the respectably dressed, bespectacled man with a briefcase who chatted amiably with the wild-looking girl in her striking, blood red jacket. No one thought it extraordinary when the pair turned off the path onto a dirt track that led them into the concealing green tangle of the *lesopolosa*—the forest zone.

They had met in the city center, just outside the public library, where he, a former schoolteacher, liked to go to read newspapers. He lived two hours away by bus, in another town, but took his pleasure from reading the papers and literary journals, roving the crowded streets of Rostov, and trying to pick up girls. This one, named Larisa Tkachenko, was a pretty blonde with little innocence left.

She was a waif from Moldavia, a republic on the Romanian border. When her parents had moved to a state collective farm in the Tselinski district of Rostov oblast, or province, she'd been handed to her grandmother to rear; later, Larisa had been sent to a Rostov boarding school. She liked to climb out the windows of her dormitory at night to spend time with draftees at a nearby army base. Even on this September day she was a truant. Allowed to take a break from helping bring in the crop on the nearby Kirov state farm, Larisa had tarried in central Rostov rather than go straight back to school. When Chikatilo noticed her, she was on her way to a bus that would take her where she was supposed to have been hours earlier.

Tkachenko's crimson jacket and perhaps something hard in her face had drawn Chikatilo the way any movement draws the attention of a wolf. He'd approached her on the street, opened an innocent conversation, and finally suggested that they find a *baza otdykha,* a parkland refreshment center for tourists, where they could have something to eat or drink. Maybe they could also find a quieter corner to be alone. The girl was willing enough; the old fellow seemed meek. She evidently didn't notice the great strength between his shoulders, which sloped like those of a boxer. They had an unspoken understanding, she believed, which had brought them into the hidden center of the wood at day's end.

Chikatilo trembled visibly. Then, unable to contain himself longer, he—the partisan, the wolf, the impotent loser—leaped on his prey, his six-foot frame immeasurably more powerful than her small body. His hands fumbled with her clothes and pulled off her trousers and underwear. Fear rose like steam from her body, exciting him. He pushed her to the ground. She struggled against him, her futile efforts like an aphrodisiac; to his ear, her terrified screams were a powerfully erotic song. He stuffed dirt into her mouth until she began to choke and punched her around the head; then, still flailing crazily at her, he grabbed her by the neck and began to strangle her. As Larisa Tkachenko writhed and thrashed, the man felt sexual stirrings—sensations that he'd rarely experienced when trying to have sex. She was dying; her fading energy seemed to flow into him, increasing his excitement and sense of total power over his prey. While her life dwindled he tore at her harder with his fingers and his teeth, ripping away flesh. As he rarely had with a woman, Andrei Chikatilo experienced, if not penetration, at least a sexual release.

The killer was still out of control. The battered and contorted body of Larisa Tkachenko, crushed in the forest litter, excited him further, and he went into a horrifying state of agitated ecstasy. He picked up the murdered girl's torn and rumpled clothes from where he'd thrown them and began to run around the body, uttering wordless, whooping cries. He flung his arms wide; some of the bloodied garments flew high into the trees. Finally he sank to his knees in front of the corpse and remained there for a few minutes, his chest heaving. Then he crept to his feet and ran away. "I felt like a partisan," he said later.

Within half an hour Chikatilo was back, no longer a guerrilla fighter but a murderer who'd returned to conceal the evidence of his crime. Working quickly, he covered the body with branches and leaves. He retrieved the clothing he'd flung with abandon and hid it among the bushes. Then he stole away.

He had learned from murdering Larisa Tkachenko: He'd learned, for instance, a bit about how to tidy up a crime scene. But that was not the most important thing. The main lesson had to do with who he really was: Andrei Chikatilo had finally seen clearly, and accepted, his monstrous sexual identity.

Tkachenko was not Chikatilo's first victim. He'd killed once before: a nine-year-old girl who naively followed the kindly-looking adult home to a squalid house he'd kept as a secret den for perverse sexual experimentation. But that had been almost three years earlier, in 1978. Although the frenzy of that attack—the cries, the pain, the fear, the blood, the power—had brought him erotic excitement and release, his mind had rejected the realization that now struck him in the woods outside Rostov-on-Don.

The manic rites around Tkachenko's corpse were Chikatilo's frenzied ritual of acceptance. The lifelong frustrations and blocked urges that had moved like lava behind his meek facade had finally found their outlet. Fantasy and reality had merged and erupted. Impotent, despised, and shunned by his peers, he'd made his life tolerable with increasingly violent sexual dreams. Now he would embark on a horrendous parody of passion. This monster was what he was *meant* to be. Killing was what he was meant to do. As he put it later, "The purpose of life is to leave your mark on this earth." Like a mad priest of death and suffering, one of the worst serial killers in modern history had embraced his calling.

More than a decade later Russia and the rest of the world still struggled to come to grips with Chikatilo's awful vocation, and the mystery of how he had followed it so faithfully for so long. In a high-ceilinged Rostov courtroom in 1992, Judge Leonid Akubzhanov, a rumpled jurist who'd driven both prosecutors and defense lawyers to despair during Chikatilo's lengthy trial, took two full days to read out the verdict and sentence against the killer, now

Rivergoing freighters take on cargo beneath a stark skyline of loading cranes at Rostov-on-Don, since the 18th century a center of Russian commerce—and organized crime.

in his fifties with the shaved head of a Russian convict. As Akubzhanov read, the accused sat slumped in an iron detention cage whose thick bars were not intended to prevent his escape but to save him from being torn apart by the outraged families of his victims.

A total of 52 times Akubzhanov declared the prisoner guilty of premeditated murder, each one gorier and more sadistic than the last. This gruesome harvest had terrorized the heartland region of the former Soviet Union and reached out thousands of miles, to Leningrad, Moscow, and even faraway Tashkent, near the rough desert of Afghanistan. Another three cases were not proved, though Chikatilo originally confessed to them; there may have been even more. With the verdict came the penalty: Chikatilo must die. The murderer reacted to the verdict by crying out, "Why me? I demand the podium! Get me a lawyer! I didn't confess to anything! Show me the corpses!" He'd evidently forgotten his own assessment, offered after his capture: "I am a mistake of nature. I deserve to be done away with."

The nightmare of the so-called Red Ripper's 12-year-long rampage was over. For the family members who'd been forced to relive—or discover—the hideous agonies that Chikatilo had inflicted on their loved ones, the death sentence did little to diminish their grief. As the litany of atroc-

During his 1992 trial a yawning Andrei Chikatilo is protected from the vengeance-minded relatives of his victims by a guarded iron cage. At right, a doctor in the standard chef-like white physician's hat helps an overwhelmed spectator through the shock of the court's relentlessly detailed descriptions of the crimes.

ities droned on throughout the six-month-long trial, relatives of the dead would sometimes rise to scream for an end to the proceedings. "We should stop all this and just liquidate the criminal," cried out the aunt of one 16-year-old victim, Yevgeny Muratov, who went to Rostov in 1988 to enroll in school and disappeared. "Too much money is being spent on supporting his life."

The survivors learned that Chikatilo had inflicted almost unimaginable pain on his victims. In virtually every case he'd etched their living bodies with light, slashing knife wounds—a kind of foreplay—then ripped at them with the blade, his fingers, and his teeth, drawing out the climactic moment of terrified death. Genitalia were hacked away, often while the victim was alive. He bit or cut off the tips of tongues, nipples, and noses, usually while the victim could feel the mutilation. Sometimes he ate pieces of the bodies. And there was his distinctive signature: Chikatilo repeatedly stabbed the eyes, following the superstition that an image of the murderer is retained on the victim's retina. Only toward the end of his killing career did he abandon that belief; his last victims lacked the trademark slashes at the eyes. Often the damage was so bad that experts had to be called in to reconstruct the faces.

Almost as remarkable as the duration and viciousness of his career of terror was Chikatilo's ability to hide his crimes—not only from authorities, but even from his own family. Despite his virtual impotence, Chikatilo married and managed to father two children. Throughout his murdering he presented himself as a doting parent and grandfather, who once angrily admonished his wife after she'd had an abortion, "How could you let a doctor kill my child!" His children had no inkling of their father's depravity, even though he'd once used his grown daughter's former apartment as a murder lair. "How could I have done that?" he reportedly asked about his crimes. "I feel pity for everybody. If I see that somebody is hurt by other people my eyes get wet. I cry watching a movie. I sob in the theater."

But if members of his immediate family missed the warning signs of Chikatilo's true nature, others did not. Years after the fact, a sister-in-law volunteered that he'd once tried to rape her and that he could scarcely keep his hands off little children. Still, even the normally suspicious police believed Chikatilo's wife, Feodosia, when she expressed shocked ignorance of her husband's crimes. It seemed that the same sexual dysfunction that drove him to murder had also placed a barrier across intimacy in his marriage. Chikatilo had even isolated himself from his family physically. In his final apartment he moved a bathtub to create a narrow, coffinlike space for himself, where, presumably, he read his cherished newspapers—and dreamed of sex and death.

A solitary monster, Chikatilo was also a paradoxical one. He was, for instance, the very opposite of the heroic partisan fighter of his fantasies. In fact, he was the epitome of the Soviet apparatchik: a drab, humorless functionary, fanatical in his devotion to failing Communist ideals and rigid in his sense of bureaucratic niceties. He was a chronic complainer who wrote scores of letters to the authorities about his unfair treatment at the hands of his peers, who almost invariably disliked him. This most vicious of murderers saw *himself* as a victim of insensitive coworkers: "In any matter—job, study, creative work—I give all of myself, but they have repulsed me from my good intentions," he said. "Because of my own character—reserved, timid, shy, especially in childhood, I am not able to adapt to this society and live my own life."

Despite the unparalleled brutality of his deeds, Chikatilo regarded himself as a pillar of Communist rectitude and morality, and he was a snob. He deplored the circumstances in which many of his victims—tramps, prostitutes, alcoholics, drifters—were living, but also viewed them as his social inferiors. "They ask, demand, and take, they are drunk from the morning onwards," he told interrogators indignantly. "The question arose of whether these degenerate elements had the right to exist."

Professionally, Chikatilo was a failure at almost everything he tried: first a despised teacher, next an incompetent factory supply clerk whose job was to patch up the gaping holes in the collapsed Soviet central planning system. Yet this same incompetent was able for years to elude the largest criminal manhunt in his country's history, to carry out many of his murders in broad daylight without ever being seen, and to keep luring strangers to their bloody doom. "Even I could not understand it," he admitted. "I think I must have had a kind of magnetism," saying later of his victims, "They followed me like dogs."

In fact, as the Soviet system decayed, the Communist world became a garden of victims for Chikatilo. Bus terminals and train stations teemed with a new underclass of alcoholics, young vagrants, prostitutes, children of broken homes, the dispossessed, the impaired. The vast Soviet wel-

Property-owning farmers called kulaks are driven from their village in 1929 during Stalin's campaign to subordinate the stubborn inhabitants of Chikatilo's native Ukraine.

fare state would once have cared for them in some minimal way, but now they drifted like dust, unable to find work, hope, or inspiration in their stagnating society. They were communism's Lost Generation, and Chikatilo had, it seemed, a particular hatred for them. "They crawl into your very soul," he said, "demanding money, food, vodka, and offering themselves for sex. These bums attract minors into their dark net." The killer's words seethed with the paranoia and sexual repression of the culture that produced him.

It was a culture that readily afforded the camouflage that helped Chikatilo elude capture for a dozen years: In a totalitarian society built on appalling crimes against millions of its own citizens, few people would make a formal complaint to authorities. Police were the enemy. They knocked on doors after midnight and took people off to labor camps in the Gulag; most Soviets had enough law in their lives. Yet the world's most feared police state couldn't catch Chikatilo, and part of the reason was that he was himself part of the establishment—a college man, a teacher, a Communist, a true believer. According to propaganda, serial killings existed only in the West; in the Soviet Union such things weren't possible. But in fact, he was a monster that the Soviet experiment had helped create.

The monster was incubated in one of Soviet dictator Joseph Stalin's great crimes against his people: the Ukrainian famine. The resulting misery had hardened into a way of life by the time Andrei Chikatilo was born on October 16, 1936, in Yablochnoye, a village of unpainted wooden houses about 100 miles east of Kiev. The name of the village meant apple, echoing the bounty that the rich black soil had always provided. But during the 1930s that fertility turned to famine as Ukraine became synonymous with horror: As many as seven million people died, most of them poor peasants like the Chikatilos.

The Soviet breadbasket was turned into a vast cemetery by a forced collectivization campaign ordered by Stalin. Under his plan, the lands of rich peasants known as kulaks passed to the state and became incorporated into collective farms. "Rich" was a relative term in those days, however, and in the atmosphere of class hatred and fanaticism that Stalin's campaign fostered, virtually any peasants who successfully farmed even a small plot of land were reviled as kulaks. Their land was taken and often they were killed; the survivors were scattered across the Soviet empire. By the late

1920s, when the collectivization program was in full swing, an estimated five to eight million people were dispossessed in that brutal fashion in a single year.

The proud farmers of Ukraine couldn't fight Stalin's Red Army and secret police, but they could resist in their own fashion. If they couldn't have their property, neither could the state. The farmers slaughtered their cattle by the millions, and they burned their harvests rather than hand them over to the Communists. Even Stalin was staggered by the stubbornness of the peasants' refusal to knuckle under—but only for a time.

Within months of the peasants' revolt, the dictator confiscated Ukraine's remaining grain to pay for the heavy machinery required by his industrial plans. By 1932 Ukraine was gripped by one of the worst famines in modern history. While continuing to plunder Ukrainian crops, Stalin forbade importing food into the stricken areas and kept starving people from fleeing their villages. Those who resisted

were shot. It was mass murder on a scale that the Nazis would later emulate, but never equal.

Yablochnoye was swept up in the horrors of the day. According to Chikatilo, his grandfather was branded as a kulak, expropriated, and banished. Tales circulated of people killing one another over food and eating the scant flesh of neighbors dead from famine. In 1933 Chikatilo's older brother Stepan died in the famine and was eaten by starving neighbors.

Anna, the mother, her affections curdled by a hard life, became domineering and cruel, chiding little Andrei for everything, including his chronic wetting of the one bed shared by the family. When he was four the boy was told about his absent elder brother and warned never to leave the house unsupervised, lest he be stolen and eaten. Whether this warning expressed the parents' real fears or was just a way of frightening a little boy into staying close to home, it had a lasting impact on young Andrei. From his earliest child-

hood he was isolated, fearful, and haunted by tales of terrible crimes. Psychiatrists would later point to the cannibalism story as the start of Chikatilo's drift toward violent murder and mutilation.

The boy's life was further filled with death by the 1941 invasion by Nazi Germany. The German panzer divisions tore easily across the open Ukrainian plain, meeting little initial resistance. Long-suffering Ukrainians at first viewed the invaders as a liberating army. Happy to encourage that delusion, the Germans welcomed deserting soldiers sympathetically and tried to recruit them against the common enemy, communism. Legions sprang up to join the Nazi forces. Chikatilo's father, Roman, however, was not among them. A landless peasant, Roman Chikatilo remained loyal to the Soviet motherland and joined the Red Army. Fighting on the Eastern Front, he was captured and spent much of the conflict in a prisoner-of-war camp outside the Soviet Union. Young Andrei did not see his father again for five

Viewing invading Germans as an alternative to Stalin's oppressive rule, Ukrainian villagers offer a plate of bread and salt, the traditional gift of welcome, to troops advancing into southern Russia in 1941.

years. Perhaps he reinvented the hapless man as the heroic partisan leader who later populated his fantasies. Meanwhile, war raged on all sides.

During the German occupation, which lasted until 1943, corpses were a commonplace, "parts of bodies everywhere," Chikatilo recalled, "children torn into pieces." But death was only part of the horror of occupation; rape abounded. Chikatilo's sister, Tatyana, born in 1943, apparently was conceived while his father was a prisoner of war. Some observers speculate that the mother may have been raped by the German invaders—and that the boy saw it and was psychologically scarred by it. Only Chikatilo knew whether the incident actually occurred, and he never talked about it.

In spite of the powerful forces working against his survival, Andrei managed to endure—if not exactly thrive—and he even attended school. He was a shy, secretive, introverted child who had problems making friends. He was often teased as a dreamer who eagerly sopped up tales of heroic Communist resistance to the Nazis. With visions of becoming a partisan himself, he doted on such patriotic epics as *Melodiya Gvardiya*, a socialist melodrama that idealized a group of young Communists who gave their lives to help win the war. But despite his youthful superhero fantasies, he later related, "I was an object of ridicule and could not defend myself."

When the war ended, Andrei's meager self-esteem suffered a heavy blow. Roman Chikatilo was liberated from prison camp by an American unit, but when he returned to Russia he was quickly tossed into a camp run by the Soviets. Stalin's boundless paranoia concerning Ukraine had been amplified by the extent of pro-Nazi collaboration during the war's early days. In the dictator's mind, surrender was a form of collaboration, and a particularly dangerous form

because it carried the added risk of anti-Socialist contamination. Chikatilo's father was luckier than many, who were shot as soon as they returned home. But the fumbling, timid son had to face the fact that the heroic parent he'd invented had been branded an "enemy of the people"—a charge that carried a weighty burden of shame.

Chikatilo manifested signs that sometimes denote a quiet but severe disturbance: At 12 he was still a bedwetter. He also was so extraordinarily shy that even though he had very bad eyesight, he was afraid to tell either his teachers or his family about the problem. Aggravated by his bad vision, his ineptitude encouraged more ridicule. His classmates taunted him for his physique, calling him *baba*, a pejorative for woman, because, they said, his breasts were too big, and making jokes about the shape of his foreskin. For the diffident Chikatilo, the crude cruelty opened deep wounds.

But as his adolescence progressed and Chikatilo got his growth, those same schoolmates dubbed him Silni Andrei—Andrew the Strong—and deferred to him physically as the toughest kid on the playground. His teachers gave him good marks in class because, despite his bad eyesight, he persevered at his studies in history and literature and displayed a phenomenal memory for long strings of information—series of large random numbers, the names of the world's Communist leaders. For, as part of his romanticization of the partisans, he'd become a fervent ideological Communist, a position he would maintain until communism itself collapsed.

Chikatilo attained enough esteem among his peers and his instructors to hold a number of responsible posts. At 16 he became editor of his school's newspaper, a sensitive political position. He also served as a member of the school committee and rose to the comparatively powerful position of student agitprop—agitation and propaganda—leader. When Stalin died in 1953, Chikatilo was the student who read aloud the endless tributes in the official Communist party organ *Pravda*. He became an activist in Komsomol, the party youth organization.

Despite Chikatilo's energy and enthusiasm, he was unable to overcome a shyness bordering on terror with females. At 16 the school achiever would still blush when merely standing next to a girl in class. Nearly a year later, when he had an initial episode of heavy petting with Tanya, a precocious 13-year-old friend of his sister, he claimed to be revolted by the experience. His acute self-consciousness was already flashing signals of sexual dysfunction—signals that vanished in the ambient static of repression.

For all the pressures and disappointments of his secondary-school years, however, Chikatilo clearly had hopes of a rosy future as he graduated. He set his sights on entering the most prestigious university in the country, the Moscow State University, studied feverishly, and went to the capital to take the entrance exams. He failed. The blow stunned him. Rather than lower his sights slightly and try for admission to another university, he enrolled at a technical college. He was convinced that what had held him back was not his own performance but his father's war record. The disappointment was another cause for repressed fury and embitterment.

The 19-year-old Chikatilo's budding sexuality was faring no better than his intellectual aspirations. While at college, he had his first major love affair, a liaison with a 17-year-old friend of his younger sister. The couple made two attempts to have sex; both times Chikatilo failed. Within two months the unconsummated affair was over.

After graduating as a communications technician—a telephone repairer—Chikatilo was ordered by the government to his first assignment, a job in the growing but barren industrial town of Nizhni Tagil, 800 miles northeast of Moscow. He was eager and willing to work, but otherwise the experience was dreadful: cold, lonely, and—again—humiliating. He tried more than once to make sexual conquests among the local girls, but he was always impotent.

The local women mocked him, and he feared that they would make his disability public. He became depressed and tried to work his way out of his dark mood by taking a correspondence course from a Moscow institute. In 1957 the state intervened in his personal woes: He was drafted for a three-year stint in the Red Army.

Putting on a uniform, however, only brought more misery. Assigned to a communications unit, Chikatilo was soon at odds with his fellow draftees. He felt that they sneered at him behind his back. His sexual misadventures continued. Some soldiers began to say he was homosexual. Finally he stopped taking leaves with his unit. Years later Chikatilo claimed that he'd been raped in the service—not as a sexual act so much as a brutal reminder of his low rank in the barracks hierarchy.

It was not until after he left the army in 1960 and returned home, however, that Chikatilo had what may have been his most indelibly remembered sexual embarrassment. On one of his infrequent dates, his body refused to respond properly. Worse, the woman talked about his failing. He bitterly recalled years later that she told everybody that he'd come back from the army "good for nothing, impotent, his 'machine' not working." But he remembered more than humiliation. "I was so ashamed when she told the local girls about me," he said. "I was very angry with that girl. I dreamed of catching her and tearing her to pieces as a revenge for my disaster." The connection between sex and murder had been made.

Now 24, Chikatilo decided not to stay in Yablochnoye. Instead, he struck a relatively short distance east and south—across the Ukrainian border into Russia and his new home, Rostov-on-Don. In that tough, teeming port city, he came upon the vast human herd on which, almost two decades later, he would begin to prey.

Residents of Rostov say that crossing the Don River bridge from the city takes one from Europe into Asia. The town was founded in 1747 as a trading and customs port, and the fertile lands around it established Rostov as a grain port. In the 19th century, with the advent of the railroads, the city became known as the Gate to the Caucasus, and waves of trans-Caucasian nationalities washed around and through it: Armenians, Georgians, fierce, hot-tempered, entrepreneurial people who brought exoticism and commerce—and violence.

Rostov became a center of Russian crime and black-marketeering. Under communism the sprawling town of docks and clapboard houses had been festooned with concrete apartment buildings and broad roadways, but it remained as rough as ever: About 300 killings a year were registered in a population of one million during the 1980s. As a crossroads, Rostov still drew the ambitious and the rootless to its railways and bus stations, seeking fortune, a kind word, a drink, a place to stay.

At first Chikatilo didn't live in the city itself. He got a job as a telephone repairman in Novoshakhtinsk, a drab little city of 200,000 at the center of one of Russia's oldest coal-mining regions some 30 miles north of Rostov. Hoping to liberate his sister from his mother's dominance, he urged Tatyana to join him in his small, one-room domain. She accepted, staying with her big brother for six months before marrying a local laborer. Left alone once more, Chikatilo settled into mature adulthood, functional in most respects, but not sexually.

Like most young men, Chikatilo was obsessed with women, but he didn't dare approach them. Because his sexual urges couldn't be denied, he satisfied them by masturbating, compulsively and often, to the point that he was unable to control the activity at all, even on the job. His coworkers were quick to notice. On a line repair job in the wooded countryside the nearsighted Chikatilo was caught unawares and nearly sank into the earth at the shouts and jokes of his colleagues. "I always thought about this," he said later, "and suffered because I realized that I was different from everyone else."

As the years passed, Tatyana also worried about her brother's solitary life. She began searching for a mate for him and introduced him to a friend who lived in Novoshakhtinsk. Feodosia, 24—three years younger than Chikatilo—was a miner's daughter, a tall, capable, confident woman. Somehow she managed to penetrate Chikatilo's immobilizing bashfulness. She found him gentle, polite, and, unlike most men of her acquaintance, obsessed with neither alcohol nor sex. They were married within two weeks, in the summer of 1963.

For the bridegroom, the wedding night was the usual debacle. Chikatilo's "machine" misfired as badly as it always had, and it was a week before his wife could persuade him to try sex a second time. Somehow they succeeded well enough to have a daughter, Lyudmilla, in 1965

and a son, Yuri, in 1969. But Chikatilo himself was later to say cryptically that the couple had "not had a full-fledged sexual act but only an imitation." Nonetheless, his wife remained a loyal partner and helpmate—although not always a sweet-tempered one. She nagged him enthusiastically, just as his mother had.

The energy that Chikatilo couldn't throw into sex went into self-improvement, and his life seemed to be on the upswing. A believer from his youth, he became an active member of the Communist party. In 1970 he abandoned his telephone company job to head a local sports center. He was tall, strong, and fond of athletics. He also liked young people. But that was just a beginning. Chikatilo had taken a few correspondence courses before marrying Feodosia and had later enrolled at Rostov State University, where he attended classes two months of the year and did the rest of his academic work by correspondence. In 1970 he earned a bachelor's degree with a specialty in Russian language and decided to become a teacher.

Educators are held in high esteem in Russia. Chikatilo's new credentials meant a major change in status, one that made his class-conscious wife especially proud. He soon found a teaching job in Novoshakhtinsk. Life in the coal mines had always been harsh and dangerous, and local family life reflected that fact. The children of Novoshakhtinsk were as tough as their fathers—and a handful even for the ablest teacher.

For Chikatilo, they proved disastrous. The aloof, introverted man eagerly flung himself into the work, but he lacked training and was unable to establish any discipline. From his first day in class he was mocked and jeered. Youngsters ran about, broke smoking rules, and generally did as they pleased. Chikatilo's response was to withdraw into frustrated silence, both from the pupils and from his fellow teachers. His colleagues remembered him as a chronic complainer.

Soon, however, they had another reason to remember him. Chikatilo may not have been able to discipline his pupils, but he began to show an extraordinary and unprofessional interest in some of them, little girls in particular. Sometimes he'd sit beside them in class, helping them with their work—but also touching them intimately. His school included a dormitory for boarding students; he took to appearing in the sleeping area without knocking, catching girls in their nightgowns or underwear. Often, the chil-

A Red Army draftee in 1958, the 22-year-old
Chikatilo poses in civilian clothes *(inset)*.
Two years later he moved to Rostov, where
he eventually earned a bachelor's degree
from Rostov State University *(below)*.

The picture of normality, Andrei and
Feodosia Chikatilo sit for a family
portrait in 1970 with their young son,
Yuri, born in 1969.

dren said, they could see him secretly stimulating himself through his pockets.

In April 1973 Anna Chikatilo died, and her son—perhaps coincidentally, perhaps because some final restraint died with her—embarked on a more overt exploration of his sexual identity. In May, while swimming with some of his pupils, he suddenly grabbed one of them, a 15-year-old, and began fondling her. Her screams, he discovered, only excited him more. He stopped only when a group of students swam over to investigate. The same month he issued an after-hours detention to a 14-year-old girl, and when the other students had left he began beating her with a ruler across the back. She tried to escape; they wrestled. Aroused by the unequal contest, Chikatilo ejaculated in his trousers and suddenly stormed out of the room, locking the door behind him. The student escaped by a window.

Until then, school authorities had tried to look the other way—in part because reporting Chikatilo's behavior to police would have brought an investigation of everyone. The Stalinist idea of collective responsibility was still a normal part of Soviet ethics; the school headmaster could expect that any punishment meted out to Chikatilo would also spill over onto him. But after the detention incident, the offending teacher was pressured into resigning. Chikatilo soon found another job—teaching at a technical school around the corner from his previous post. He stayed there for four years and somehow managed to control his molesting impulses, but he was no more popular than he'd been in the past. When an order came for staff cuts, he was among the first to go.

Once again, the taciturn instructor had little trouble finding a job, this time at a technical school in Shakhty, another tough mining town a few miles to the east of Novoshakhtinsk. The school trained boys from the age of 15 in mining—not exactly Chikatilo's area of expertise—so he wound up running the school's live-in hostel for students. His wife was also taken on staff. The new supervisor's main task was to look after the youngsters' moral development. He soon proved as much of a disaster as before. Neither students nor teachers respected him; they called him Goose because of his gangling build and protruding Adam's apple. He remained aloof and threw his energy into Communist party activities.

His sexual obsessiveness resurfaced. One autumn night in 1978, the supervisor of morals entered the boys' dormitory and leaned over the bed of a 15-year-old named Shcherbakov, pulled back the sheets, and attempted oral sex. The boy awakened and the teacher fled, but not unseen. From then on, Chikatilo was at the mercy of his students, who taunted him with threats and jeers.

Incredibly, the incident led to no disciplinary action against the perpetrator. Despite his aberrant sexuality, Chikatilo became more respectable, as he began writing a column for the local Communist party newspaper on political and moral topics. The only person who showed much concern about his behavior was Feodosia. Although she'd shrugged off tales of his molestations earlier, she now tried to get him to see a psychiatrist or a sex therapist. He refused.

Chikatilo's obstinacy was not simply an aversion to treatment: He was not much inclined to meddle with his psyche because he was beginning to enjoy it. He was building a secret identity for himself, one that allowed him to revel in his fantasies of power and sexual gratification without fear of being caught. Not long after moving to Shakhty, he'd bought a small, tumble-down house on the edge of town, little better than a hut. He didn't live there, but he had plenty of time to visit, since his schedule at the school called for him to be on duty for only a single 24-hour shift every three days.

The house on Mezhevoi Pereulok was his secret trysting place, where he brought prostitutes, drunks, and drifters drawn from public toilets, streets, parks, and railway stations, to trade sex for food, drink, or money. Although Chikatilo's impotence had become a permanent feature of his married life, his sexual urges were as undiminished as the chronic dysfunction of his "machine." In a bid to push himself to potency, his drives and his anger impelled him to try ever more outlandish sexual techniques. He was drawn in particular to domination—the domination of little girls. Unlike adult women, they gave him a sense of being in complete control. He polished his blandishments, and at least once, he lured a pair of six-year-olds back to Mezhevoi Pereulok and assaulted them. He'd crossed a crucial psychological frontier. Without being entirely conscious of it, Chikatilo had begun to hunt.

Prey was everywhere. In a society where serial killing was ideologically impossible—Communist doctrine said that only corrupt capitalistic cultures could produce such monsters—children were not taught to fear adults.

They saw nothing threatening in a mild, slope-shouldered, goose-necked 41-year-old teacher.

After work on the evening of December 22, 1978, Chikatilo had a stroke of luck. On Mezhevoi Pereulok he met Yelena Zakotnova, a pretty blonde child who had tarried at a friend's house after school. Now she was on her way home. Yelena was nine. She chatted easily with Chikatilo, who fell into step beside her on the street. She also said she wanted to fix her hair. The friendly man had a solution: Use the mirror at his place, which was only a few steps away. The trusting little girl followed him.

The sun sets early in the Shakhty winter, and it was dark when Chikatilo ushered Yelena into his run-down lair. They stepped inside — and Chikatilo was immediately transformed. He threw himself on the girl, pushing her to the floor. He ripped off her clothes, and rubbed against her, but he remained impotent. In frustration, he penetrated her with his finger, causing her to bleed. Aroused by the sight of blood, he began stabbing her and experienced a powerful orgasm. He had to have another. Swept away, he stabbed her repeatedly, fondling her at the same time. Finally, he strangled her.

As the killing fog lifted, Chikatilo realized the enormity of his deed. He panicked, then regained control. He pushed the girl's clothes back on and put her into a sack. Looking out the door to make sure he wasn't seen, he carried the small body across the street and ran to a nearby stream. He heaved the bloody burden into the water and threw the child's schoolbag after her. Yelena Zakotnova drifted away. The bag fell on the opposite side of the creek.

Two days later Yelena's remains were discovered only a short distance from her schoolbag. Police began a door-to-door search of the area. Their attention was soon drawn to Chikatilo's squalid dwelling. A neighbor had noticed the light on at night, which was unusual, since he normally carried out his sexual liaisons during the afternoon and early evening, then returned home to Feodosia. Neighbors had also seen enough strange women and girls going in and out of the shack to have some idea of what the man was up to. An interview with Chikatilo left police suspicious. A check of his background, and the circumstances of his sudden departures from previous jobs, heightened their interest. But Feodosia said her husband had been home on the night of December 22, the night that Yelena had disappeared. After eight or nine questioning sessions, police attention suddenly shifted to another suspect who lived on the run-down lane.

Aleksandr Kravchenko, 25, had committed a similar killing several years earlier in the Crimea and had escaped execution because he was — barely — a minor. He'd served 6 years of a 10-year prison sentence. Kravchenko was caught in Shakhty during a burglary attempt and arrested. Then, after some intensive interrogation, he confessed to Yelena's murder. Chikatilo was forgotten.

Just as suddenly as he'd confessed, however, Kravchenko suddenly denied the murder, claiming police had beaten the confession out of him. The only material evidence against him was some grass on his clothing that matched traces found on Zakotnova. The prosecution's main witness was Kravchenko's wife, who said — possibly because of police pressure — that he'd admitted the crime to her. Police ignored some evidence that might have cleared Kravchenko, including a witness who told them that she'd seen a middle-aged man with glasses talking to a girl who looked like Yelena at a bus stop near the top of Mezhevoi Pereulok. She said she thought the man had been trying to persuade the child to do something.

The judge who tried Kravchenko found him guilty but sentenced him to 15 years in jail rather than to death — a clemency that recognized, perhaps, the flimsiness of the evidence. Prosecutors, however, appealed the sentence all the way to the Soviet Supreme Court — and won. Six years later, in 1984, Kravchenko was executed by a firing squad.

As Kravchenko was being arrested and tried, the real killer was digesting a mixture of emotions roused by his first murder. There was shock, coupled with the intense pleasure called forth by the girl's agony and her blood. Morally ambivalent, Chikatilo both loved and hated his deed. He also knew that he would do it again if the opportunity arose. But this killing had also been a very close call; the brush with capture had terrified him. It had also alerted his employers, who already suspected him of perversion.

For the next three years fear and caution inspired Chikatilo to quell his horrible urges. Then, in 1981, the headmaster at his school suggested that he resign voluntarily, as part of a mandated staff cut. Chikatilo was cut loose, freed from his responsibilities, his past, his joint job with his wife. He was free to start everything again. Just as abruptly as he'd become a teacher, he abandoned his profession. Perhaps his reputation made it impossible for him to find another teaching job; perhaps he'd decided to submerge into

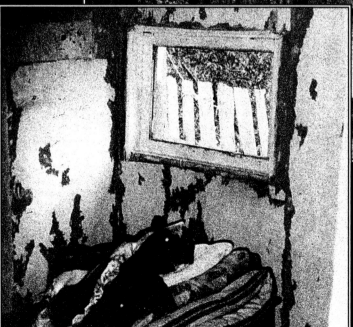

Impotent but sexually obsessed, Chikatilo purchased this run-down shack on Shakhty's Mezhevoi Pereulok to use as a trysting place for the women and children he lured into its shabby interior *(inset)* with promises of food, drink, or money. It was here that Chikatilo finally began to murder.

Chikatilo enticed his first victim, nine-year-old Yelena Zakotnova, back to his squalid hut and brutally murdered her, then threw her body into this branch of the nearby Grushevka River. Her book bag landed on the opposite bank. A shack much like Chikatilo's can be seen in the background.

YELENA ZAKOTNOVA

Soviet society, where he'd be freer to follow his deadly instincts. In any case, he took a sudden, voluntary drop in status. In March 1981 he became a supply clerk for a Shakhty industrial concern.

There was shrewd method in Chikatilo's downward mobility. In the unwieldy Soviet system, supply clerks were people of peculiar influence who often gleaned special advantages from their positions. Chikatilo's job, in essence, was to make an unworkable industrial economy work by scrounging the parts, materials, and supplies that were always unavailable under central planning. Called pushers, these arch-scroungers spent little time in the office and a lot on the road, cajoling and persuading reluctant suppliers to come across with whatever was needed to keep a particular industry going. They were a kind of human substitute for the laws of supply and demand.

The rigid, uncommunicative Chikatilo had none of the necessary salesman's qualities. But Chikatilo was not looking for professional success; he was intrigued by the possibilities the job offered his secret life. He had no time clock to punch. He had to travel extensively—sometimes on short trips to pick up supplies, but sometimes on long ones. No one would know exactly where he was or what he was up to. The loss of status bothered him, but he muted that by burying himself in Communist party hack work and evening classes in Marxism-Leninism. He told his few friends that he was still a teacher.

Chikatilo's new job soon fulfilled its hidden promise. Only six months after becoming a pusher he met Larisa Tkachenko near the Rostov library. An hour later, poised like a mad wolf over her bloody body, he discovered what he had irrevocably become.

Just as Chikatilo's first murder had been followed by a three-year pause, the slaughter of Larisa was followed by another, briefer, hiatus. Nine months passed before Chikatilo ventured out on another hunt.

On June 12, 1982, Lyuba Biryuk's mother asked her to go from their home to the nearby village of Donskoi to buy food. The bright, well-behaved 13-year-old girl did her shopping; a boy later remembered seeing her on the bus to town, clad in a blue dress and a pair of white sandals. But then Lyuba decided to walk home instead of taking the bus. On the way she met Andrei Chikatilo. He quickly engaged the teenager in conversation. What was her name? Where

was she going? His questions were neutral and harmless. Behind a screen of disarming small talk, he hungered.

The unlikely couple crossed the road and walked along a path hidden by bushes. Unable to restrain himself further, Chikatilo sprang, forcing the girl to the ground. He ripped off her clothes, tried to rape her, and failed. He covered her mouth with one hand and began to cut and slash her body with the other, which held a knife. Her blood and muffled screams brought Chikatilo to orgasm; then Lyuba Biryuk died. He covered the body with trash, bundled up the girl's simple garments and her shopping bag, and threw them into the woods. He slipped away. By the time the corpse was discovered two weeks later, the hot, wet Russian summer had reduced it to little more than a skeleton.

Whatever inhibitions had once restrained Chikatilo now ran before the flood of his enthusiasm for death. Already he was ranging all over the region. His next victim, Lyuba Volobuyeva, 14, was murdered on July 25 while the supply clerk was on a business trip to Krasnodar, a city 150 miles south of Rostov. Traveling in the nearby Agdey district on August 13, he slaughtered a nine-year-old boy, Oleg Pozhidayev. Back in Shakhty only three days later he surprised and killed Olga Kuprina, 16, then paused for a couple of weeks before killing Irina Karabelnikova, 18, and Sergei Kuzmin, 16, seven days and a mile apart, outside Shakhty.

Karabelnikova was another of the sad bits of social flotsam that Chikatilo was learning to recognize at a glance. The product of a broken home, she first lived with her father, a coal miner, then with her mother, before moving into a youth hostel. She met a soldier and nearly married, but finally did not. When Chikatilo found her in Shakhty, she was lonely and at loose ends. She agreed to go off with him for sex, presumably expecting to be paid. Her body lay in the forest near the train station for two weeks before it was discovered.

On December 11 Chikatilo committed his final crime of 1982, murdering 10-year-old Olga Stalmachenok, who was not at all the type that he would later claim to despise. A well-loved child from Novoshakhtinsk, she was on her way home from school when the bus broke down and she had to wait at the station for another one. Years later, several witnesses disclosed that they'd seen the girl walking past with a man who held her hand and looked like her father or grandfather.

But there was also another intriguing clue. At the time the

girl disappeared, Rostov police received a postcard addressed to "Parents of the Missing Child." "Don't get upset," its message taunted. "She is not the first and not the last. Before New Year we need another 10." The postcard directed police to look for the child's body in a specified place, and was signed "Sadist—Black Cat." Olga's body was found four months later, far from where the postcard told police to look.

As the number of murders grew, so, apparently, did Chikatilo's mania for killing. He went into almost constant motion. Unlike many psychopathic killers, he never forced his company onto his would-be victims. He would strike up a light conversation, tossing out small talk. If he met the slightest resistance, he moved on. The very lightness of his approach helped render him invisible: Who could remember the polite middle-aged man who appeared at an elbow,

uttered a few pleasantries, then vanished? When he did hook victims, Chikatilo took extraordinary—but always unobtrusive—pains to get them alone. If those efforts failed, he didn't pursue.

Mousily anonymous himself, Chikatilo had an unmistakable signature as a murderer: slashed eyes, evisceration, severed genitals and reproductive organs. The remains showed puzzling variations on this grisly theme, however, and Rostov area police hadn't begun to associate the victims until December 1982. Then the investigation started to coalesce into a search for a single killer, and police began speaking grimly of the lesopolosa murders.

Part of the delay was due to the fact that the Soviet police system, at all levels, was ill equipped for the job of finding a murderer who killed often, over a vast area. Clues and suspects went onto file cards, not computers; errors were

covered by falsified records; and attention to business was often spotty. Police, like many of their compatriots, were often more interested in finding food than finding criminals. The Soviet compartmentalization of responsibility, its taste for secrecy, and the country's simmering antagonisms also worked for Chikatilo, keeping news of murders in one jurisdiction from leaking into others. Finally, there were problems of turf among the many layers of Soviet law enforcement, reaching from national police down through provincial and local levels, and often overlapping. Jurisdictional problems were rife.

Despite the competition and infighting among various crime-fighting fiefdoms, there eventually came to be an organized effort to pursue the serial slayer. Mikhail Gregoriyevich Fetisov, the big, friendly chief of criminal investigations for the Rostov district, established a task force to catch the lesopolosa killer. At about the same time, Fetisov added a new detective to his Division of Especially Serious Crimes: Viktor Vasiliyevich Burakov, a tough 36-year-old cop with the face of a wrestler and a growing reputation in forensic analysis.

Born in 1946 on a farm in Bryansk, a few hundred miles northwest of Rostov, Burakov had risen within the system, graduating at the head of his class from the High Investigations Academy in Volgograd in 1978. Because of his high marks he was assigned to the difficult post of leading the Analysis Team in violent Rostov-on-Don. It was Burakov

Hunting for prey in a land where relatively few people own cars, Chikatilo searched among the hordes of commuters streaming through Rostov's local bus station *(above)* and train station *(below)*.

Long forest strips, or *lesopolosas,* border a highway near Rostov-on-Don. Planted to prevent soil erosion, the strips became synonymous with murder when mutilated victims began turning up among the trees.

---

who, seeing the winter-preserved remains of little Olga Stalmachenok in a field in April 1983, sensed that her slayer was a serial killer.

If detectives suspected that a monster was killing in and around Rostov, they kept their suspicions to themselves. In typical Soviet fashion, they told the public nothing. Instead, Operation Lesopolosa steamrolled on, following one false trail after another. Immense resources were thrown into analyzing the Black Cat postcard and comparing it with thousands of other letters written by workers, bureaucrats, and virtually everyone employed in the region. The grand effort triggered by the message drew a blank, and for a good reason: Black Cat was a hoax.

Local cops decided that the killings were so horrible that only someone mentally retarded could have carried them out—a breathtaking feat of wrongheaded deduction. Rather than look for a clever, active killer, the police concentrated on the weak-minded. Their first targets were a pair of young men named Yuri Kalenik and Valery Shaburov, residents of a nearby hostel for the mentally handicapped, or *internat,* who'd been arrested for trying to steal a bus. Under interrogation—means unspecified—Kalenik confessed to raping and killing 11 people, 7 of whom were lesopolosa victims. Despite his handicaps—and perhaps with some coaching from police—he identified several of the murder sites to investigators' satisfaction. With an admitted killer in hand, the authorities called off the hunt, and Burakov, somewhat skeptically, began tying off the loose ends. Rostov's ordeal seemed to be over.

For six months after Olga Stalmachenok's murder, Chikatilo did not kill again, constrained by the rigors of the Russian winter and perhaps frightened by the heightened police activity. His bland, faintly repulsive, everyday existence proceeded as it always had. Although he occasionally showed sparks of good humor, flirting and joking with a few women in the office, Andrei the supply clerk was as reviled as Andrei the teacher had been. His bosses found him incompetent and gave him tongue-lashings virtually every day.

In a coincidental national counterpoint to Chikatilo's professional decline, the Soviet economy was entering its final phase of breakdown. Authorities were trying to lash the foundering system into some sort of respectable performance, and as failure followed failure, supply pushers like Chikatilo came under fire as never before. Yet as the criticism mounted he took it all meekly, convinced that he was being picked on unfairly, but determined not to fight back. Mostly he longed to get out of sight. "God, it would be better if I went away on a trip again," he told one of his few friends at the factory. "At least when I am on the road, there is no one always telling me off."

Colleagues remember him sitting at his desk, writing with concentration in a little exercise book, so absorbed that he failed to answer when spoken to. Someone who peeked over his shoulder saw only rows of small crosses—the neutral doodles of a man whose mind was elsewhere. His behavior was also becoming openly odd. For example, he would leave with a driver on a supply pickup, then abandon him without explanation, even passing up rides in the process. He carried a bag with him everywhere. Office snoops once opened it and discovered a change of clothing and underwear. As a joke they

added a brick. Chikatilo said nothing, as usual. But his demons gathered. "If something was wrong in my life and my work," he explained later, "then I found myself again at the train station or in the forest, and so all that would start. That frustration pressured me all the time and it was boiling inside of me every day, every hour."

Finally he sought the relief that only killing could give him. Laura Sarkisyan, 16, an Armenian teenager, was murdered in late June or early July 1983, though police had to take Chikatilo's word for it: Her body was never found. She was soon followed by Irina Dunenkova, 13, whose mutilated corpse was discovered in a deserted stretch of woods on the edge of Rostov near the airport, an area known as Aviators' Park.

Although the police couldn't have known it, Irina Dunenkova offered a powerful clue to the killer's identity. She'd known Chikatilo years earlier, when she and her older sister Tatyana had gone several times to the killer's sexual lair in Shakhty. Irina suffered from Down syndrome, and at the time Chikatilo hadn't tried to molest her. But he recognized her immediately when he met her again at the Rostov rail station in July. She'd become a vagrant, shabbily dressed, dirty, and with barely enough money to buy a snack. She went

with him easily. He took her to the park, tried to have sex, failed—and pulled out his knife. Her body was not discovered for a month.

An older tramp, Lyudmilla Kutsyuba, 24, met the same fate later in the month near a small railway stop in Shakhty. Then it was the turn of Igor Gudkov, a boy of only eight. He too was found in Aviators' Park.

After Igor's death the Rostov police and prosecutor's office created a special 16-man team to crack the case. But Chikatilo continued unhindered. Even as the mentally defective Kalenik was being grilled, the killer hacked apart at least one more woman in the neighboring area. While Burakov began his "mopping up" after Kalenik's confession, Chikatilo struck again, this time murdering a 19-year-old prostitute on the edge of Shakhty on October 27. Two days after Christmas he murdered a 14-year-old schoolboy, Sergei Markov, near Shakhty.

The police response was to arrest two more internat boys, who also quickly pleaded guilty. The sad farce continued. On January 10, 1984, an 18-year-old alcoholic vagrant named Natalya Shalapinina turned up horribly mutilated in Aviators' Park. Her nose and upper lip had been cut off,

along with a finger from her left hand. A month later a 44-year-old derelict, Marta Ryabenko, was found hideously ripped on virtually the same spot. Within a week of her murder police arrested an alcoholic man, first charging him with a rape in the woods nearby. He too confessed.

No one questioned these confessions. Ritualized admissions of guilt had been a routine part of Soviet law enforcement since Stalin's time. Indeed, since the days of totalitarian purges, the fact of arrest was usually considered more than sufficient evidence of guilt. Despite the Soviet Union's accelerating drift toward openness, the accumulated distortions of the despotic legal system were still very much in play. Moreover, the police had deflected any criticism by clamping down completely on the news, leaving the highly developed Russian grapevine to pass the word of murders—often in a very distorted form. Rumors spread that the killings were the work of a cannibal gang, that Rostov mobsters were using children's lives as chips in a bet, and even that the killer traveled in a posh black Volga sedan with the license plate CCO—the initials of the Russian words for Death to Soviet Children.

Meanwhile, the true murderer, oblivious to the blunder-

Chikatilo led at least two of his Rostov victims
along this lonely path into the stands of acacia
trees in Aviators' Park.

ing attempts to capture him, kept ratcheting up the stakes for his pursuers. In March 1984 another body was found on the edge of an outlying housing estate in Novoshakhtinsk. Dima Ptashnikov, 11, had been a bright youngster with a passion for stamp collecting and poetry before he was stabbed 54 times and afflicted with Chikatilo's usual grotesque mutilations. But this time, investigators got a minor break. Near the body, they found a footprint on muddy ground. It told them that the killer had large feet. Then a witness came forward, saying she had seen the boy walking with a man in his fifties, anywhere from five feet ten inches to six feet tall, wearing glasses and carrying a bag. The man walked with a slight limp. Investigators later learned that Chikatilo was having problems with blood vessels in one of his legs at the time.

The police were not the only ones hobbled by typically Soviet problems—Chikatilo himself was having a very Soviet kind of trouble at work. Earlier that spring he'd been fired from his job—or at least pressured to resign—for theft. Whether he committed the deed was questionable, but he was so intensely disliked at work that no one felt like speaking up for him.

The trouble had started just after the New Year, when he'd gone with a truckdriver on a routine mission to pick up supplies in Moscow. After their arrival, the inept pusher pulled his usual disappearing act, telling the driver that he'd meet him back at the factory hostel where they were staying. He did the same thing three nights running. When he and the driver returned to Shakhty, they brought back rolls of linoleum and other materials; a bookkeeper later charged that more than 200 feet of the floor covering—two rolls—were missing.

Pilferage was a way of life in the Soviet Union—but so was covering up. When the theft was reported, Chikatilo was hauled in to explain. The stubborn clerk insisted that he'd done nothing wrong—and stayed away from work for a couple of weeks. It was the chance his bosses had been waiting for. Despite the intercession of Feodosia, they charged Chikatilo with theft of state property. The same night, the body of Marta Ryabenko was discovered.

Chikatilo was looking for a new job, but he had even more time on his hands than usual. One May day he met Tatyana Petrosyan at the Shakhty railway station. He'd known her six years earlier when she was 24 and had con-

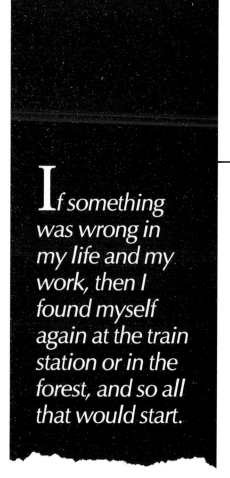

If something was wrong in my life and my work, then I found myself again at the train station or in the forest, and so all that would start.

sented to come back to his decrepit love nest for a tryst. Petrosyan, who sold pies at the station, was married, with a young daughter, Svetlana, and may have been mildly retarded. Her relationship with Chikatilo hadn't lasted long, and the intervening years had not been kind to her. Her husband had eventually found out about her various infidelities and left her with only a little alimony. Her main memory of Chikatilo, aside from his sexual failings, was that he'd been mildly kind to her. They agreed to arrange a date. Eventually Chikatilo suggested a picnic. He also suggested that she bring her daughter, now 11, along.

The threesome linked up on the train and got off at a little stop in Sady, a remote spot surrounded by dense woods. It seemed a romantic enough place, although the setting didn't matter—Petrosyan was drunk. After a 10-minute walk she was blearily amenable to Chikatilo's suggestion that she lie down. He'd brought little Svetlana a doll. She took it and wandered off into the forest.

As usual, sex was a fiasco, and the drunken Petrosyan was scathing about Chikatilo's performance. "Call yourself a real man?" she sneered. That was enough—more than enough—for what the unemployed clerk had in mind. He reached into his bag and pulled out a kitchen knife. Then he slammed the handle like a blackjack into the side of her head. As her screams rose, he stabbed her again and again. She died far more quickly than most of his victims. Then he rose naked and bloodstained—to see Svetlana. The terror-stricken child suddenly saw a roaring horror rushing in her direction, knife in hand. She turned and ran, covering just a few yards before Chikatilo rammed the knife into her. She lived only a few seconds. It was the only time he'd ever killed in front of a witness, and that may have explained the special attention he gave to little Svetlana's bleeding corpse. When police discovered it nearly two months later, the head lay several yards away.

The pressures Chikatilo faced as a result of the theft charge undoubtedly roused his worst demons. That summer marked the most murderous period of his career. Within weeks after the Petrosyan double murder, three more people—Yelena Bakulina, 22; Anna Lemesheva, 20; and Dima Illarionov, 13—died under his knife. Lemesheva's death was particularly brutal. Another social loser, she'd accepted an invitation from Chikatilo, with a tacit invitation to sex on the side. She was found with her uterus chopped out and thrown into the bushes near a small railway station near Shakhty.

Even in a closed society, such horrors could not be kept quiet forever. In June, Vladimir Kazakov, a veteran prosecutor from Moscow, arrived in Rostov, with orders to review the case. He found the police in a state of angry confusion, some holding that the murders were the work of a gang of internat boys. Others, noting the presence of semen on some of the dead boys' bodies, argued that there must be two killers, one of them a deranged homosexual. Few thought that more than six of the murders could be linked. Kazakov found at least 23 related killings, most of them in the area bounded by Rostov, Shakhty, and Novoshakhtinsk. He thought the confessions from the various people accused of some of the murders to be incredible: One man had confessed to a murder that occurred after he'd been arrested and jailed.

There was, Kazakov was convinced, a single killer on the loose, even though that person violated all the normal rules of serial murder by choosing victims of both sexes and a variety of ages. But the disfiguring wounds, especially around the eyes, were a clear signature. He called in more experts from Moscow, and they analyzed semen samples found on the victims for blood grouping. According to their laboratory analysis, the semen had come from a man with the rare AB blood grouping—a type found in only six percent of the population.

Moscow decided to put the cases under the control of a special task force. The capital also opened a probe into local police procedure that resulted in allegations of unspecified "contraventions of legality"—Soviet for bad investigative work. By way of compensating, Fetisov, the investigations chief for Rostov, put more than 200 people on the case and created a special criminal investigations subunit: the Department of Serious Crimes of a Sexual Nature. Viktor Burakov was asked to head the new office, familiarly called the Killer Department.

On August 1, 1984, Chikatilo found a new position, and a promotion to boot, as head of the supply department at Spetzenergoavtomatika, a heavy-machinery factory in Rostov. But that bit of economic relief didn't brake his killing. That evening he met Natalia Golosovskaya, 16, a respectable girl from the boondocks, at a bus stop near Rostov's airport. The bus didn't arrive and Chikatilo suggested a walk—and a shortcut through the thick surrounding woods of Aviators' Park. Everything else followed his usual grisly pattern—except that Chikatilo didn't linger long after the girl died. The murder had taken place only a few hundred yards from a busy school; one of the students even thought he heard screams. The next day the body was found under a pile of leaves.

Five days later Lyudmilla Alekseyeva was waiting for a bus to take her to a neighboring town to visit relatives. Chikatilo led her to what he called a better bus stop by way of a wooded path. Her death was one of his worst: Perhaps to extend the duration of his excitement, Chikatilo took special pains to keep her alive as long as possible as he stabbed her 39 times, amputated her nose and upper lip, and removed her sex organs.

The next day the supply pusher was on his way for a week's stay in Tashkent, capital of Uzbekistan, on a quest for equipment switches. The old Central Asian city was filled with Muslim women, modestly clad and veiled. Even here, Chikatilo found a victim. He soon struck up an acquaintance on a river beach with a woman whose headless body was discovered the day after he flew back to Rostov. The case of that mysterious death was solved only when Chikatilo confessed, and the woman's identity was never known. The second victim of his business trip was identified as Akmaral Saidalieva, 10, a runaway from Alma-Ata, capital of neighboring Kazakhstan. Given the sorry state of police communications, and the pervasive Soviet reluctance to communicate, authorities didn't even know that the bodies bore damage that identified them as the work of a killer who normally stalked hundreds of miles away.

Back in Rostov, Chikatilo waited only a couple of weeks before striking again. His intention on August 28 was merely to go shopping, but as he walked along the road he met Aleksandr Chepel, a boy of 11 whose parents had recently moved from the center of the city to a new high-rise complex on the edge of town. Aleksandr missed his old friends; he'd walked into town to play with them and was now walking home. He waited at a bus stop, but the rush-hour vehicles, filled to overloading, didn't pick him up. A kindly man suggested that they take a shortcut to a better stop. The route led across the Don River to the secluded left bank where Chikatilo had murdered Lyuba Alekseyeva. Now he killed again, inflicting mutilations so horrendous that the child's father fainted when he saw his son's body in the morgue five days later.

With the death of young Aleksandr, something like panic began to sweep through the region. Some 30 people had been murdered in the same hideous way, and even if press accounts didn't play up that fact, the rumor grapevine began to vibrate at top speed. Finally, the drowsing newspapers stirred. An article in the local Communist party daily, signed by a ranking Interior Ministry official, praised socialism's success at cutting the crime rate—and almost in passing took note of Chepel's death. "We assure the populace," the official wrote, "that the killer will be found in the near future." In the Soviet Union such oblique language meant that the lid was blowing off the case.

Not soon enough, however, for Irina Luchinskaya, 24, an attractive and promiscuous woman who still lived with her mother in Rostov but never turned down a chance for a good time. On September 6 she went off to work, warning her mother that she'd be home late. She was going to a *banya,* or steam bath, ostensibly for health reasons, but really because it was a place to socialize and drink. She never got there. As she waited at a Rostov bus stop, a middle-aged man suggested they go off into the woods for "relaxation." She complied—and died.

That should have been Chikatilo's last murder. His continuing trail of blood had once again brought him to the attention of the Moscow prosecutor's office, and to Viktor Burakov, the same official who'd linked his first six killings as the work of one man. Burakov brought into the case a Rostov psychiatrist, Aleksandr Bukhanovsky, who was a Soviet rarity—a psychiatrist specializing in homosexuals, transsexuals, and others whose deviations were supposed to be impossible under communism. The killer, Bukhanovsky said, was likely to appear normal, to be married, and to hold a regular job. He was not completely out of control; if threatened, he could suppress his urge to murder.

As if on cue, the killings stopped, but not because the ripper had put away his knives. On September 14, 1984, five days after Bukhanovsky released his profile, Chikatilo was hauled in as a suspect in the lesopolosa murders.

Convinced that bus stops and railway stations played key roles in the stalking pattern of the murderer, Burakov had concentrated his forces at those locations. In late August, Rostov police detective Aleksandr Zanasovsky had noticed a middle-aged man, dressed in a suit and carrying a bulky briefcase, in the Rostov bus station. What caught Zanasovsky's attention was that the man was approaching dozens of women, apparently trying to pick them up. As Zanasovsky watched, the suspect walked up to one after another and spoke briefly to each, moving on almost immediately if he got a negative reaction. Then the fellow had gone outside and tried the same thing at a bus stop.

The fascinated police officer finally stopped him for questioning. Asked his name, the man replied, "Andrei Chikatilo." What was he up to? "I was waiting to go home and

was bored," was the reply. "I wanted to talk to someone. I like young people. I used to be a teacher." There was no reason to hold him, so the officer let him go. And yet, in his gut, Zanasovsky sensed that this was the killer that everyone was looking for.

Two weeks later Zanasovsky spotted Chikatilo again, this time at a local bus station. The policeman followed him for hours, boarding a trolley, crossing to another bus, then another, and another. All the while Chikatilo kept talking and smiling at women. Finally, as night fell, the suspect returned to Rostov's main drag, Bolshaya Sadovaya Street, and began walking in and out of cafés. Then he headed to the city's modest Maksim Gorky Park. He was looking more and more restless and agitated. He returned to the railway station, sitting next to various females and talking, often getting sharp rebuffs, until 3 a.m. Then he went back to the bus station, where he finally persuaded a 19-year-old to give him oral sex, her head concealed under his jacket. The couple parted. Chikatilo, still hunting, headed for the city's streets.

Zanasovsky had seen enough. He walked up to the rangy, slope-shouldered supply clerk and arrested him on suspicion. Chikatilo's entire face, the policeman later recalled,

Partially concealed, the brutally mutilated remains of 24-year-old Irina Luchinskaya lie in Aviators' Park, where Chikatilo had lured her for sex.

broke out into a sweat, but he soon recovered his composure. Loudly protesting his innocence and demanding to know the charges against him, Chikatilo was led to the market police post and his briefcase was searched. Inside were lengths of rope, a kitchen knife with an eight-inch blade, and a jar of petroleum jelly. Surely, the authorities had their killer.

In custody, Chikatilo claimed he was guilty of nothing more suspicious than missing a bus and trying to spend the night in the railway station. The knife, he explained, he used on the road to slice sausage; everybody carried a knife. He offered no explanation for the other articles. Police had him held on a petty harassment charge that carried a 10-day jail sentence. Then they began furiously checking. They soon discovered that their man had been questioned in connection with the 1978 murder of nine-year-old Yelena Zakotnova, a killing for which another man had been executed. They also discovered that Chikatilo's shoe size matched the footprint found near the body of 11-year-old Dima Ptashnikov and that the suspect fit a rough description from a witness who'd seen the boy in the company of a middle-aged man. Investigators took a blood sample, hoping to match it with semen traces found in Ptashnikov's body. Laboratory analysis showed that Chikatilo's blood group was the rather common type A, not the AB indicated by the killer's semen. To their dismay, police found their prime suspect exonerated.

In fact, Chikatilo had been spared by a stroke of technical luck. Blood groups are identified from substances called antigens that are attached to red blood cells and signal the body's immune system that the cells are friendly. These same antigens are usually present in other body fluids, permitting blood type to be determined from saliva, semen, or even tears. But in about 20 percent of the population, the gene that produces the soluble substances is absent. Called nonsecretors, these people show no blood type signal anywhere but in their blood. Had Chikatilo been a nonsecretor, his semen should have shown no blood type whatever. Yet the biological laboratory at Moscow's Bureau of Forensic Medicine consistently got a type AB indication from the semen he left on and in his victims.

Svetlana Gurtovaya, director of the biological lab, reported later, in 1988, that such puzzling differences in blood types could result from a previously unknown phenomenon, which she called "paradoxical secretion"—the existence of antigens in the body fluids that don't correspond to antigens in the blood. Another, perhaps more credible, possibility, later reported by a French scientist, was that the chemical used in Soviet blood analyses, while adequate for typing blood, sometimes produced a false B signal when used to test semen. Thus, Chikatilo's A blood group, if present in his semen, could have been chemically skewed to reflect an AB grouping.

Most Western experts sneer at the Soviet results, noting that blood grouping is a sensitive laboratory process in which many things can go wrong—contamination by some bacteria, for example, can produce a spurious B grouping. In fact, in the West blood typing has been largely replaced by analysis of genetic material. Forensic scientists believe that the problem was what it first seemed: sloppy laboratory work. Given the number of wrongful arrests in the case—and the fact that 21 more people would die before Chikatilo was finally brought to justice—Western investigators also point out that the Russian authorities have a large stake in insisting that anything other than incompetence was the cause of the debacle.

Even as their case against Chikatilo was disintegrating, in fact, the thwarted lesopolosa task force embarked on yet another tangent. Following the notion that the dead boys must have been killed and raped by a homosexual assailant, they began dragging Rostov's clandestine population of gay males out into the light. In Soviet society at large, most sexual activity was furtive and quick; for homosexuals, it was a very dangerous game indeed. In the Soviet Union, homosexuality was viewed as unstable and aberrant behavior, punishable under harsh sodomy laws imposed by Stalin and still on the books half a century later.

A longtime party policeman not much inclined to sympathy for what he saw as aberration, Burakov used a known homosexual as an informer and rounded up hundreds of gay Rostov men, most of whom had managed to keep that part of their lives secret. Even after the detective was satisfied that the killer could not be homosexual, the roundup continued, rolling like a juggernaut across hundreds of lives. In all, 440 men were investigated, and 105 of them were convicted under Soviet antisodomy laws. Three men chose suicide instead, collateral casualties of Chikatilo's rampage.

During this misguided campaign, the real killer waited in custody. The only crime investigators could pin on Chikatilo was the pending linoleum theft charge, and they were unable to develop new evidence linking him to murder. No matter how strongly men like Zanosovsky believed Chikatilo was the killer, the discrepancy between his blood type and that found in the semen samples was insurmountable—it seemed to prove, scientifically, that Chikatilo could not be their man after all. Remarkably, the Rostov police never bothered to obtain a semen sample from their prisoner. On December 12, 1984, having served three months in jail, the forest zone ripper was sentenced to a year of hard labor for theft—and immediately freed. "It was all the same to me," he told them years later. "I died so many times . . . and so many times I revived."

After his narrow escape Chikatilo immediately sought out new territory. He settled on the city of Novocherkassk, a heavy industrial center of 200,000 people about 25 miles northeast of Rostov, and an important historical site. For centuries, Novocherkassk had been the seat of the Don Cossacks, the tough horseback fighters who served the czar. After the Bolshevik Revolution, they paid heavily for those loyalties. They were massacred and exiled by Lenin and Stalin, and their identity was ordered expunged. The city also had a more recent history of rebellion. In 1962 local workers rose up against Moscow to protest wage cuts and price increases. Dozens were shot in putting down the strike, the details kept secret for more than two decades. For Chikatilo, however, the important thing about the city was that he was able to find work there as a metal supplier, and he was able to reassemble his family life, blaming his brief jail stint on the vindictiveness of his former bosses. Feodosia concurred, unaware that the police had suspected him of murder.

In March 1985 the Soviet Union acquired a new leader, Mikhail Gorbachev, and a new direction. For those in pursuit of the serial killer, the change of regime meant the replacement of the Moscow prosecutors whom Vladimir Kazakov had assembled in Rostov—another singular break for Chikatilo, as it stalled the investigation.

But caution also restrained the ripper. When, after six months, Chikatilo struck again, he compounded the mystery. In late July 1985 he went on a business trip to Moscow. The World Youth Festival was taking place; the city was stuffed with outsiders. Traveling by train to Domodedovo, the city's long-haul airport for the southeastern

U.S.S.R., he was approached by an 18-year-old named Natalia Pokhlistova. She asked him if he had anything to smoke or drink—a clear hint that something was available in return. Chikatilo bartered for sex; she agreed. Near the airport, they left the train and walked into the woods, where he stabbed her 38 times and strangled her. She was found the next day by a mushroom picker.

Vladimir Kazakov was one of the first to hear of the body. He rushed to the morgue, identified the wounds as the work of the serial killer, and immediately arranged a check of all airline tickets and hotel rooms in the capital. Thousands of names were looked over. The effort turned up nothing, partly because none of the information was computerized—each of thousands of airline tickets had to be logged by hand. In fact, this net might have brought in Chikatilo, had he followed his plan to fly to Moscow. But, because of the crush of the Youth Festival, he'd ended up going by rail, where there were no passport checks. Then, while in the city, he'd stayed at a factory hostel, not a hotel, and missed the police dragnet. The killer had inadvertently handed his pursuers another red herring to trail: For a time they believed their man had moved to Moscow.

Chikatilo didn't correct their error until late summer. Then, on August 27, he picked up a vagrant, Inessa Gulyaeva, at the Shakhty bus station. Another 18-year-old, she jumped at the offer of a bed at his cottage in return for sex in the woods. He left her tattered body about 500 yards from the bus station, signaling Rostov police that their quarry was back in town. Gulyaeva was his 34th slaying, his last for the year.

Troubled by the chronic failure of Rostov police to bring the murderer to justice, Moscow once more stepped in. In November 1985 the Chief Procurator of the Russian Republic appointed Chief Inspector Isa Kostoyev, director of Moscow's Department of Crimes of Special Importance, to supervise the hunt. Kostoyev had built a reputation as a tough—almost an irresistible—interrogator. Although he didn't know it, he also had something in common with the man he would finally help snare: Like Chikatilo, he had suffered at the hands of Joseph Stalin.

In 1944 Stalin had ordered the Ingush, an entire Islamic nation within the Soviet Union, from their fertile home in the Caucasus into exile in the remote desert of Kazakhstan. Then only about 18 months old, young Kostoyev was taken east by his parents in this so-called resettlement, a journey

that killed many of the Ingush. Exile, and the hard life that followed, still burned in Kostoyev's memory—along with a powerful hatred of the Soviet dictator. Given the implacable dislike that still exists between Caucasians and Russians, it was probably never in the cards that Kostoyev and the Russian Burakov would hit it off. To Burakov, Kostoyev remained the bossy intruder from Moscow. To Kostoyev, Burakov remained a bungling parody of a Russian cop.

With only the vaguest of psychological profiles to go on, Kostoyev set up an index of suspects that eventually included 25,600 names, laboriously compiled by hand, since the Russians did not have Western-style police computers. Chikatilo's card was high on the list: number nine. But it noted that he was excluded from the investigation on account of his blood type. Tens of thousands of others had to be checked, including more than 5,800 men with previous convictions, 10,000 mentally ill people with potential for violence, and more than 160,000 intercity truckdrivers.

Investigators also looked for people with special skills. By this time, Chikatilo had become a maestro among sadists. Forensic studies showed that he still bit and slashed his victims, but with bloodthirsty precision, the better to prolong their agony while he mutilated their living bodies. So informed was his knife work that police thought he might be a professional; slaughterhouse workers were included in the search.

As the task force constructed its grand house of file cards, it managed to solve 95 murders, 245 rapes, and 140 assault cases—but not the case at hand. Then, just as Kostoyev came on the scene, the murders again seemed to stop. For Rostov police, 1986 was a disconcerting year: An intolerant Ingush from Moscow had taken over; Burakov suffered a

Apartment number 68 in this crumbling, prewar
Novocherkassk building at 36 Gvardeiskaya Street was
Chikatilo's home from 1985 until his final arrest.

mild nervous breakdown; and there were no murders with the lesopolosa signature. As 1987 opened, the manhunt poised like a destroyer listening for a silent submarine. But there was nothing.

Chikatilo was indeed running silent. He'd reverted to form at his job in Novocherkassk. Once again he was a supply officer, head of the factory's ferrous metals department. Once again his bosses hated his work and let him know it, revelations he suffered in silence. The dressings-down were particularly painful this time, for his daughter, Lyudmilla, worked in the same factory and sat in on the criticism sessions. Eventually, however, she left. Chikatilo hung on for nearly five years, for, in every other respect, his job was very much to his liking; it took him out of town to other hunting grounds.

The killer surfaced in May 1987, when he murdered 13-year-old Oleg Makatenkov. The boy was dumped in the woods near Revda, in the Ural Mountains. Another slaying took place in Leningrad. Neither was connected to Chikatilo until after his final arrest. The next year, 1988, he killed three times, all closer to home. One victim was a nine-year-old boy, Aleksei Voronko. Another was 16-year-old Yevgeny Muratov, who had traveled overnight to Rostov to enroll in a vocational school. The next morning he left by train. Chikatilo was aboard. Somehow, he persuaded the youngster to disembark at a deserted station north of Shakhty, to help him carry luggage to his nonexistent cottage. The body was discovered eight months later by playing children.

In 1989 the Soviet Union was literally coming to pieces as Mikhail Gorbachev's democracy-from-above began to tear apart the Communist system of control. Chikatilo seemed almost to mimic the national disintegration, for he too was losing control. Only that can explain his extraordinarily reckless decision early in 1989 to kill a streetwalker indoors, in a Shakhty apartment formerly occupied by his daughter, Lyudmilla. The victim was Tatyana Ryzhova, the daughter

ALEKSEI KHOBOTOV

The body of 10-year-old Aleksei Khobotov was not found until Chikatilo himself led police investigators to a shallow grave he'd dug for himself.

of a collective farm worker, who had been transformed in adolescence from a bright, studious child into the runaway consort of petty criminals. At the beginning of March she returned to Shakhty as a drunken vagrant. Chikatilo spotted her immediately at the train station and offered her a drink if she would go with him to tenement block 206, a crumbling thin-walled high-rise. His daughter had long since left town with her own family. Chikatilo had held on to the apartment for his son's return from military service—and, in the interim, to give himself a secret love nest. It had been years since he'd had one.

Once again, sex was a failure; Tatyana grew argumentative and demanded 500 rubles before she would leave. She screamed. Chikatilo silenced her with a punch. Then, as she revived and began again to scream, he stabbed her in the mouth to shut her up and kept on stabbing. But as his mind cleared, he realized that he'd trapped himself with a corpse in a bloodstained room in the middle of a crowded building. Grabbing a strong-bladed knife, the killer improvised. First he hacked off the corpse's arms and legs. Then he wrapped them in her clothes and cleaned up the apartment with a mop. Scrounging outside the building, he found a sled, packed it with his grisly burden, and began hauling Tatyana's remains in the direction of the railway tracks. As he staggered along, the sled jammed, and a passerby stopped to lend him a hand. After the man was out of sight, Chikatilo stuffed his bundles into a large pipe near the railway. The girl's remains were found 10 days later.

By now, Gorbachev's policy of *glasnost,* or openness, was in high gear, and Russians had a blaring, sensationalist press that let them know that a dangerous serial killer was in their midst—and had been for a decade. Authorities had noticed that the slow, local trains called *elektrichka*—a favored mode of mass transportation in a car-poor country—figured in a number of the disappearances, which now rated massive press publicity, and decided to blanket the line with force. More than 500 police were posted in stations, as passengers on trains, or in the woods alongside railway tracks, posing as picnickers or mushroom pickers. Police-women decoys traveled on trains; they were given special training in karate. Chikatilo never fell for the bait—perhaps he never even noticed it. But he somehow managed to maintain his anonymity, even though the years he had spent in the vicinity made it highly likely that he would run across people he knew.

At one point he finally did. The bookkeeper from his Novocherkassk factory was amazed one weekend to discover her secretive colleague on a weekend train to the countryside, still wearing a suit and tie. She remembered him as a man obsessed, moving quickly from car to car, his eyes darting to all sides. He was carrying a large black nylon bag. Spotted later by another fellow worker, Chikatilo explained that he still had a cottage in Shakhty that he liked to visit. He ignored questions about the bag.

Chikatilo killed four more people that summer, three of them little boys, and one as far away as the town of Kolchugino, east of Moscow. Psychologists would later explain that sadists of his type frequently switch from female to male victims as their psychosis reaches its final stages. If so, Chikatilo was hitting a psychotic peak: Of his 16 murders from 1988 onward, 11 were boys. And, incredibly, his methods were becoming more cruel—the bodies often showed deep wounds in the abdomen through which the murderer had removed internal organs while the victims still lived.

VIKTOR PETROV

Lured from the Rostov train station by Chikatilo, 13-year-old Viktor Petrov was found murdered in the city's nearby botanical gardens.

The murderer's psychosis also revealed itself in signs of a self-destructive recklessness, as on the day in May 1989 when Chikatilo spotted eight-year-old Sasha Dyakonov walking along a Rostov street. It was the day after Sasha's birthday. Chikatilo had been in town looking for wallpaper. Spotting the small boy by the roadside, he didn't bother to make one of his usual pitches. Instead he walked silently beside him for a time, then suddenly swept him into a stand of bushes. He left the boy's stabbed body only five feet from the road, but it wasn't discovered for 65 days.

On August 28 the killer made another opportunistic move when he struck up a conversation with 10-year-old Aleksei Khobotov outside a Shakhty video store. Western videos were all the rage in the new Soviet Union; Chikatilo lied and said that he had some. He walked the naive boy home through a graveyard. Two years earlier, feeling low, he'd dug himself a grave in a clutch of blackthorn a few yards from the cemetery. When he and the boy reached the site, he hit the youngster with a hammer, sliced open his abdomen, and cut off his genitals. Then he threw the body into the pit and buried it. Aleksei was not found until after his killer's arrest.

Only two weeks into 1990—a year when the killer would take eight lives—Chikatilo slaughtered Andrei Kravchenko, an 11-year-old Shakhty child, after luring him with more talk of movies. Two other boys were murdered near the Rostov botanical gardens. One of the pair, 13-year-old Viktor Petrov, died in late July under especially haunting circumstances. He was traveling with his mother and younger brother Sasha at the Rostov train station when Chikatilo, loitering there as he often did, made a move toward Sasha. Petrov's mother spotted the man and shouted for him to go away. The family had missed its train and slept in the station. At 1:30 a.m., Viktor got thirsty and asked his mother for money for a nearby mineral-water dispenser. He never returned. The hunter had waited for him.

Another 11-year-old, Ivan Fomin, was staying with his grandmother in a house overlooking the city beach at Novocherkassk, when Chikatilo overtook him in August. He killed the boy savagely, as a wolf might, in a stand of reeds almost within view of other bathers.

Bit by bit, Chikatilo's megalomania, perhaps amplified by the great power he wielded over his bleeding victims, manifested itself in more mundane ways. Always a crank letter writer, the clerk had become deeply involved in a feud with Georgian neighbors—Chikatilo called them Assyrians, after their biblical forerunners—near the apartment he was keep-

As a younger son watches, Oleg Fomin *(above)* points to the area where the remains of his 11-year-old son, Ivan, were found among the reeds at the Novocherkassk city beach. A captain of the local prison guards, Fomin organized a massive search the day after his son disappeared. Found two days later, the body was so mutilated that the father, although a hardened prison guard, fainted when he saw it. The family erected a personalized headstone *(left)* for Ivan and made a small shrine for him in their home *(right)*.

ing for his son. The neighbors were building a garage and toilet outside the apartment complex. Chikatilo began firing off letters to local Communist party officials denouncing the project. Then Chikatilo decided to take the matter up with President Gorbachev himself and made a special trip to Moscow to see him. He failed, needless to say, but in the process camped out in Red Square with a variety of other protestors, chiefly refugees from ethnic conflicts. After a few days, he returned home—and resumed killing.

Vadim Gromov, 16, was a mentally handicapped school dropout who spent endless hours riding back and forth around Shakhty on the elektrichka, where he was almost a fixture to local residents. He stood out like a piece of bait to the stalking Chikatilo, who'd developed an expert eye for the types who made the easiest victims. On October 17 Chikatilo struck up a conversation with Gromov and was soon able to lure the simple lad with the promise of drink at a nonexistent cottage. The killer took him into the woods north of Shakhty, to virtually the same spot where he'd murdered Yevgeny Muratov in 1988. Everything was as

before, except perhaps more bloody. Then, straightening his clothes, the killer went back to his train station and rode home. So far as his bosses at work were concerned, he'd been far away, on a job in the city of Kharkov.

Enraged and energized by Gromov's death, the police task force sent about 60 officers to Shakhty. They arrived just in time to hear news of the disappearance of another boy, 16-year-old Viktor Tishchenko, who had gone to the railway station to pick up some tickets a day earlier and never returned. His body turned up on November 3.

For once, there was a witness: The ticket agent reported that a middle-aged man had lurked behind the lad as he purchased his tickets. The agent's daughter added another clue: She'd seen a man on a train recently try to pick up a boy too. He had failed and moved to another compartment.

Chikatilo didn't realize it, but he was stalking inside a trap engineered by Burakov—a tactic that, in typical Russian fashion, traded the possibility of casualties for a chance to envelop and destroy the enemy. With Fetisov's approval, a snare was made using hundreds of law-enforcement per-

176

sonnel along railway lines—except in a narrow area near the tiny country station at Donleskhoz, not far from where Gromov's body was found. Like a predator running before beaters, the murderer, Burakov believed, would now be driven by the police presence to hunt only in that narrow, seemingly unprotected area. When the murderer lured his next victim into the forest, they would have him.

On November 6—the day before the annual celebration of the Bolshevik Revolution—a police sergeant on the Donleskhoz platform spotted a middle-aged man in a gray suit walking out of the woods carrying a bag with a shoulder strap. He had leaves on his clothes, a bandage on his finger, and a red stain on his cheek, as though he'd wiped away some blood. The suspicious cop asked him for identification papers. Andrei Romanovich Chikatilo. He wrote down the name and ID number and at the end of the day filed a report. But it was holiday time: The report sat on a desk in the nearby town of Krasny Sulin for almost a week.

On November 12, their holiday over, police investigators returned to Donleskhoz to go back over the Gromov mur-

der site. One detective poking around in the bushes suddenly saw a piece of blue nylon hanging from a branch. It looked like the pocket from a coat. Because the area had already been picked clean by police, the scrap could mean only one thing: The killer was back in the forest zone.

The next day, 40 police and 20 dogs formed a line at the railway track and began pushing into the woods. About 50 yards from their starting point, they found the body of a young blonde woman under a pile of leaves, horribly mutilated. A month later, she would have been buried until spring. Svetlana Korostik, 22, had been stabbed in the stomach and her genitals amputated. The tip of her tongue and her nipples had been cut off. The lesopolosa murderer had struck again—inside the police snare.

By chance, Fetisov was in the area when the woman's body was found. After visiting the murder site, he hurried to the Krasny Sulin police station, which had been responsible for the Donleskhoz surveillance. Breathing fire, he demanded an explanation. Two of the three officers on duty, it transpired, had wandered off to find something to eat.

Enraged, Fetisov asked to see the reports that should have gone to Burakov but had languished through the holiday. As he shuffled through the papers, he came upon a name he half-remembered. He phoned Burakov in Rostov to tell him. The detective, sensing that the hunt might finally be over, went back to his card index and took another look at number nine: Andrei Chikatilo.

Suddenly a lot of seemingly unconnected images formed a legible picture: Chikatilo's 1984 arrest; the knife and rope found on him at that time. His employment records began turning up other coincidences, such as the fact that he'd been in the Ukrainian town of Ilovaisk on May 14, 1988, when young Lyosha Voronko was murdered. Further digging turned up the long-buried facts about his sexual behavior as a schoolteacher and his brush with suspicious authorities after the 1978 murder of Yelena Zakotnova. As they ferreted out Chikatilo's dark secrets, the police kept him under continuous surveillance.

As police watched Chikatilo hunting through the crowds of Novocherkassk, however, they began to worry that he would detect them and escape their net. Worse, the police feared that they might fail to catch him in the act, allowing him yet another victim. Rather than take that risk, on November 19 they decided to arrest him.

The next afternoon, three detectives stepped out of an unmarked car in Novocherkassk and walked up to Chikatilo outside a café. As another officer videotaped the bust, they handcuffed their quarry and pushed him into an unmarked car. Chikatilo did not resist arrest, perhaps because he knew he was finished. They drove him back to the central police station in Rostov, where mug shots and blood samples were taken. Then they searched the bag he'd been carrying. Inside were two lengths of rope, a nine-inch kitchen knife, and a pocket mirror. Pressed about his movements on November 6, Chikatilo denied traveling anywhere. No one believed him.

As for the seemingly intractable problem of blood type, the police got another break: Forensic experts from Moscow believed Chikatilo exhibited paradoxical secretion, in which blood and body fluids show different groupings. Although not widely accepted, their testimony was enough to remove the last remaining element of doubt about him.

The killer was now beyond the point of no return. He'd become one of the players in Russia's age-old theater of interrogation, in which prosecutor and criminal have tested each other since czarist times. The task of acting out the drama with the lesopolosa killer fell to Isa Kostoyev, whose law-school thesis, authored almost 30 years earlier, had been on the tactics of interrogation. In the ensuing interactions between the two men, Kostoyev gently led Chikatilo to the idea that the state had an airtight case against him, and that a man who'd done what he had must surely be insane. In Russia, as in most countries, legal insanity meant that one could neither control nor understand the consequences of one's actions. A confession would spare Chikatilo a bullet in the brain and put him in a hospital where people would listen and help. A week of such persuasion produced nothing.

But soon Chikatilo began to make oblique admissions—of his weakness for "perverted sexual displays"; of his impotence; of his fascination and hatred for the human flotsam he saw in rail and bus stations and on trains. "I used to watch them as they walked away to secluded places," he said. Then he admitted in detail his sexual advances toward students when he was a teacher. Finally, in an elliptical statement, he talked about the "dangerous and serious nature" of the offenses that had led to his arrest. "I am ready to give evidence of the crimes that I committed, but please do not torment me with the details, because my psyche could not cope with this," he said. "Everything which I have done makes me tremble." He was no longer claiming blanket innocence; but he hadn't confessed to murder.

The police put on a new kind of pressure. Chief investigator Kostoyev called in the prescient Rostov psychiatrist, Aleksandr Bukhanovsky, who had drawn up such an accurate profile of the killer years before. Bukhanovsky agreed to help as long as he was not obliged to get a confession,

keep his own notes, or provide any confession made to him as evidence. In return, he was willing to encourage Chikatilo to cooperate. Within hours after the two men met, the accused murderer was pouring out tales of bitterness and persecution. Toward the end of the day, he admitted for the first time that he'd committed murder. Evidently, the killer cracked after listening to Bukhanovsky read his insightful profile of the man he had called X. *(See box, page 181.)*

The next day Chikatilo was charged with 36 murders and, over the following week, admitted to 34 of them. But to the consternation of his captors, he didn't stop there. His confessions continued. He admitted killing Yelena Zakotnova in 1978, then added another 19 killings to the list. In some cases, police had never found a body. One was that of Aleksei Khobotov, the 10-year-old Chikatilo had buried in his own grave. The killer led authorities to the spot. After that, he took investigators on a series of gruesome scavenger hunts to various murder sites.

Still, Chikatilo could not yet use the words "murder" or "killing"; instead he said that he did "this" or "that." Over time, he also began to admit such practices as chewing on sexual organs that he'd removed. Throughout, Chikatilo continued to insist that he'd never set out with the deliberate

After emerging from the woods near this desolate train platform at Donleskhoz, Chikatilo was questioned about a red smear on his face—an exchange that later led to his arrest on November 20, 1990, when the killer finally stood for police cameras *(right).*

intention of murdering anyone, but to have sex. It was only when his chronic dysfunction brought mockery or scorn that he'd gone into a frenzy. In other words, the deaths had really been the victims' fault.

No one believed that Chikatilo had not hunted in order to kill. The encounters between Chikatilo and his victims may have been opportunistic and accidental, but so were those of wolves and sheep. His every other preparation reeked of care, caution, and planning. He was a sadistic professional, adroit enough to keep his wife in the dark about his entire career as a murderer. In fact, when Feodosia first heard the reason for her husband's arrest, she refused to believe it. "He is not capable of killing a man," she remarked. "He isn't capable of killing a chicken." Only after Chikatilo led the police to Aleksei Khobotov's grave did she accept the truth—and look with horror on the sharp-bladed knives that her husband had scattered casually among their household cutlery.

Feodosia met Chikatilo only once again, to get his signature authorizing her use of their family savings account. "If only I had listened to you, Fenyuchka," he muttered. "If only I had followed your advice and got treatment." Before his trial started she moved away from Novocherkassk with the help of authorities, under a new name.

Building the case against Chikatilo took 16 months, much of it taken up with psychological tests at the Serbsky Institute in Moscow, where he was found sane enough to try for his crimes. His trial began April 14, 1992. His first appearance in court provoked pandemonium as the relatives of victims screamed and tried to push their way past guards to his protecting cage. It took 10 minutes before Judge Akubzhanov was able to make himself heard.

As the trial began, Chikatilo made it clear that he did not intend to make the process easy. On the first day of the trial, he pulled a pornographic magazine from his pocket and waved it briefly. Then he took to interrupting the proceedings with interjections and shouts until his removal from the courtroom became almost a daily ritual. He called for a new defense attorney and began claiming that he was a political prisoner. He abruptly recanted his earlier confession of the Zakotnova murder, then denied five more killings, including those of Larisa Tkachenko and Olga Stalmachenok. In June he suddenly stripped in court. When he was returned to his cage after several days he was handcuffed—but still managed to get his pants off near the end of the trial. On

the final day, he sang the Communist *Internationale.* Such antics aside, Chikatilo spent much of his trial sitting in his cage in a daze of abstraction, now and then stretching his face in a canine yawn.

But as the judge prepared to withdraw from the courtroom for the final time to consider his verdict, reality brushed up against Chikatilo in a form that he appeared to understand. A man rose from the public gallery, put his hand in his pocket, and pulled out a small chunk of metal. With all his might he threw the largely symbolic missile at Chikatilo's head but missed, hitting the prisoner in the chest. The courtroom guard rushed toward the assailant but stopped when the rest of the crowd quickly formed a protective ring around him. The man was Volodya Alekseyev, whose sister Larisa had suffered special horrors in 1984. The commander of the guard detachment took a level look at the pale, trembling man and his grim fellows, and decided that the incident had never happened.

On October 15, 1992, Andrei Chikatilo was sentenced to death. Unless the Russian appeal process offers a reprieve, Chikatilo will be taken from his prison cell and walked along the gray stone corridors to a room all prisoners know, where he will be made to kneel while he hears his sentence read. The executioner will draw his Makarov automatic and fire a single, nine-gram bullet into the back of Chikatilo's head. A quick and merciful end for the forest zone killer, perhaps—but, finally, an end. ◆

Portrait of X

At first, Andrei Chikatilo *(below, left)* faced his interrogation by Moscow chief investigator Isa Kostoyev *(below, right)* almost calmly. For 8 of the 10 days allowed for questioning by Soviet law, Kostoyev battered the killer's defenses, to little effect.

Seated in the bare room beneath a stern portrait of KGB founder Feliks Dzerzhinsky, Chikatilo would not confess his crimes. Although the sadistic murderer of more than 50 girls, boys, and women would speak indirectly of his early molestations, he remained quiet about the killing. According to some observers, he broke his silence only on the ninth day, November 29, when he was visited by Rostov psychiatrist Aleksandr Bukhanovsky and heard himself described by an informed stranger.

At the behest of Viktor Burakov, one of the principal investigators on the case, Bukhanovsky had prepared two profiles of the leso-polosa killer, one in September 1984 and the other in July 1987. Although they are imperfect, in retrospect the descriptions have the ring of prophecy.

Writing in 1984, Bukhanovsky inferred that the killer was sexually crippled and unable to have a normal relationship with a woman. His world would be friendless, internal, and sealed off even from those closest to him. But he was not a stupid man—indeed, the killer possessed enough intelligence to plan his murders and elude capture.

In his second profile, where he referred to the killer as X, Bukhanovsky described the murders as a twisted analog of sex. X, he wrote, had likely been isolated from childhood, and had spent a painful adolescence marked by constant humiliations and jeering peers. The subject's largely internalized existence would have coalesced entirely around his autoerotic fantasies. He would not be much for drink or drugs, and he very likely possessed a puritanical streak.

On the other hand, Bukhanovsky believed, X might have fathered a family—in fact, a dominating wife could be a factor in the equation. X would relish the power of being a teacher, a supply clerk, or a secret policeman, or he would welcome the isolation of an academic life. He would be a bit above average height, rather strong, and in his late forties or early fifties. And while he experienced sex urges powerful enough to make him kill, he was abysmally impotent and utterly self-absorbed.

To Andrei Chikatilo, this portrait of himself by a man he'd never known must have been devastating. But it must also have suggested to the killer that in Bukhanovsky, at last, there was someone who understood him—someone he could talk to about those "things" he'd done.

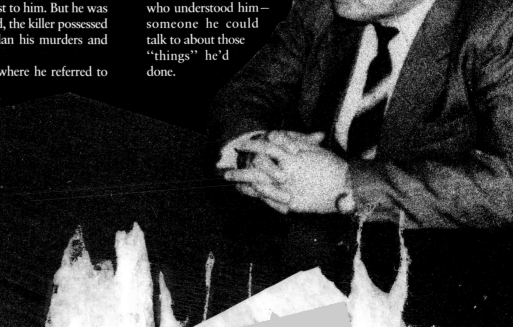

Andrei Chikatilo raises his
weak eyes to the light on
October 15, 1992, the day
he learned he had to die
for his terrible crimes.

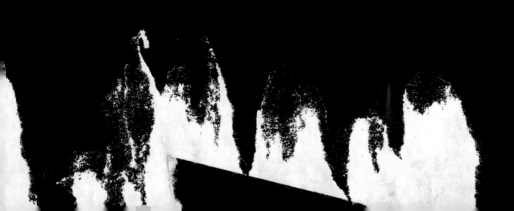

Acknowledgments

The editors thank the following for their valuable assistance:

Michael Aluffi, Watsonville Police Dept., Watsonville, Calif.; Hugh Aynesworth, Dallas, Tex.; John Backderf, Cleveland, Ohio; Dr. Judith Becker, Tucson, Ariz.; Prof. Frederick Berlin, Johns Hopkins Medical School, Baltimore, Md.; Yuri Bespalov, Rostov-on-Don, Russia; Justice Roger Boren, Los Angeles, Calif.; Sheriff Jim Boutwell, Williamson County Sheriff's Office, Georgetown, Tex.; Gerald Boyle, Esq., Milwaukee, Wis.; Dean Brett, Esq., Bellingham, Wash.; Dr. Aleksandr Bukhanovsky, Rostov-on-Don, Russia; Viktor Burakov, Rostov-on-Don, Russia; Billy Capshaw, Hot Springs, Ark.; Peter Chang, Santa Cruz, Calif.; Margaret Cheney, Hollister, Calif.; Jim Conner, Santa Cruz Police Dept., Santa Cruz, Calif.; Gary Craig, *Democrat and Chronicle,* Rochester, N.Y.; Andrew Crain, Santa Cruz Police Dept., Santa Cruz, Calif.; Robert Cullen, Chevy Chase, Md.; Arthur Danner III, District Attorney, Santa Cruz, Calif.; Paul Decker, Assistant Superintendent, Florida State Prison, Starke, Fla.; Kurt Ellison, *Watsonville Register-Pajaronian,* Watsonville, Calif.; Dave Ernst, New York State Parole Board, Albany, N.Y.; Gail M. Ewing, Assistant Library Director, *Palm Beach Post,* West Palm Beach, Fla.; Vic Feazell, Austin, Tex.; Peter Ford, Library Manager, *Democrat and Chronicle,* Rochester, N.Y.; Irene Garcia, *Madera Tribune,* Madera, Calif.; James A. Jackson, Santa Cruz, Calif.; James Kearney, Section Chief of Scientific Analysis Section, Federal Bureau of Investigation, Washington, D.C.; Bob Knudsen, Acme, Wash.; Prof. Mike Kukral, Athens, Ohio; Richard Lourie, Newtonville, Mass.; Michael McCann, District Attorney, Milwaukee, Wis.; Gregg O. McCreary, Supervisory Special Agent, Federal Bureau of Investigation, Quantico, Va.; Rick McIlwain, Florida State Attorney's Office, Fort Pierce, Fla.; David Martinez, Police Dept., Pueblo, Colo.; Mike Masters, Long Island, N.Y.; Terry Medina, Chief, Watsonville Police Dept., Watsonville, Calif.; Jim Mitchell, Reno, Nev.; Capt. Swen Nielson, Police Dept., Provo, Utah; Fred Nolte, Bellingham, Wash.; Ed Richards, Williamson County Sheriff's Office, Georgetown, Tex.; David Rodriguez, Northampton, Mass.; Frank Salerno, Burbank, Calif.; Georgia Scharenberg, Bath, Ohio; Charles Scherer, Santa Cruz, Calif.; Susan Scherer, Corralitos, Calif.; Anne Schwartz, Milwaukee, Wis.; Joseph Scislowicz, Information Officer, Wisconsin Dept. of Corrections, Portage, Wis.; Brad Shellady, Rock Island, Ill.; Charles Siragusa, Rochester, N.Y.; J. Leslie Sopko, *Democrat and Chronicle,* Rochester, N.Y.; Robert E. Stone, Port St. Lucie, Fla.; Dr. Andrei Tkachenko, Serbsky Institute, Rostov-on-Don, Russia; Glenn Toriumi, University of California at Santa Cruz Police, Santa Cruz, Calif.; Rita Valdivia, *Madera Tribune,* Madera, Calif.; Richard F. Verbrugge, San Jose, Calif.; Russ Vorpagel, Sacramento, Calif.; Terry Wright, Bellingham, Wash.

Bibliography

Books:

Baumann, Ed, *Step into My Parlor.* Chicago: Bonus Books, 1991.

Belli, Melvin, and Danny R. Jones, *Belli Looks at Life and Law in Russia.* Indianapolis: Bobbs-Merrill, 1963.

Biondi, Ray, and Walt Hecox, *The Dracula Killer.* New York: Pocket Books, 1992.

Burn, Gordon, *Somebody's Husband, Somebody's Son: The Story of the Yorkshire Ripper.* New York: Viking, 1984.

Cheney, Margaret, *Why—The Serial Killer in America.* Saratoga, Calif.: R&E, 1992.

Conquest, Robert, *The Harvest of Sorrow.* New York: Oxford University Press, 1986.

Conquest, Robert, ed., *Agricultural Workers in the U.S.S.R.* New York: Frederick A. Praeger, 1969.

Conradi, Peter, *The Red Ripper.* New York: Dell, 1992.

Cullen, Robert, *The Killer Department.* New York: Pantheon, 1993.

Dallin, Alexander, *German Rule in Russia: 1941-1945.* Boulder, Colo.: Westview Press, 1981.

Damio, Ward, *Urge to Kill.* New York: Pinnacle Books, 1974.

Dolot, Miron, *Execution by Hunger.* New York: W. W. Norton, 1985.

Eddowes, Michael, *The Man on Your Conscience: An Investigation of the Evans Murder Trial.* London: Cassell, 1955.

Egger, Steven A., *Serial Murder: An Elusive Phenomenon.* New York: Frederick A. Praeger, 1990.

Farrell, Barry, *The Journalism of Barry Farrell.* Ed. by Steve Hawk. Berkeley, Calif.: Creative Arts Book Co., 1989.

Jaeger, Richard W., and M. William Balousek, *Massacre in Milwaukee.* Oregon, Wis.: Waubesa Press, 1991.

Kennedy, Ludovic, *Ten Rillington Place.* New York: Simon and Shuster, 1961.

Levin, Jack, and James Allen Fox, *Mass Murder: America's Growing Menace.* New York: Plenum Press, 1985.

Leyton, Elliott, *Hunting Humans.* New York: Pocket Books, 1986.

Louis, Victor, and Jennifer Louis, *The Complete Guide to the Soviet Union.* New York: St. Martin's Press, 1991.

Lourie, Richard, *Hunting the Devil.* New York: HarperCollins, 1993.

Lunde, Donald T., *Murder and Madness.* San Francisco: San Francisco Book Co., 1976.

Lunde, Donald T., and Jefferson Morgan, *The Die Song: A Journey into the Mind of a Mass Murderer.* New York: W. W. Norton, 1980.

Nicholson, Michael, *The Yorkshire Ripper.* London: W. H. Allen, 1979.

Noble, John, and John King, *U.S.S.R.: A Travel Survival Kit.* Hawthorn, Australia: Lonely Planet, 1991.

O'Brien, Darcy, *Two of a Kind: The Hillside Stranglers.* New York: New American Library, 1985.

Phillips, Conrad, *Murderer's Moon.* London: Arthur Barker, 1956.

Randall, Francis B., *Stalin's Russia.* New York: Free Press, 1965.

Ressler, Robert K., Ann W. Burgess, and John E. Douglas, *Sexual Homicide.* Lexington, Mass.: Lexington Books, 1988.

Ressler, Robert K., and Tom Shachtman, *Whoever Fights Monsters.* New

York: St. Martin's Press, 1992.

Schwartz, Anne E., *The Man Who Could Not Kill Enough.* New York: Carol, 1992.

Schwarz, Ted, *The Hillside Strangler.* Garden City, N.Y.: Doubleday, 1981.

Smith, Hedrick, *The New Russians.* New York: Random House, 1990.

Tolstoy, Nikolai, *Stalin's Secret War.* New York: Holt, Rinehart and Winston, 1981.

West, Don, *Sacrifice unto Me: The 21 Santa Cruz Murders.* New York: Pyramid Books, 1974.

Wilson, Colin, *Written in Blood.* New York: Warner Books, 1989.

Wolf, Marvin J., and Katherine Mader, *Fallen Angels.* New York: Facts on File, 1986.

Yallop, David A., *Deliver Us from Evil.* London: Macdonald Futura, 1981.

Periodicals:

Alford, Jeffrey, "Missing Iowa Girls Linked to South Florida Killings." *Palm Beach Post,* May 16, 1973.

Allen, Teresa, "A Nightmare Unravels." *Bellingham Herald,* Dec. 30, 1979.

Allison, Ralph B., "Difficulties Diagnosing the Multiple Personality Syndrome in a Death Penalty Case." *International Journal of Clinical and Experimental Hypnosis,* Apr. 1984.

Apple, R. W., Jr., "Truck Driver in Britain Confesses at His Trial to Killing 13 Women." *New York Times,* Apr. 30, 1981.

"Articles Found in Schaefer Home Detail Disappearances of 2 Women." *Palm Beach Post,* May 15, 1973.

Aynesworth, Hugh:
"Caught Up in a Web." *Dallas Times Herald,* Apr. 14, 1985.
"Lifesaving Confession." *Dallas Times Herald,* Apr. 15, 1985.
"Lucas Gets Death on His Word Only." *Dallas Times Herald,* Apr. 15, 1985.

Aynesworth, Hugh, and Jim Henderson, "Henry Lee Lucas: Mass Murderer or Massive Hoax?" *Dallas Times Herald,* Apr. 14, 1985.

Barron, James, "Milwaukee Police Once Queried Suspect." *New York Times,* July 27, 1991.

Barron, James, and Mary B. W. Tabor, "17 Killed, and a Life Is Searched for Clues." *New York Times,* Aug. 4, 1991.

Bastable, Jonathan, "Smiling Rostov Ripper Chills Blood of Those Left to Mourn." *Sunday Times,* Apr. 19, 1992.

Battin, Richard, "Mass Murder Suspect Fantasized Killings as a Child." *Mercury-News,* Nov. 4, 1973.

"Bianchi Given Six Life Sentences." *Bellingham Herald,* Oct. 22, 1979.

Blake, Gene:
" 'I Stand Mute,' Buono Says in Penalty Phase." *Los Angeles Times,* Nov. 17, 1984.
"Jury Gives Buono Life Sentence for 9 Murders." *Los Angeles Times,* Nov. 19, 1983.

"Bluebeard on the Beach." *Time,* May 28, 1973.

Borders, William, "Yorkshire Ripper Claims Student in North England as 13th Victim." *New York Times,* Nov. 20, 1980.

"Bound Girls' Escape Sets Off Strange Chain of Events." *Palm Beach Post,* May 13, 1973.

Briggs, Peter B., "Place, Jessup Girls Found Death at the Beach." *Palm Beach Post,* May 13, 1973.

"Briton Ordered to Trial in the 13 'Ripper' Deaths." *New York Times,* Feb. 21, 1981.

Carpenter, Aurea, "Serial Crime and Punishment." *Times Saturday Review,* May 9, 1992.

Carroll, Rick, "DA's Grim Vow at Kemper Trial." *San Francisco Chronicle,* Oct. 24, 1973.

Clark, William:
"Christie Is Absolved of Crime He Admitted." *New York Times,* July 15, 1953.
" 'Pretty Lucky' to Escape." *Palm Beach Post,* May 14, 1973.

Coleman, Daniel, "Clues to a Dark Nurturing Ground for One Serial Killer." *New York Times,* Aug. 7, 1991.

"Crazed Ripper Pleads Guilty." *New York Post,* Apr. 29, 1981.

Dalrymple, James:
"Book Stirs Hate Feud for Wife of Ripper." *Sunday Times* (London), June 2, 1991.
"Ripping Yarns." *Sunday Times* (London), Dec. 23, 1990.
"Death Try by Kemper Fails Again." *San Jose Mercury,* Oct. 29, 1973.

Donovan, Dick:
"Gerard Schaefer: Murder Suspect Is Portrayed by Classmates as a Loner They Didn't Care to Know." *Palm Beach Post,* May 20, 1973.
"Gerard Schaefer, to Parents and to Wife, a Loving, Gentle Person." *Palm Beach Post,* May 13, 1973.

Ellison, Jayne:
"Photos Seized at Schaefer's Mother's Home." *Palm Beach Post,* May 15, 1973.
"Schaefer Found Guilty of Murder." *Palm Beach Post,* Sept. 28, 1973.
"6 Dead; 28 May Be: A Trail of Butchered Girls." *Palm Beach Post,* May 13, 1973.
"Strange Arsenal Found in Probe of Deaths." *Palm Beach Post,* May 14, 1973.

Farr, Bill, "Memos Cite Holes in Strangler Case." *Los Angeles Times,* July 26, 1981.

Fein, Esther B., "True Crime, and Publishers, in Russia." *New York Times,* Aug. 17, 1992.

"15 Life Terms and No Parole for Dahmer." *New York Times,* Feb. 18, 1992.

"Fire Delays Kemper Trial; Suicide Try." *San Jose Mercury,* Nov. 6, 1973.

Foderaro, Lisa, "A Serial-Murder Trial, on TV, Grips Rochester." *New York Times,* Dec. 1, 1990.

"God Told Me to Kill: Ripper." *Daily News,* May 12, 1981.

Goldberg, Carey, " 'I Was like a Crazed Wolf.' " *Los Angeles Times,* Apr. 18, 1992.

Gorney, Cynthia, and Paul Taylor, "The Lucas Puzzle." *Washington Post,* Apr. 15, 1985.

Gortmaker, Linda, and Hilary Hylton, "Newspapers Taken in Search." *Palm Beach Post,* May 15, 1973.

"Grandson 'Upset'—Kills Two." *San Francisco Examiner,* Aug. 29, 1964.

"Grisly Fremont Find: 2 Headless Corpses." *San Jose Mercury,* Feb. 16, 1973.

"Guilty Plea by Dahmer and a 16th Life Sentence." *New York Times,* May 2, 1992.

" 'Hang Him!' " *Time,* Jan. 19, 1981.

Hanley, Robert:

"Parole Board under Scrutiny in Murder Suspect's Release." *New York Times,* Jan. 13, 1990.

"Paroled Killer Accused in Deaths of 11 Women in Rochester Area." *New York Times,* Jan. 6, 1990.

"Rochester Slaying Suspect Is Called Kind but Violent." *New York Times,* Jan. 13, 1990.

Hauptfuhrer, Fred, "Olivia Reivers Has Reason to Wonder: Was She the Yorkshire Ripper's Last Date?" *People,* Jan. 26, 1981.

Hazlett, Bill:
"Abuse by Buono, Bianchi Claimed." *Los Angeles Times,* Mar. 10, 1982.
"Bianchi Had Celebrity List, Court Told." *Los Angeles Times,* Apr. 9, 1982.
"Buono Admitted Killings, Jury Told." *Los Angeles Times,* Mar. 3, 1982.
"Ex-Wife Tells of Threat by Buono." *Los Angeles Times,* Apr. 6, 1982.
"Witness to Testify that Buono Played Role in 'Talent Scout Scheme.'" *Los Angeles Times,* Mar. 8, 1982.

Henderson, Jim:
"California Confessions Accepted Despite Holes." *Dallas Times Herald,* Apr. 15, 1985.
"DPS Chief Says Some of Lucas' Admissions False." *Dallas Times Herald,* Apr. 17, 1985.
"Lubbock Murder Not Resolved in Many Minds." *Dallas Times Herald,* Apr. 14, 1985.
"Memory or Fantasy?" *Dallas Times Herald,* Apr. 15, 1985.

"Henry Lee Lucas Confesses, so a Murder Verdict Is Voided." *New York Times,* Sept. 2, 1984.

"The Hillside Stranglers." *Murder Casebook,* Vol. 2, Part 18, 1990.

Hinkle, Tom, "Former Sheriff Hired and Fired Murder Suspect Schaefer." *Palm Beach Post,* May 20, 1973.

Honig, Tom, "Kemper's Kill Method Revealed at Trial." *Santa Cruz Sentinel,* Oct. 26, 1973.

"'How Say You?'" *Time,* May 11, 1981.

Hudson, Elizabeth, "Victim of Own Hoax, Willing Confessor Awaits Death." *Washington Post,* Dec. 2, 1990.

Hylton, Hilary, and Linda Gortmaker,

"3 Missing Fort Lauderdale Women's Cases Probed." *Palm Beach Post,* May 13, 1973.

"Insanity Defence in Christie Case." *Manchester Guardian* (England), June 23, 1953.

Kaiser, Robert G., "Britons Again Weigh Murder Case of 1950s." *Washington Post,* Oct. 13, 1966.

"Kemper's Fantasies of Killing." *San Francisco Chronicle,* Nov. 1, 1973.

"Killer in Texas Sentenced to Die." *New York Times,* Apr. 14, 1984.

"Killer of Woman, 80, Is Given 75 Years after Plea of Guilty." *New York Times,* Oct. 2, 1983.

Lacayo, Richard, "Master of Cant and Recant." *Time,* Jan. 12, 1987.

Lewis, Anthony, "Britain Pardons a Man Hanged in 1950 for Murder of Daughter." *New York Times,* Oct. 19, 1966.

Loudon, Bennett J., "2nd Trial in Wayne Still On." *Democrat and Chronicle,* Dec. 14, 1990.

"Lucas Sentenced to Die." *New York Times,* June 4, 1984.

"Macabre Discovery on Cliff." *San Jose Mercury,* Jan. 11, 1973.

McKnight, Keith, "The Dahmer Chronicles." *Akron Beacon Journal,* Aug. 11, 1991.

"Man Said to Have Killed 150 Stands Trial in Texas Death." *New York Times,* Mar. 12, 1984.

"A Mass Murderer Reconsidered." *Time,* Apr. 29, 1985.

Masters, Brian, "Dahmer's Inferno." *Vanity Fair,* Nov. 1991.

"Mattox Says Lucas Crimes Overstated." *Dallas Times Herald,* Apr. 16, 1985.

Miller, Ron, "4 Coeds Who Thumbed Way to Grisly Deaths." *San Jose Mercury,* Feb. 24, 1973.

"Milwaukee Officers Dismissed." *New York Times,* Sept. 9, 1991.

"Monster of the Rivers." *Murder Casebook* (London), Vol. 6, Part 82, 1991.

Morales, Hector:
"Schaefer-Linked Writings Detail Execution Methods." *Palm Beach Post,* May 18, 1973.
"Stone: Single Suspect in Death of 2 Girls." *Palm Beach Post,* May 15, 1973.

Murray, James, "Twisted Fan Club Who Believe the Ripper Is Innocent." *Today,* May 18, 1992.

"Officers Tell Jury of Letting Dahmer Keep Boy." *New York Times,* Feb. 13, 1992.

Orne, Martin T., David F. Dinges, and Emily Carota Orne, "On the Differential Diagnosis of Multiple Personality in the Forensic Context." *International Journal of Clinical and Experimental Hypnosis,* Apr. 1984.

"Paroled Killer Indicted in Deaths of 10 Women." *New York Times,* Jan. 24, 1990.

Partlow, Bob:
"Bianchi Pleads Guilty." *Bellingham Herald,* Oct. 19, 1979.
"Bianchi's Childhood a Tale of Tragedy." *Bellingham Herald,* Oct. 24, 1979.
"Emotional Ordeal Finally Over." *Bellingham Herald,* Oct. 20, 1979.
"Murder Story Draws National Attention." *Bellingham Herald,* Jan 21, 1979.

Partlow, Bob, Sue Smith, and Eric Brazil:
"From LA to Bellingham: A Study in Murder." *Bellingham Herald,* Jan. 13, 1980.
"Women Trapped: Murder Pattern Developed." *Gannett News Service,* Jan. 16, 1980.

Prichard, Peter, "The Double-Initial Murders." *Democrat and Chronicle,* Sept. 22, 1976.

Purnell, John M., "Briscolina, Farmer: Death Cut Short Travel Dreams." *Palm Beach Post,* May 13, 1973.

Rais, Guy, "'Seriously-Ill' Ripper Moved to Broadmoor." *Daily Telegraph* (London), Mar. 28, 1984.

Rakhayeva, Yulia, "The Rostov Killer Awaiting a Verdict." *New Times,* Sept. 1992.

Randolph, Eleanor, "Russian Convicted of Murdering 52." *Washington Post,* Oct. 15, 1992.

Rattner, Steven, "Briton Is Given 13 Life Sentences for the 'Yorkshire Ripper' Murders." *New York Times,* May 23, 1981.

Reynolds, Ruth, "The Strangler of Notting Hill." *Sunday News* (London), Aug. 9, 1953.

"The Rillington Place Murders." *Mur-*

der Casebook* (London), Vol. 1, Part 4, 1990.

" 'Ripper' Confession Read: Killing Was an Addiction." *Daily News,* May 7, 1981.

"Rochester Jury Convicts Parolee in Serial Killings." *New York Times,* Dec. 14, 1990.

Rohrlich, Ted, "She and Bianchi Conspired to Frame Buono, Girlfriend Claims." *Los Angeles Times,* June 22, 1983.

Rosenbaum, Ron, "Dead Reckoning." *Vanity Fair,* Sept. 1990.

Schmemann, Serge:
" 'Citizen Ch.': Russia Opens Files on Serial Killings." *New York Times,* Apr. 4, 1992.
"The Man in the Iron Cage: A Russian Horror Story." *New York Times,* July 30, 1992.

"A Serial Killer Gets a Sentence of 250 Years." *New York Times,* Feb. 2, 1991.

Smith, Sue:
"Bianchi's 'Personalities' Taped Their Stories." *Rochester Times-Union,* Oct. 25, 1979.
"The Kenny Bianchi They Knew." *Rochester Times-Union,* Jan. 29, 1979.

Smith, Sue, Bob Partlow, and Eric Brazil, "Bianchi Was Diagnosed as a 'Deeply Hostile Boy.' " Gannett News Service, Jan. 14, 1980.

Smith, Sue, Eric Brazil, and Bob Partlow, "Bianchi Came to California in Search of a Dream." Gannett News Service, Jan. 15, 1980.

Sopko, J. Leslie:
"Murder x 10." *Democrat and Chronicle,* Dec. 14, 1990.
"Psychiatrists May Be the Key Factor in Shawcross Verdict." Gannett News Service, Sept. 17, 1990.
"Shawcross Says Cops Ask Him to Help Solve Deaths." *Democrat and Chronicle,* Aug. 2, 1992.

Stumbo, Bella, "The Final Act: Years in the Making." *Los Angeles Times,* Nov. 15, 1983.

Sunde, Scott, "Dallas Police Doubt Lucas, but Suburbs Listening." *Dallas Times Herald,* Apr. 16, 1985.

"Suspect in 165 Killings Convicted in 2nd Murder." *New York Times,* Nov. 10, 1983.

"Suspect in Slayings Indicted in 9th Case." *New York Times,* Jan. 12, 1990.

"Suspect in 10 Sexual Murders Is Portrayed as Unremorseful." *New York Times,* Sept. 22, 1990.

"Texas Jury Sentences Drifter to Life for Slaying Girlfriend." *New York Times,* Nov. 11, 1983.

"Texas Murder Count Dropped." *New York Times,* Dec. 31, 1986.

"The 13th Victim." *Time,* Dec. 1, 1980.

Toufexis, Anastasia, "Do Mad Acts a Madman Make?" *Time,* Feb. 3, 1992.

Treen, Joe, and Constance Richards, "A Monster Caged at Last." *People,* Oct. 19, 1992.

"Twice Commended for His Police Work." *Daily Telegraph & Morning Post* (London), June 26, 1953.

"Visions of Murder." *Murder Casebook* (London), Vol. 8, Part 116, 1992.

Walsh, Edward:
"Ghoulish Details Dominate as Dahmer Trial Begins." *Washington Post,* Jan. 31, 1992.
"Killings Open Old Wounds." *Washington Post,* Aug. 1, 1991.
"Man Describes Hours-Long Ordeal before Police Apprehended Dahmer." *Washington Post,* Feb. 1, 1992.
"Mass Killer Said to Plan 'Temple' Made of Victims." *Washington Post,* Feb. 5, 1992.

Warren, Marcus, "None Suspected Kindly Russian Was Killer of 55." *London Daily Telegraph,* Apr. 20, 1992.

Watkins, John G., "The Bianchi Case: Sociopath or Multiple Personality?" *International Journal of Clinical and Experimental Hypnosis,* Apr. 1984.

West, Don:
"Judge Puts Kemper in 'for life.' " *San Francisco Examiner,* Nov. 9, 1973.
"Kemper Tells Why He Stopped Killing." *San Francisco Examiner,* Oct. 26, 1973.
"Psychiatrist: Kemper Sane." *San Francisco Examiner,* Oct. 27, 1973.
"Why Boy Went on Rampage." *San Francisco Chronicle,* Aug. 29, 1964.

Wilson, Don, "Distraught Kemper Halts Trial." *San Jose Mercury,* Nov. 1, 1973.

Womack, Helen, "Russians Hear Grim Truth of 55 Serial Killings." *The Independent* (London), Apr. 16, 1992.

"Woman Is Charged with Trying to Copy the 'Hillside Strangler.' " *New York Times,* Oct. 4, 1980.

"The Wrong Man." *Time,* Oct. 28, 1966.

"The Yorkshire Ripper." *Murder Casebook* (London), Vol. 1, Part 1, 1989.

"Yorkshire Ripper Gets Life." *Daily News,* May 23, 1981.

Zeigler, Michael, "After 18 Years, Victim's Mother Receives Justice." *Democrat and Chronicle,* Dec. 14, 1990.

Other Sources:

Affidavit of Bellingham Police Captain Duane Schenck, Whatcom County Superior Court, State of Washington vs. Kenneth A. Bianchi, Sept. 18, 1979.

Allison, Ralph B., M.D., Psychiatric Report to Judge Jack S. Kurtz, State vs. Kenneth A. Bianchi, Whatcom County Superior Court, Bellingham, Wash.

Bianchi, Kenneth A., Chronological Medical History and Reports of Six Court Appointed Experts on the Issues of Competency to Stand Trial and Sanity; State vs. Kenneth A. Bianchi, Whatcom County Superior Court, Bellingham, Wash.

Bianchi, Kenneth A., letters, résumé, papers, etc., Exhibits from People vs. Angelo Buono, Los Angeles Superior Court.

Criminal Complaint #F-912542, State of Wisconsin vs. Jeffrey L. Dahmer, filed Aug. 22, 1991, and Sept. 11, 1991.

Dahmer, Jeffrey L., Confession, Bath Police Dept., Bath, Ohio.

Dahmer, Jeffrey L., Psychiatric Report by Dr. Park E. Dietz, University Hospital of Cleveland, Cleveland, Ohio.

Faerstein, Saul J., M.D., Psychiatric Report to Judge Jack S. Kurtz, State vs. Kenneth A. Bianchi, Whatcom County Superior Court, Bellingham, Wash.

Kemper, Edmund Emil, III, Interview in Pueblo, Colo., by Santa Cruz, Calif., Sheriff's Dept. Investigator Michael Aluffi and Santa Cruz Police Lt. Charles Scherer (transcript), Apr. 24, 1973.

"The Lucas Report." Jim Mattox, Attorney General of Texas, Apr. 1986, Austin, Tex.

Mulliken, John (London), *Life* dispatch, July 25, 1953, New York.

Oakland Park, Fla., Police Dept. Report OR #73-2815, Apr. 4, 1973.

Pilcher, Joe, "Insanity Defense," *Time* dispatch, Oct. 2, 1981, New York.

Psychiatric Examination Reports to Madera County, Calif., Superior Court Judge Jack L. Hammerberg, Sept. 18, 1973, on Edmund Emil Kemper III, by Robert A. Kinsey, M.D., Fresno, Calif.

Psychiatric Examination Reports to Madera County, Calif., Superior Court Judge Jack L. Hammerberg, Sept. 18, 1973, on Edmund Emil Kemper III, by Paul Levy, M.D., Fresno, Calif.

Pueblo, Colo., Police Dept., Supplementary Offense Reports, Serial No. MUR-221, Apr. 24, 1973, by Officers David Martinez and James P. McCoy.

Range, Peter (Stuart, Fla.), "Crime of the Century—Take One, Take Two, and Take Three," *Time* dispatches,

May 17, 1973, New York; "Crime of the Century—Take Four," *Time* dispatch, May 21, 1973, New York.

St. Lucie County, Fla., Sheriff's Office Report by Lt. Pat Duval, Apr. 1, 1973.

Santa Cruz, Calif., Office of the District Attorney, Investigation Report, Case No. 73-847, by Inspector R. F. Verbrugge, May 4, 1973.

Santa Cruz, Calif., Police Dept., Supplementary Offense Report, Case No. 161770, re Phone Calls Received at Desk, Apr. 23-24, 1973 (transcript of three telephone conversations with Edmund Emil Kemper III).

Schaefer, Gerard, Three Untitled Short Stories, no dates.

Sheriff of Broward County, Fla., undated list of exhibits marked "Juvenile Confidential," C-60993.

Still, Larry (London), "Timothy Evans—Take I," *Time* dispatch, Oct. 20, 1966, New York; "Timothy Evans—Take II and Take III," *Time* dispatch, Oct. 20, 1966, New York.

Szczesny, Joe (Detroit), "Lucas Recant," *Time* dispatch, Apr. 18, 1985, New York.

Testimony of Nancy Ellen Trotter and Paula Sue Wells, July 25, 1972, Stuart, Fla.

Voigt, George (London), *Time* dispatch, Mar. 28, 1953, New York.

"Yorkshire Ripper," *Time* dispatch, Jan. 9, 1981, New York.

Television Programs:
"50 Weeks of Planned Killing: A Profile in Mass Murder." San Francisco: KGO-TV, 1978.

"Interview with the Man from the Cage." *Moscow News,* Nov. 29, 1992.

"The Mind of a Murderer, Parts I and II." *Frontline,* #206, Mar. 19, 1984 (transcript).

"Mind of a Serial Killer." *NOVA,* #1912, Oct. 18, 1992.

Mitchell, Jim, interview with Angelo Buono (transcript), WCBS, June 22, 1982.

"Murder: No Apparent Motive." New York: Rainbow Broadcasting Co., 1984.

20/20 Interview with Chikatilo—ABC, 1992.

Index

Picture Credits

The sources for the illustrations that appear in this volume are listed below. Credits for the illustrations from left to right are separated by semicolons; from top to bottom they are separated by dashes.

Cover: AP/Wide World Photos, New York. **4, 5:** Don McCullin. **6:** AP/Wide World Photos, New York. **8, 9:** Third Coast, Milwaukee, Wis. **11:** *Akron Beacon Journal,* Akron, Ohio. **12, 13:** AP/Wide World Photos, New York—*Akron Beacon Journal,* Akron, Ohio; *Cleveland Plain Dealer,* Cleveland, Ohio. **14, 15:** *Akron Beacon Journal,* Akron, Ohio. **16, 17:** © David Rodriguez/Sygma, New York. **18:** *Milwaukee Journal,* Milwaukee, Wis. **19:** AP/Wide World Photos, New York. **20, 21:** Marshall Cavendish Ltd., London, © photos Richard Gibson. **22:** Bob Enters. **23:** AP/Wide World Photos, New York. **25:** Reuters/Bettmann, New York, inset, AP/Wide World Photos, New York. **26, 27:** *Milwaukee Journal,* Milwaukee, Wis. **29:** AP/Wide World Photos, New York. **31:** Marshall Cavendish Ltd., London, © photo Richard Gibson, inset, Reuters/Bettmann, New York. **33:** Milwaukee County Sheriff's Department, Milwaukee, Wis. **34, 35:** *Milwaukee Journal,* Milwaukee, Wis. **36, 37:** AP/Wide World Photos, New York; private collection. **38, 39:** Jeffrey Phelps/*Milwaukee Sentinel,* Milwaukee, Wis. **40:** AP/Wide World Photos, New York. **42-44:** Bellingham Police Department, Bellingham, Wash. **45:** *Bellingham Herald,* Bellingham, Wash. **46:** Bellingham Police Department, Bellingham, Wash. **47:** *Bellingham Herald,* Bellingham, Wash. **48:** Phil Schofield, private collection. **51:** Jim Mitchell. **52, 53:** Private collection. **54:** Jim Mitchell, inset, private collection. **55:** Phil Schofield, private collection. **56-63:** Private collection. **65:** Private collection—AP/Wide World Photos, New York. **68-71:** AP/Wide World Photos, New York. **72, 73:** UPI/Bettmann, New York. **75:** Bellingham Police Department, Bellingham, Wash. **76-78:** AP/Wide World Photos, New York. **79:** Private collection. **81:** UPI/Bettmann, New York. **83:** AP/Wide World Photos, New York. **84:** Syndication International, London. **86:** Hulton Deutsch Collection, London; Syndication International, London. **88:** Syndication International, London. **89:** AP/Wide World Photos, New York. **90, 91:** Private collection. **92:** UPI/

Bettmann, New York. **94, 95:** Private collection. **96:** UPI/Bettmann, New York. **98:** Topham Picture Source, Edenbridge, Kent, England. **99, 100:** Varley Picture Agency, Leeds, Yorkshire, England. **102-105:** AP/Wide World Photos, New York. **106:** UPI/Bettmann, New York. **107:** AP/Wide World Photos, New York. **109:** *Democrat and Chronicle*/The Gannett Company, Rochester, N.Y. **110:** UPI/Bettmann, New York. **113:** *Watsonville Register-Pajaronian,* Watsonville, Calif. (2)—bottom left, private collection. **114:** UPI/Bettmann, New York. **115:** Sam Vestal/*Watsonville Register-Pajaronian,* Watsonville, Calif. **118, 119:** *Madera Tribune,* copied by Van Neely. **120, 121:** © Marshall Cavendish Ltd., London, Photo Mastersearch/Robert Oliver. **122, 123:** Marshall Cavendish Ltd., London, © photo Richard Gibson. **125:** AP/Wide World Photos, New York; *Watsonville Register-Pajaronian,* Watsonville, Calif. (2). **127:** UPI/Bettmann, New York. **129:** *Watsonville Register-Pajaronian,* Watsonville, Calif. **130, 131:** *San Jose Mercury,* San Jose, Calif. **132, 133:** Marshall Cavendish Ltd., London, © photo Richard Gibson, insets, *Watsonville Register-Pajaronian,* Watsonville, Calif. (2). **134, 135:** AP/Wide World Photos, New York. **138, 139:** *Watsonville Register-Pajaronian,* Watsonville, Calif. **140:** UPI/Bettmann, New York. **142:** County of Santa Cruz District Attorney, Santa Cruz, Calif. **143:** Private collection. **144:** AP/Wide World Photos, New York. **146, 147:** TASS from Sovfoto, New York. **148:** Reuters/Bettmann, New York—Sovfoto, New York. **150, 151:** RIA-Novosti/Sovfoto, New York. **152:** Service Cinéma des Armées, courtesy Time Inc. Magazines Picture Collection. **155:** Constance Richards—Issa Kostaev and Richard Lourie, *Hunting the Devil* © 1993. **156:** Issa Kostaev and Richard Lourie, *Hunting the Devil* © 1993. **159:** From *Hunting the Devil* by Richard Lourie, © 1993 by Richard Lourie. Reprinted by permission of HarperCollins. **160:** Issa Kostaev and Richard Lourie, *Hunting the Devil* © 1993. **162-167:** Constance Richards. **170:** East News/Sipa Press, New York. **173:** Constance Richards. **174, 175:** Issa Kostaev and Richard Lourie, *Hunting the Devil* © 1993. **176, 177:** Sipa Press, New York. **178-181:** Issa Kostaev and Richard Lourie, *Hunting the Devil* © 1993. **182, 183:** Reuters/Bettmann, New York.

Time-Life Books

EDITOR-IN-CHIEF: Thomas H. Flaherty

Director of Editorial Resources:
 Norma E. Shaw (acting)
Executive Art Director: Ellen Robling
Director of Photography and Research:
 John Conrad Weiser
Editorial Board: Dale M. Brown, Janet Cave,
 Roberta Conlan, Robert Doyle, Laura Foreman,
 Jim Hicks, Rita Thievon Mullin, Henry
 Woodhead

PRESIDENT: John D. Hall

Vice President and Director of Marketing:
 Nancy K. Jones
Editorial Director: Russell B. Adams, Jr.
Director of Production Services: Robert N. Carr
Production Manager: Prudence G. Harris
Director of Technology: Eileen Bradley
Supervisor of Quality Control: James King

Editorial Operations
Production: Celia Beattie
Library: Louise D. Forstall
Computer Composition: Deborah G. Tait
 (Manager), Monika D. Thayer, Janet Barnes
 Syring, Lillian Daniels
Interactive Media Specialist: Patti H. Cass

Time-Life Books is a division of Time Life
Incorporated

PRESIDENT AND CEO: John M. Fahey, Jr.

© 1993 Time-Life Books. All rights reserved.
No part of this book may be reproduced in any
form or by any electronic or mechanical means, including information storage and retrieval devices
or systems, without prior written permission from
the publisher, except that brief passages may be
quoted for reviews.
First printing. Printed in U.S.A.
Published simultaneously in Canada.
School and library distribution by Silver Burdett
Company, Morristown, New Jersey 07960.

TIME-LIFE is a trademark of Time Warner Inc.
U.S.A.

Library of Congress Cataloging in Publication Data
Compulsion to Kill/by the editors of Time-Life
Books.
   p.   cm. — (True crime)
 Includes bibliographical references and index.
 ISBN 0-7835-0016-5
 1. Serial murders—Case studies.
I. Time-Life Books. II. Series.
HV6515.C64 1993
364.1'523—dc20   93-17273
                                         CIP
 ISBN 0-7835-0017-3 (lib. bdg.)

TRUE CRIME

SERIES EDITOR: Laura Foreman
Administrative Editor: Jane A. Martin
Art Director: Christopher Register
Picture Editor: Jane Jordan

Editorial Staff for *Compulsion to Kill*
Text Editors: Carl A. Posey (principal),
 John Sullivan
Writer: Robin Currie
Associate Editors/Research: Jennifer Pearce
 (principal), Vicki Warren
Assistant Art Director: Brook Mowrey
Senior Copyeditors: Elizabeth Graham (principal),
 Colette Stockum
Picture Coordinator: Jennifer Iker
Editorial Assistant: Donna Fountain

Special Contributors: Douglas J. Brown, John
Clausen, Jim Halpin, Jane Huseby, R. Curtis Kopf,
Ken Myers, Katharine N. Old, Georgia Pabst,
Catherine Harper Parrott, Igor Pshchichkov, Robin
Tunnicliff, Tony Wassell (research); John Clausen,
George Constable, George G. Daniels, Margery
duMond, Jane Gruenebaum, George Russell (text);
John Drummond (design); Mel Ingber (index).

Correspondents: Elisabeth Kraemer-Singh (Bonn);
Christine Hinze (London); Juan Sosa (Moscow);
Christina Lieberman (New York); Maria Vincenza
Aloisi (Paris); Ann Natanson (Rome). Valuable as-
sistance was also provided by Liz Corcoran,
Caroline Wood (London); Constance Richards
(Moscow); Elizabeth Brown, Katheryn White
(New York).

Consultant:
Robert K. Ressler is a criminologist and the director
of Forensic Behavioral Services, a Virginia-based
consultancy. A 20-year veteran of the Federal Bureau of Investigation, Ressler is an internationally
known expert in the area of violent criminal offenders, especially serial and sexual homicide; it was he
who coined the term serial killer. He is also a specialist in criminal-personality profiling, crime-scene
analysis, sexual assaults, and hostage negotiation.
During his 16 years at the Behavioral Science Unit
at the FBI Academy in Quantico, Virginia, Ressler
helped create the agency's National Center for the
Analysis of Violent Crime, and the nationwide Violent Criminal Apprehension Program, or VICAP. He
holds a Master of Science degree in police adminis-
tration from Michigan State University. His publications include two textbooks, *Sexual Homicide: Patterns and Motives* and *Crime Classification Manual,*
and his 1992 autobiography, *Whoever Fights Monsters.* Before taking up his FBI career, Ressler served
in the U.S. Army military police criminal investigation division in Washington and Vietnam and recently retired with the rank of colonel after 35 years
of total active-duty and reserve service.

Other Publications:
WEIGHT WATCHERS® SM
 RECIPE COLLECTION
THE AMERICAN INDIANS
THE ART OF WOODWORKING
LOST CIVILIZATIONS
ECHOES OF GLORY
THE NEW FACE OF WAR
HOW THINGS WORK
WINGS OF WAR
CREATIVE EVERYDAY COOKING
COLLECTOR'S LIBRARY OF THE UNKNOWN
CLASSICS OF WORLD WAR II
TIME-LIFE LIBRARY OF CURIOUS AND
 UNUSUAL FACTS
AMERICAN COUNTRY
VOYAGE THROUGH THE UNIVERSE
THE THIRD REICH
THE TIME-LIFE GARDENER'S GUIDE
MYSTERIES OF THE UNKNOWN
TIME FRAME
FIX IT YOURSELF
FITNESS, HEALTH & NUTRITION
SUCCESSFUL PARENTING
HEALTHY HOME COOKING
UNDERSTANDING COMPUTERS
LIBRARY OF NATIONS
THE ENCHANTED WORLD
THE KODAK LIBRARY OF CREATIVE
 PHOTOGRAPHY
GREAT MEALS IN MINUTES
THE CIVIL WAR
PLANET EARTH
COLLECTOR'S LIBRARY OF THE CIVIL WAR
THE EPIC OF FLIGHT
THE GOOD COOK
WORLD WAR II
HOME REPAIR AND IMPROVEMENT
THE OLD WEST

*For information on and a full description of any
of the Time-Life Books series listed above, please
call 1-800-621-7026 or write:*
Reader Information
Time-Life Customer Service
P.O. Box C-32068
Richmond, Virginia 23261-2068

This volume is one of a series that examines
the phenomenon of crime. Other books in the
series include:
Serial Killers
Mass Murderers
Mafia
Unsolved Crimes